Traitor, Outlaw, King

Traitor, Outlaw, King

Part One:
The Making of Robert Bruce

Fiona Watson

Copyright © 2018 Fiona Watson

All rights reserved

ISBN: 9781719899192

fionawatsonhistorian.wordpress.com

To Archie

With grateful thanks and fond memories

Map of Scotland

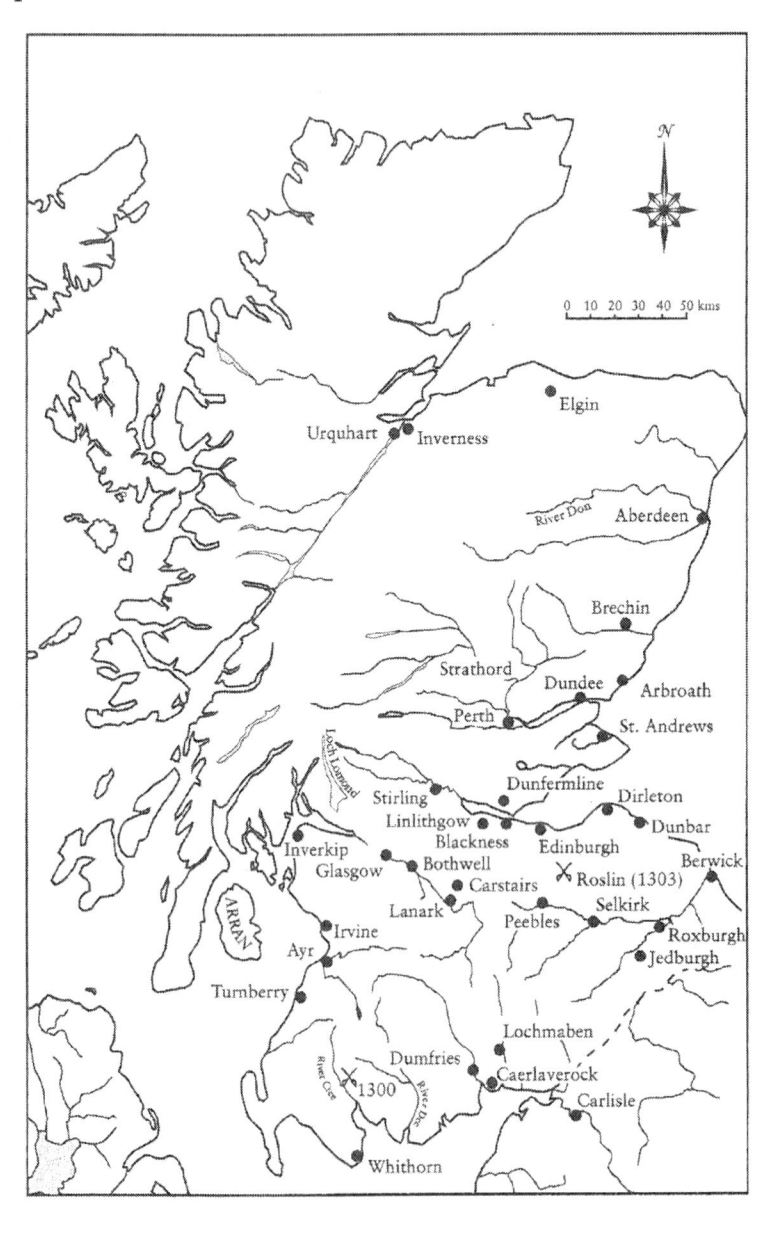

CONTENTS

Map of Scotland vi
A wee word about the Bruces 1
Prologue 5
Chapter One 8
    Figure 1: the Scottish and English royal families, 1058-1219 11
    Figure 2: the Bruces of Annandale 15
Chapter Two 19
    Figure 3: line of descent from David, earl of Huntingdon 22
Chapter Three 33
    Figure 4: the Scottish royal family and its relationship with the English royal family to 1290 37
Chapter Four 48
Chapter Five 59
Chapter Six 71
Chapter Seven 83
Chapter Eight 101
Chapter Nine 117
Chapter Ten 131
    Figure 5: John Comyn's descent from King Donald III 136
    Figure 6: King Robert's family 160
INDEX 166
BIBLIOGRAPHY and SHORT GLOSSARY 193
PICTURE CREDITS 200
ACKNOWLEDGEMENTS 202
ABOUT THE AUTHOR 204
NOTES 206

A WEE WORD ABOUT THE BRUCES

The statue of Robert the Bruce at the entrance to Edinburgh Castle [Ad Meskens].

The story I would like to unfold for you on these pages is not a pretty one. Few come out of it with their honour intact and King Robert isn't one of them, despite what his propaganda would have us believe. But perhaps he wouldn't have lasted long in the predatory politics of medieval Britain if he had. It's also fair to say that he was far from unusual across most of human history in trying to exploit every inch of advantage, every favourable connection, to enhance his family's position even if he was ultimately – and shockingly - prepared to go further than most to get what he believed was rightfully his.

And while it's easy to dismiss him as self-seeking, as entirely focused on the glory, riches and honours that he would later deny were his inspiration, we cannot know for sure that he did not also burn with righteous indignation at the way in which the ancient kingdom of

Scotland was treated by Edward I of England. This is not meant to excuse the terrible things Bruce did, to romanticise what was nasty, brutal and cunning as well as remarkable, statesmanlike and generous about him. But in his incredible self-belief and his determination never to give up, as well as the formidable skills of leadership that eventually brought him such extraordinary success, he joins a long list of heroes whose careers were won at the cost of the spilling of much blood and whose brutal tactics are something I, for one, wish never to witness in real life.

King Robert, in other words, shares many of the attributes of a Napoleon or a Julius Caesar. But while he is honoured in his homeland, his story has not yet resonated around the world in the same way as theirs have, or even that of his compatriot, Sir William Wallace. In some ways, it's not difficult to understand why. Wallace, unlike Bruce, is not tarnished by the well-founded suspicion that he acted in pursuit of his own vaulting ambition but rather sought to remedy a terrible injustice inflicted upon his native land for the greater good. The fact that Sir William failed and suffered a cruel death only made his sacrifice the greater, the paying of this ultimate price enhancing his posthumous reputation and deservedly so. But if Robert Bruce had not succeeded where Wallace failed, then that sacrifice would have been in vain. We may suspect King Robert's motives, but we cannot deny his achievements.

And yet this extraordinary man did not come out of nowhere, even if there was a moment, around the turn of 1306-7, when it appeared that way. Though Bruce can seem almost superhuman in the fight against England, his early career – the subject of this first book on his life - was full of failure, even hubris, though still touched with his characteristic energy. In that he was very like his grandfather, who left no stone unturned in promoting his claim to the Scottish throne after the death of the Scottish king, Alexander III, without a male heir in 1286. And King Robert's grandfather in turn had much in him of the very first Robert Bruce who came to Britain from Normandy around 1100, armed with formidable determination, ingenuity and an unquenchable desire to succeed. This is the story of seven generations of ambitious men – and the women who stood alongside them – as they schemed and fought for their place in an uncertain world.

And so, dear reader, to understand King Robert and the times through which he lived, we must confront those who came before him. But in doing so we immediately hit a problem. Our Robert was the seventh lord of Annandale, and all of his predecessors bar one shared his name. To try to make sense of this glut of Roberts, I have given them a number. Thus the first Robert Bruce of Annandale is Robert (1). As the man who brought the family to Britain and transformed their fortunes, he deserves a proper mention, but we will not dwell for long on Roberts (2-4), who continue in much the same vein. However, Robert (5) – the future king's grandfather – is well worth getting to know, for it is with him that the search for a throne begins. And then there is Robert (6) – the first Bruce earl and our Robert's father. He is something of a disappointment, but nonetheless his liking for his southern English estates and his interest in the Celtic dimensions of his Scottish earldom of Carrick both left an important imprint on his famous son, who is Robert (7) or – when it seems safe to do so – just plain Robert.

But no man is an island and our Robert was shaped by a number of those he encountered on the bumpy road to the crown. Two of the most important were also the most surprising. In 1296 King Edward of England, in one shattering moment, seemed to put paid to the Bruces' ambitions whilst also transforming Scotland from an independent kingdom of many centuries duration to an appendage of a wider English empire that stretched from the northern tip of mainland Britain all the way to Bordeaux in mid-western France. A powerful, competent and highly respected monarch, Edward was restlessly intelligent and ruthlessly interventionist. He was, in other words, exactly the kind of king whose methods Robert often sought to emulate, even as he rejected his authority. There were perhaps rather more similarities between the two than we might wish to admit, not least in their unswerving determination to serve their own interests.

Head of Scotland's most powerful family, John Comyn of Badenoch was Robert Bruce's equal in ambition. But by 1306 Comyn far outstripped Bruce in experience, success against Edward I and political influence within Scotland. He was also nephew of the king – John Balliol – whom the Scots had been fighting to restore, as well as having a perfectly respectable claim to the throne of his own, through an eleventh-century Scottish monarch. For all those things, he had to die if Robert were to have any chance of fulfilling the destiny to which he believed he was entitled. Comyn's murder set off the chain of events that certainly propelled Robert on to the throne, but only by unleashing a civil war that changed Scotland forever and nearly finished off the Bruces – and perhaps Scotland with them – once and for all.

King Robert's reign, then, was forged in a furnace of bloody ambition and we should not be fooled by the intensity of Bruce's desire for the crown into imagining that he alone had right on his side. Nor should we be surprised – when winners write history, the past becomes another country even for those who lived there. But if this book is mostly a story of failure, then out of that failure was born something quite unexpected, something extraordinary that really did change the course of history. What comes next – how an outlaw without even a horse became a brilliant military leader and a country was reconquered for its king – will be revealed in the second part of this story …

Prologue

Pilkington Jackson statue of Robert the Bruce, Bannockburn [Kim Traynor].

Let Scotland's warcraft be this: footsoldiers, mountains and marshy ground; and let her woods, her bow and spear serve for barricades. Let menace lurk in all her narrow places among her warrior bands, and let her plains so burn with fire that her enemies flee away. Crying out in the night, let her men be on their guard, and her enemies in confusion will flee from hunger's sword. Surely it will be so, as we're guided by Robert, our lord.[1]

With these words, perhaps written around 1308, the Scots turned their backs on the 'rule book' of medieval warfare and disappeared into the hills and bogs where they would not only be safe, but might sow the seeds of the destruction of their enemies. They did so in the firm belief that their future success was guaranteed by the guidance and leadership of one man – their lord and king, Robert the Bruce.

It is easy to forget – since we can look back and see that their faith was justified – just how revolutionary this form of sustained warfare was. And yet only a year or so earlier few would have given Bruce much chance of staying alive, never mind driving his many foes out of what he had the temerity to call his kingdom. Robert's transformation from 'King Hobbe' – the outlawed murderer and usurper reduced to skulking around the far-flung wilds of Scotland on his little 'hobby' horse – to a ruler of international renown seems more fitting for a work of fiction than fact.

Today he sits high above us, a look of reassuring intensity on his face as he surveys the route taken by Edward II of England's invading army, the one he is about to beat at Bannockburn. Robert the Bruce, immortalised in Charles Pilkington Jackson's 1964 statue, is every bronze inch the hero, a warrior king astride his splendid war-horse and carrying his famous battle-axe, the one that would soon split the head of a reckless English knight who dared to challenge him in single combat.

I wonder what Bruce would have thought of this, perhaps the most famous of his modern incarnations. He would surely have been surprised to see himself astride a mighty destrier, such a conventional symbol of knightly power and prestige, but one that, for most of his career, King Robert had no use for. At the same time, I suspect he would have been astonished and delighted in equal measure to find himself portrayed in so unequivocally triumphant a pose, to know at last that the rhetoric carefully crafted throughout a reign forged in the fallout of an act of shocking and polarising violence has stood the test of time. For this ruthless, driven genius deserved every bit of opprobrium poured on his head by Scots and English alike, even as he also inspired gratitude and devotion among his contemporaries and future generations. In one instant Bruce pulled his country apart and almost destroyed it in his obsessive quest for the throne; but in time he proved that he was the one – perhaps the only one – to put Scotland back together again not just as it was, but free of the disruption and humiliation of English occupation, a confident, independent kingdom once more, even if the scars of war ran deep.

But this is no fairy tale. There was no room for doubt in his mind, whether it was his right to wear the crown of Scotland, stolen from the Bruces - so far as he was concerned, by John Balliol and Edward I - or the need to persevere with the fight, deep into England or across to Ireland, long after many of his subjects had grown weary of his military preoccupations as they struggled with the repercussions of years of war, famine and disease. He was neither untarnished hero nor irredeemable villain, but a mixture of the two; a man who forged his own destiny and that of an independent Scottish nation even as he was prepared to see both die in the trying. He was in many ways the greatest king to rule Scotland, a genius in war and a ruthlessly effective politician who rose like a phoenix from the ruins of his own dismal early career. But he could so very easily have been Scotland's last.

Chapter One

In the beginning

In which the first Robert Bruce arrives in England from Normandy and proves useful to the English and Scottish kings, which brings him extensive lands in both kingdoms. Most of the time, this is an excellent way of acquiring more property and good marriages, but the first two Roberts suffer when the kings of England and Scotland go to war. Nevertheless, by 1200 the Scottish branch of the family is doing well on both sides of the border, even if their main focus is north of it.

Guisborough Priory by Thomas Girton, 1801

They came to the British Isles, those tough, determined Bruces, from Brix on the plains of the Cotentin in north-west Normandy.[2] The first Robert Bruce crossed the Channel in the service of his lord – Count Henry of the Cotentin, youngest son of England's first Norman king, William the Conqueror. In 1100 this Henry took advantage of the unfortunate death while they were out hunting of his elder brother, William II of England, to have himself crowned before his eldest brother, the Duke of Normandy, could stop him.

By 1103 Robert (1) already held more than a hundred manors mostly in the county of Cleveland in North Yorkshire. Henry had given them to him not so much as a reward for past services, but in the hope and belief that Bruce could tighten the crown's grip on a part of England whose lords were not keen to acknowledge the authority of William the Conqueror and his sons. Such independence was even more marked beyond Yorkshire, however, a situation that Henry intended to remedy himself. But the presence of trusted men like Bruce living nearby was key to making any royal intervention last longer than a short-lived military campaign. Robert (1) was clearly an energetic, capable man whom the English king knew from experience in the Cotentin could be trusted to get a job done, a ruthless determination that was handed down to future generations. It was certainly a trait to be found in his great-great-great-great-grandson, Robert (7), the future king.

The rest of Robert (1)'s lands in North Yorkshire were probably acquired in the next decade or so through marriage with a local heiress, the other tried-and-tested way for an ambitious knight to expand his holdings. By 1120 he was by far the most wealthy and powerful landowner in Cleveland. Encouraged by his success, the king then granted him lands some thirty miles further north in the district of Hartness (called Hartlepool today) with its port. Robert (1) was now master of a cohesive swathe of territory that ran from the coast through the valley of the River Tees and on up into the hills.[3]

No doubt in order to give thanks for the remarkable improvement in his family's fortunes as well as marking his position as a prominent English baron, Robert (1) founded an Augustinian priory at Guisborough 'to the honour of God and the holy Virgin Mary' in 1119. He gave the canons he brought there a generous 10,000 acres of his lands with their meadows, pastures, waters, moors and groves, along with a mill and everything they needed to build their new home. Bruce also became Henry's justice, or chief representative, in the north of England, sometimes attending the king's council meetings as an important, if still only modestly wealthy, nobleman and royal servant.[4]

But of far more significance in the long run – though it wouldn't have seemed that way at the time – was Robert (1)'s friendship with another unexpected king, David I of Scotland. David was the youngest of seven sons of Malcolm III [see *Figure 1*], but had to flee to England on his father's death in 1093 when his uncle seized the throne. Henry took the prince under his wing and it was presumably at the English king's court that Robert (1) first met the young Scot.

Prince David's family fortunes soon changed and his older brothers all became kings of Scotland in turn, bringing him a gift of lands stretching across the far south of the Scottish kingdom by 1113. But in 1124 the last of his brothers died. Though two of them had produced a son of their own, neither young man was brother-in-law and protégé of Henry I of England. It therefore seemed prudent to the Scottish aristocracy to allow David to take the throne at the ripe old age of forty rather than risk invasion from south of the border.

Even before he became king, David remembered the friends he had made in England, especially a man with a proven track record in bringing Norman methods – in land management, administration, architecture and military organisation – to 'difficult' areas. What Robert (1) had done for King Henry in promoting royal authority in Yorkshire, David hoped Bruce would do for him from the great estate he gave him in Annandale in south-west Scotland, which had, until recently, been part of the independent kingdom of Strathclyde. The Yorkshire baron was more than just a regional enforcer, however; he was David's mentor before and after he became king, offering advice and friendship as they both established themselves north of the border.[5]

There was no question of Bruce relocating permanently to Scotland, though the fact that he could devote so much time to Annandale and to David suggests that he had a firm enough grip on his Yorkshire estates to be able to leave them for considerable periods. Robert (1) presumably ordered the construction of a new residence at Annan to serve as the administrative heart of his latest acquisition. Perhaps made of timber to begin with and set on a formidable earth and stone mound, the castle stood watch over a ford on the River Annan that lay on its western flank.[6] This river provided easy access to the Solway estuary that separated Scotland from England a few miles to the south.

Figure 1: the Scottish and English royal families, 1058-1219

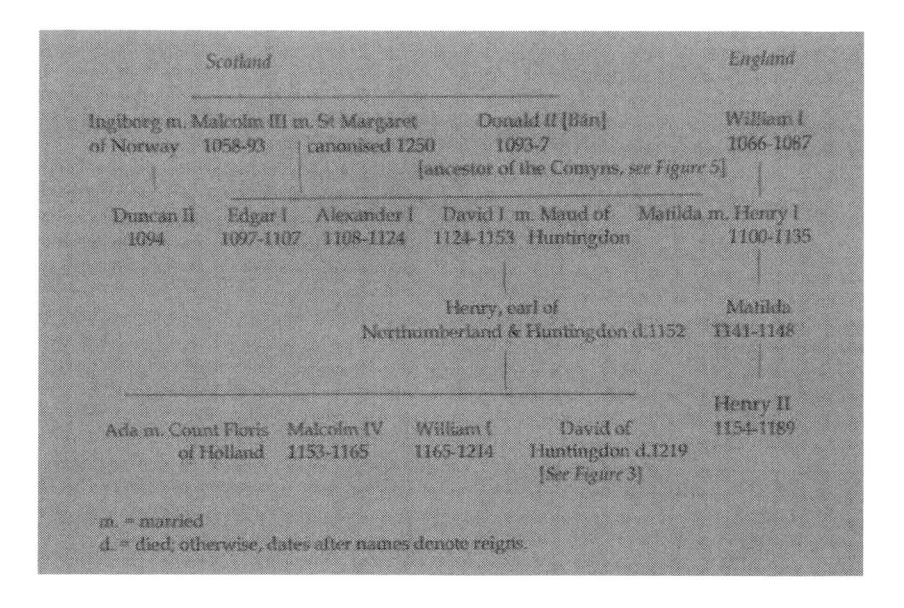

```
                            Scotland                                          England

Ingiborg  m. Malcolm III  m. St Margaret        Donald II [Bán]              William I
of Norway   1058-93       canonised 1250        1093-7                       1066-1087
                                                [ancestor of the Comyns, see Figure 5]

Duncan II   Edgar I    Alexander I    David I m. Maud of    Matilda m. Henry I
1094        1097-1107  1108-1124      1124-1153 Huntingdon            1100-1135

                                      Henry, earl of                   Matilda
                                      Northumberland & Huntingdon d.1152   1141-1148

                                                                       Henry II
Ada m. Count Floris   Malcolm IV   William I    David of               1154-1189
of Holland            1153-1165    1165-1214    Huntingdon d.1219
                                                [See Figure 3]

m. = married
d. = died; otherwise, dates after names denote reigns.
```

Given David's close relationship with Henry and Robert (1)'s own connections to them both, it wasn't the protection of Scotland's border with England that made Bruce so useful. Rather it was the need to keep an eye on the strange and disconcerting – from a Norman point of view – land of Galloway to the west. Colonised many centuries before by Norse-Gaels (a hybrid of Scandinavians and Celts), its lords resisted absorption into the kingdom of Scotland even if they usually chose to give their loyalty to its kings. And while David's father, Malcolm III, had most certainly been a Gael, the Scottish king and those he grew up with regarded the Gaelic language and culture as bizarre at best but more often as downright barbaric.

Proving himself useful to more than one royal master brought considerable rewards to Robert (1) but, as he approached his seventies, relations between Scotland and England began to unravel, putting him in an awkward situation. In 1135 King Henry I died, survived by only one legitimate child – a daughter – by his first wife, King David's elder sister. Though Henry had named this daughter as heir to England and

Normandy, her male cousin immediately crossed the Channel and was crowned king. For the next eighteen years, civil war stalked England.

In time-honoured fashion, King David saw in England's weakness an opportunity to grab more territory for himself. Scottish kings – like any other - had long viewed their borders as 'flexible' and their success in moving them is amply illustrated by the fact that their kingdom had once reached only as far as the River Forth, but now stretched a further eighty miles south into what had previously been English territory. There was surely no reason, as far as they were concerned, why the border could not be moved again, an ambition underlined by the fact that David's own father had died trying to stake a claim to lands in English Northumberland. Mustering an army in the late summer of 1138, the Scottish king crossed the border, claiming to be riding out in support of his niece, Henry's daughter. With the civil war busy raging in the south and David soon in control of Northumberland, it was left to the archbishop of York to raise the men of Yorkshire against him.

One of those was Robert (1), described as 'a man aged and of great resources, scant of speech but speaking with a certain dignity and weight,' an entirely predictable description of an elderly knight. As a Norman, he had a very low opinion of the native Scots, a prejudice that, like any other, we should not take too seriously; Scottish Gaels may have had a very different language and culture – some of them as yet scorned to wear armour as too unmanly for a warrior, for example – but that did not make them savages. Nevertheless, the old adventurer admonished his 'great friend,' the Scottish king, for his foolish, even self-destructive, behaviour during abortive peace negotiations. He poured particular scorn on David's baffling reliance on the kind of men whom any self-respecting knight should keep at a safe distance. 'Since when, I ask you,' Bruce scolded, 'have you found such trust in the Scots that you can so confidently divest and deprive yourself of the counsel of the English, the help of the Normans…? Do you think, O King, that the heavenly Majesty will look on with favourable eyes when you seek to destroy those who won your kingdom for you and yours and made it secure?'[7] When the chips were down, Robert (1) had only one master, and it wasn't his friend, the king of Scots.

Since He clearly could not have done otherwise, God denied David victory at the Battle of the Standard on 22 August 1138. The Scottish army was mostly composed of infantry – as it would be over 160 years later when commanded by King Robert the Bruce – and even David fought on foot, though on this occasion so did most of the horsemen opposing him. The Scots were divided into four lines, the leading one manned by the men of Galloway with their long spears. Despite attacking first with terrifying yells – a strategy that had already brought them success earlier in the campaign – they were beaten back by English archers and the Scottish army began to disintegrate.[8] However, since He also works in mysterious ways, His heavenly Majesty then turned a blind eye to the Scottish king taking over Cumberland and much of Northumberland anyway, though the English kings got them back again after David's death fifteen years later.

Despite this hiccup in Anglo-Scottish relations – which probably resulted in the temporary confiscation of Annandale – Robert (1) was soon back in David's company and favour. In 1141, only three years after the battle of the Standard, Earl Henry, the Scottish king's eldest son, dealt with a dispute involving the monks of Durham 'in the presence of my father and Robert Bruce and others of his barons …'[9] Robert (1) died within the year and was buried in his priory of Guisborough. Among his many successes was the raising to manhood of two sons, Adam and Robert, who now took on the task of further improving the family fortunes over the next generation and producing, God willing, healthy sons of their own.

Following Norman custom, Adam, the eldest, inherited the family's lands in England, while Robert got Annandale in Scotland. Indeed, this second Robert seems to have lived north of the border for some years already, perhaps as a companion of Earl Henry. Certainly what his father failed to mention in his outraged speech to David I before the battle of the Standard was that his younger son – though probably little more than a boy - was in the Scottish army ready to fight against his father and older brother. Or perhaps to protect their Scottish interests, should that prove necessary.[10]

This short excursion into the life of the first Robert Bruce lets us glimpse a career focused not on the opportunities limited by the borders of his native land, but on the various possibilities dangled before him by powerful individuals, wherever they might lead him. It was a similar story with kingship, or at least the route to it in both England and Scotland, which, on opportune occasions, might be as much about combining some of the right credentials with a heavy dose of ruthless determination, good luck and good contacts as strict, well-defined rules.

Of course, in the two centuries that separated the first Robert Bruce from his great-great-great-great-grandson – our King Robert – Western

European society changed. Rules tightened; royal government became more efficient, its embrace more far-reaching even in Scotland – whose kings left far more power in the hands of their nobles than did the kings of England – impacting further on people's lives, both positively and negatively. And identities changed too as kingdoms evolved from loose communities of interest - distinct groups with their own laws and customs - to increasingly coherent entities bound together by the king's law. The king's way of doing things slowly became the way things should be done throughout his domains and in Scotland by 1200 it became important to the Scottish monarch and his advisors to present the different peoples within his kingdom as a single, natural unity, anciently put together as part of God's plan.[11]

But just because it suited kings and writers of history to emphasise cohesion within the evolving states of medieval Europe doesn't mean that contradictory instincts suddenly disappeared. Princes, nobles and entrepreneurs continued to behave just like the first Robert Bruce, seizing on any opportunity to expand their wealth and prestige, for otherwise they might fall behind and be unable to protect and provide for their relatives and those lesser folk who looked to them for jobs and other forms of support and protection.

And why should it matter whether those opportunities lay across a border or even relied on the application of force, if necessary, for surely no-one would succeed unless they had God on their side? In this the Bruces were no different from anyone else and they were all only following the example set by their rulers. As the family grew wealthier and more important during the twelfth and thirteenth centuries, the only potential cloud on the horizon was the trying possibility that their lords, the kings of Scotland and England, would go to war with one another. There would be other occasions when members of the family had to choose sides, just as father and son had done at the battle of the Standard. But it didn't seem to do them much harm. Not yet.

****

In the decades following Robert (1)'s death, his descendants did indeed continue to feather both family nests with more lands and advantageous marriages. But it was the junior Scottish branch, rather than the Yorkshire one, that proved the more successful in climbing the social ladder. The Scottish Bruces were also remarkably blessed in one important respect –

their ability to produce sons generation after generation. The direct line passed unbroken from the first Robert Bruce, who was born about 1070, down to his great-great-great-great-great-grandson, David – King David II of Scotland – who died childless three hundred years later in 1371.

Figure 2: the Bruces of Annandale

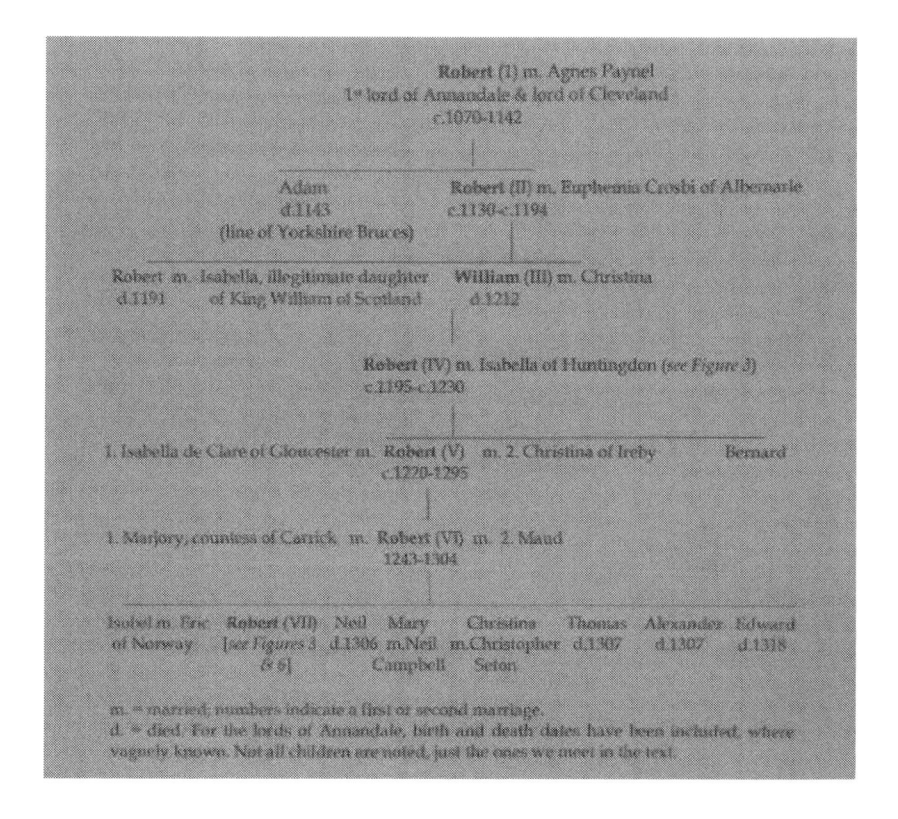

```
                    Robert (I) m. Agnes Paynel
                1st lord of Annandale & lord of Cleveland
                            c.1070-1142
                                |
        Adam                Robert (II) m. Euphemia Crosbi of Albemarle
        d.1143                      c.1130-c.1194
    (line of Yorkshire Bruces)
                                        |
    Robert m. Isabella, illegitimate daughter    William (III) m. Christina
    d.1191    of King William of Scotland         d.1212
                                                    |
                        Robert (IV) m. Isabella of Huntingdon (see Figure 3)
                                c.1195-c.1230
                                        |
    1. Isabella de Clare of Gloucester m. Robert (V) m. 2. Christina of Ireby    Bernard
                                c.1220-1295
                                        |
    1. Marjory, countess of Carrick m. Robert (VI) m. 2. Maud
                                1243-1304
                                        |
    Isobel m. Eric  Robert (VII)  Neil  Mary     Christina     Thomas  Alexander  Edward
    of Norway    [see Figures 3  d.1306  m.Neil   m.Christopher  d.1307  d.1307    d.1318
                    & 6]                Campbell  Seton

    m. = married; numbers indicate a first or second marriage.
    d. = died. For the lords of Annandale, birth and death dates have been included, where
    vaguely known. Not all children are noted, just the ones we meet in the text.
```

But the bedrock of their fortunes was the 250,000 acres (378 square miles)[12] of lucrative real estate that formed the lordship of Annandale. Though there was good arable land along the Solway coast and the lush valley of the River Annan, much of the estate was hill country up to 2223 feet (667 metres) high, ideal for producing one of the most lucrative commodities of the later Middle Ages. With the rise of the great cloth-making towns of Flanders from the twelfth century, Flemish and German merchants came to Scotland to buy up large quantities of wool, giving landowners a very lucrative incentive to stock as much of their land as possible with the hardy little native sheep, as well as looking to acquire more pasture where they could. It was also good for hunting, that great aristocratic pastime.

In return, the Bruces owed the Scottish crown the service of ten knights, the right to hold land then largely equated with the provision of men for royal armies. However, Scotland's kings agreed that they would not interfere in the lordship's internal affairs except in cases of murder, rape, robbery and arson (the 'four pleas of the Crown'). Even then, no royal official would cross Annandale's boundaries, but one of Robert's own knights was appointed to deal with these heinous crimes, answering to the royal justices based at nearby Dumfries.[13] Such sweeping powers could be seen as a sign of trust as much as of royal weakness. Men like Robert (1) and David I understood each other and wanted the same things – a powerful Scottish monarchy and the rewards that came with it for both of them.

The Bruces of Annandale, then, were more or less complete masters of their extensive Scottish domains but they still had lands and family in Yorkshire and chose to be buried at Guisborough. That they viewed the border as no barrier is amply illustrated by the fact that Robert (2) gifted the revenues of six of his Scottish churches to the Yorkshire priory,[14] which probably explains why the chronicle produced at Guisborough is remarkably well informed about Scottish affairs, including the activities of the future king, Robert (7).

The Bruce castle at Annan soon proved less than adequate, however, parts of it supposedly being washed away along with a good portion of the town in the mid-twelfth century. It was said that this disaster was the work of St Malachy, an Irish bishop who had accepted hospitality from Robert (II), but went on to curse him for hanging a thief that the saint had asked to be pardoned.[15]

Be that as it may, Robert (2) certainly built another fortress at Lochmaben thirteen miles north-west. This castle was also defended by water, sitting as it did on a narrow neck of land between two small lochs [lakes]. It seems to have been bigger too, the main structure – this time certainly made of stone – sitting on a mound that was 'unusually large and oval in plan.'[16] There was certainly no lack of funds to invest in what was an increasingly costly element of lordly expenditure.

Nevertheless, the next three generations of Bruces had a far less cosy relationship with the kings of Scots than the first lord of Annandale; they preferred to devote their energies to forging and keeping strong ties with their own senior tenants and near neighbours.[17] The knights of Annandale were a conspicuously close-knit bunch whose loyalty and service stretches across the generations. A later charter granted between 1211 and 1233 gives us a brief glimpse of this inner circle, of those who helped the Bruces to manage their estates, who stood behind their decisions and often carried them out, as well as riding with them to war - the Johnstones, Mauleverers, Corries, Jardines, Crosbies, Kirkpatricks, Herries and Levingtons.[18] Some of their descendants would still prove conspicuously loyal to their lord several generations later, turning their backs on the future king while his father ruled Annandale, but following him on his perilous path towards the throne and beyond once he became their seventh lord.

Annandale, then, made its owners powerful members of the aristocracy, prompting some of the highest in Scotland and even England to consider them as worthy sons-in-law. Robert (2) married a niece of the important Yorkshire nobleman, William, earl of Albemarle; but in 1183, his eldest son was honoured with the hand of no less a lady than an illegitimate daughter of David I's grandson, King William.[19] At the same time, the Bruces of Annandale clearly didn't think of themselves as particularly 'Scottish;' they were above all part of a western European aristocracy united by a common language (Norman French) and religion, as well as a shared culture of knightly virtues and lordly rights and responsibilities. These responsibilities included serving with their retinues among the men-at-arms of the English and Scottish armies for their lands in both kingdoms.[20] But within forty years of the battle of the Standard, the Bruces found themselves having to choose between two masters once again.

In 1173-4 King William I of Scotland used the outbreak of another civil war in England to try to regain the swathe of territory south of the border that his grandfather David I had held until his death twenty-one years earlier. Robert (2) was appalled. Like his father, he was of the view that his primary duty was to the 'bigger' king, Henry II of England, to whom both he and King William had sworn oaths of loyalty as English landowners. The price was almost certainly the loss of his two castles of

Annan and Lochmaben as the border was put on a war footing to guard the most westerly approach between Scotland and England.[21]

But this time invasion spelt disaster. On 13 July 1174 the Scots once more encountered a force hastily assembled from among the men of Yorkshire at Richmond only some thirty miles from the Bruces' English estates. King William was eager for battle, spurring his horse with the words: 'Now we will see who the knights are.' His answer came almost immediately as he was unhorsed, taken prisoner and carted off in chains to face an aging and irate Henry II of England in Normandy.

And this time the English king refused to slap William on the wrist and make him retake his oath of homage and fealty, the standard, futile response to previous Scottish attempts to take more English territory. Henry wanted cast-iron guarantees, demanding in what was set down as the Treaty of Falaise that the Scottish king swear homage not just for his English lands, which was entirely proper, but for his kingdom, which was not, an oath also meant to be binding on his successors. His ransom was set at 40,000 merks (about £22 million today[22]) and his nobility had to promise to turn against their king if he were to invade again. Finally – in a stinging and unprecedented intervention – a string of castles from Berwick on the eastern Border to Stirling right in the heart of Scotland was supposed to be handed over to Henry's 'mercy.' Twenty-one Scottish nobles, including William's own brother, David, Earl of Huntingdon, and four earls were to be sent to England as hostages for their king's good behaviour.[23]

But William survived this dreadful humiliation and only fifteen years later managed to purchase a renunciation, known as the Quitclaim of Canterbury, of the whole degrading set of terms forced upon him from Henry II's son, Richard I. Nevertheless, he could not afford to destabilise the south-west by permanently getting rid of the Bruces and decided to woo Robert (2) back into loyal service on the vulnerable border with the marriage of his illegitimate daughter to the lord of Annandale's son. The family had weathered yet another storm.

Chapter Two

Social climbing

In which the Bruces join the lesser ranks of the Scottish royal family and acquire rich lands in southern England, becoming very wealthy and well-connected Anglo-Scottish noblemen. Meanwhile, relations between the two kingdoms improve so that there is no longer any question of the Bruces having to choose between their two royal masters. But the dangers of restricting inheritance of lands, property and titles to sons or grandsons begin to haunt the Scottish royal family, who vehemently deny claims of overlordship from English kings when they go south to swear oaths of loyalty for their English lands.

Seal of David, earl of Huntingdon, grandson of David I of Scotland, c.1160.

It was the fourth Robert Bruce of Annandale who secured the marriage that would propel his descendants into the history books. At some point after 1210, he was given permission to marry Isabella, second daughter of David, earl of Huntingdon, grandson of David I and King William's younger brother [see *Figure 3*]. Though Earl David was, since the birth of Prince Alexander in 1198, no longer heir to the throne, his daughters were still excellent catches and Isabella's elder sister married Bruce's western neighbour, Alan, lord of Galloway, while her younger one settled for an English lord, Sir Henry Hastings. But none of them had any inkling as to just how momentous these matches would ultimately prove to be.

For King William, marrying his brother's daughters to lords of the south-west (Annandale and Galloway) was supposed to bind them closer to the Scottish crown, just as the marriage of Robert (2)'s eldest son with William's daughter was meant to wean the Bruce family off their habit of siding with England's kings. There was, of course, no guarantee that the strategy would work, but this time it did. Robert (3) had remained loyal when the aging Scottish king rode out with his army against King John of England in 1209, even supplying one of his younger sons as a hostage for William's good behaviour; seven years later, Robert (4) joined a Scottish force occupying Cumberland as the new Scottish king, Alexander II, marched down through England, also against King John. The third and fourth lords of Annandale were now more loyal to their Scottish, rather than English, interests simply because these were by far the more important. But that was about to change.

Robert (4) and Isabella of Huntingdon had a son about 1220. When the boy was about ten, his father died, but his mother lived on for several decades, her great landed wealth giving her the luxury of not remarrying. As niece of King William of Scotland and great-granddaughter of David I, Isabella presumably instilled in her eldest son what it meant to be a member of the wider Scottish royal family. It was certainly something that 'Robert the Noble' – as Robert (5) was known for most of his life – felt very keenly.[24]

All the same, some of Robert (5)'s later wealth and status came to him through sheer luck. In 1237 the vagaries of medieval life and death struck once again when Isabella's youngest sibling and only brother, John, earl of Huntingdon, died without leaving any children of his own. Isabella and her sisters divided up amongst them his great English estates as well as the lucrative properties in Scotland given to their father, Earl David, by his brother, King William.

When his mother died in 1252, Robert (5) inherited her share of these lands. In Scotland this meant the prosperous trading port of Dundee on the east coast and part of the rich arable lordship of Garioch in Aberdeenshire eighty-five miles to the north; in England they amounted to a nice package of lands that included Writtle and Hatfield Broadoak in

Essex deep in the grain-rich south. The marriage between Isabella of Huntingdon and Robert (4) ultimately pushed the Bruces back into a much closer relationship with English kings. Now they became prominent cross-border nobles in the mould of their forefather, Robert (1), with all the opportunities – and potential conflicts – that serving two masters naturally brought with it.[25]

But there was potentially far more to this inheritance than mere lands. In March 1238, only nine months after John of Huntingdon's childless death, the king of Scotland, Alexander II, lost his wife. Whatever his personal feelings towards his dead queen, Alexander's major concern was the fact that he and Joan had, like John, failed to produce any children, never mind the son they – and the kingdom – needed above all else. Into this potentially disastrous breach supposedly stepped young Robert (5).

Admittedly Robert's mother was the *second* daughter of Earl David of Huntingdon, who represented the nearest alternative line of succession should the main royal line fail. But her elder sister Margaret, married to the lord of Galloway, had produced only a girl, Dervorguilla. Naturally, at a time when the king must protect his people at the head of an army, an adult male was preferable to a woman even of the senior line and so Bruce was chosen as Alexander's heir, for the short-term at least, in front of a gathering of Scottish magnates – or so Robert (5) claimed half a century later, though he could show nothing to prove it.[26]

In fact, the king soon married again and fathered a son three years later, putting paid to any momentary flight of fancy that Robert (5) might inherit a crown. But even before that happy event, indeed even before Bruce was allegedly named as heir to the throne, Dervorguilla of Galloway gave birth to a son of her own. Her husband was John Balliol, an important nobleman with extensive estates in the north-east of England centred on Barnard Castle. At this point in time, neither the Bruces nor the Balliols had any particular reason to imagine that the direct line of descent from David I would fail. But in the event that it did, the arrangement supposedly agreed between Alexander and Robert (5) in 1238 would inevitably face a challenge from Bruce's tiny Balliol cousin from the elder line once Dervorguilla's son had grown to manhood.[27]

Nevertheless, as a scion of the royal house of Scotland, Robert (5) was sufficiently attractive to marry into a top-rung English family two years later. Isabella de Clare's father was the earl of Gloucester, while her mother was a daughter of the earl of Pembroke who, as her second husband, married Richard of Cornwall, King Henry III's brother. Through this second Isabella, the Bruces acquired yet another southern English property, the village of Ripe in Sussex. Together, these southern English estates provided far easier access to the seat of English government at Westminster – and therefore to the English king himself – than the Bruces' northern English lands ever could.

Figure 3: line of descent from David, earl of Huntingdon

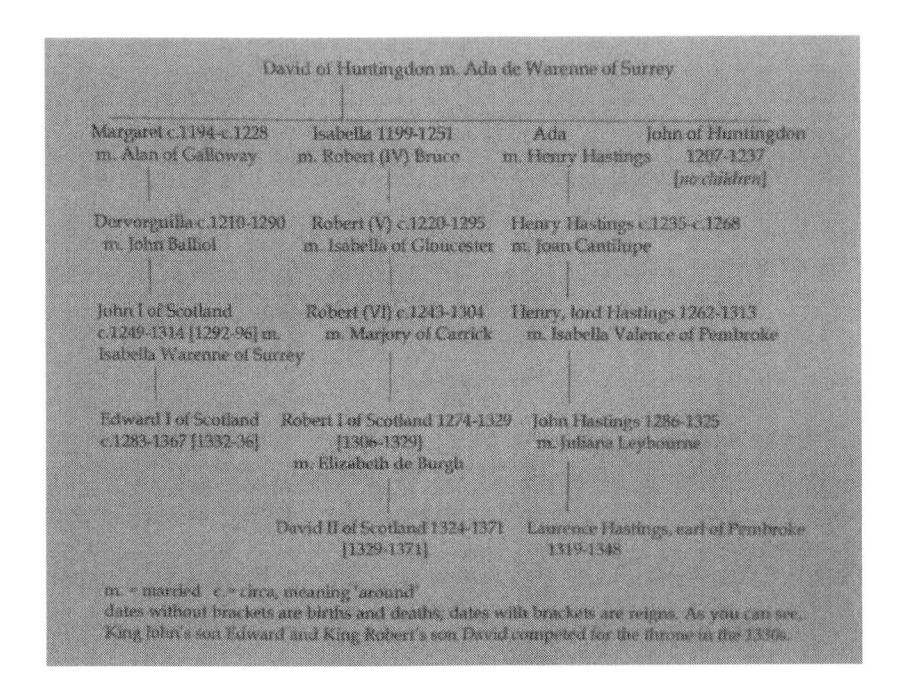

```
                David of Huntingdon m. Ada de Warenne of Surrey
                                      |
   ┌──────────────────┬──────────────────┬──────────────┬──────────────────┐
Margaret c.1194-c.1228  Isabella 1199-1251   Ada           John of Huntingdon
m. Alan of Galloway     m. Robert (IV) Bruce  m. Henry Hastings  1207-1237
                                                              [no children]
       |                        |                    |
Dervorguilla c.1210-1290  Robert (V) c.1220-1295  Henry Hastings c.1235-c.1268
m. John Balliol           m. Isabella of Gloucester  m. Joan Cantilupe
       |                        |                    |
John I of Scotland        Robert (VI) c.1243-1304  Henry, lord Hastings 1262-1313
c.1249-1314 [1292-96] m.  m. Marjory of Carrick   m. Isabella Valence of Pembroke
Isabella Warenne of Surrey
       |                        |                    |
Edward I of Scotland      Robert I of Scotland 1274-1329  John Hastings 1286-1325
c.1283-1367 [1332-36]     [1306-1329]                     m. Juliana Leybourne
                          m. Elizabeth de Burgh
                                |                           |
                          David II of Scotland 1324-1371   Laurence Hastings, earl of Pembroke
                          [1329-1371]                       1319-1348
```

m. = married c. = circa, meaning 'around'
dates without brackets are births and deaths; dates with brackets are reigns. As you can see, King John's son Edward and King Robert's son David competed for the throne in the 1330s.

****

During the 1230s and 1240s, Robert (5) could often be found acting as a typical lord of Annandale, holding courts, making and receiving grants of property, usually in the company of local families, as well as local churchmen and members of his own household, including his steward, Sir Robert Herries, his clerk, William of Annan, and his physician, Adam of Kirkcudbright.[28] By 1243, he had also fulfilled one of his most important responsibilities by fathering a son. A year later, he was one of those Scottish nobles who swore that Walter Comyn had not attacked King

Henry of England's lands in Ireland, coming third on the list of witnesses after two earls.[29] A few months later, he did the same for Alexander II, who promised not to make war against Henry in return for an agreement that the English king's four-year old daughter would marry the Scottish king's three-year old son. Once again Robert (5)'s status as a major Scottish landowner was confirmed by his place as first after the earls.[30]

And yet he was clearly not at the heart of Scottish government and politics, but that was presumably out of choice. This was in marked contrast to another family of Norman extraction which also came to England from Normandy before moving into Scotland. The Comyns, like the Bruces, arrived in the north in the reign of David I. However, as the descendants of Norman clerks rather than landowners, they did so by serving the king directly, William Comyn becoming the Scottish king's chancellor – responsible for the issuing of charters and other aspects of state bureaucracy – around 1133.

They were well rewarded for their service, their landholding portfolio reaching further and further north over the following decades until, by 1212, another William Comyn acquired Buchan in the north-east of the kingdom through marriage with its heiress, the first Scot of non-native origins to bag himself an earldom [see *Figure 5*]. This William seems to have spent much of his time attending the king when he wasn't putting down unrest in other parts of the north, extending his own holdings into the strategically vital lordship of Badenoch at the same time.[31] Such energetic and proactive royal service was a rather different approach to acquiring wealth and power from that adopted by the Bruces.

But even Robert (5) was forced into politics during the difficult minority of Alexander III, who succeeded at the age of only seven after his father's unexpected death in the summer of 1249. The possibility of a boy-king, not to mention a woman or girl, was the price to be paid for restricting the crown to sons or grandsons, a custom that took root in Scotland after the death of David I in 1153. This was the first time that the issue had come out into the open. It was, despite everything, a sign of political maturity, a decisive acceptance of the crown's authority even if the king himself was not able to wield it effectively, in this case because of his age. In the past, such weakness would have tempted a brother or cousin to seize the throne for himself.

To be fair, the Scots were not alone in finding minorities tricky as kingdoms across Western Europe faced the somewhat inevitable tendency for such political vacuums to be filled by factions that an adult king should usually be able to control. Given that Alexander III was not going to reach formal adulthood for quite some time (thirteen years, as it turned out), the internal tussle for power was fairly inevitable.

In the immediate aftermath of Alexander II's unexpected death, Alan Durward, Scotland's senior lawman (justiciar) and husband of the new king's illegitimate half-sister, took the initiative, presiding over the boy's inauguration at Scone. But Walter Comyn, earl of Menteith – son of the Comyn earl of Buchan – was not going to let Durward take the spoils that went with control of the king so easily. However, he had a problem – though a powerful and wealthy nobleman, he scarcely wielded the natural authority of the most senior and long-established earls of Scotland such as Fife or Strathearn; nor was he a member of the extended royal family which might have justified any attempt to act in Alexander's name.

But he knew a man who was. Around the end of July, only two weeks after Alexander's inauguration, Walter Comyn was at Dryfesdale in Annandale only a few miles from Lochmaben castle, along with his half-brother, Alexander, earl of Buchan, and his cousin John, the lord of Badenoch [see *Figure 5*]. Given Robert (5)'s royal blood, Comyn must have gone to him for help, a request that the lord of Annandale considered in his 'full court,' some of his loyal knights at his side.[32]

Robert (5) chose not to throw in his lot with the Comyns, who soon stole the young king away from Durward without his help anyway. In truth, the normal business of government continued much as it had done before the old king's death. There were even carefully orchestrated displays of national unity, such as the ceremony at Dunfermline Abbey in 1250 to reinter in a specially-designed tomb the remains of Margaret, wife of Malcolm III and mother of David I, who had just been made a saint.[33] The Scots had to make the most of this honour as the pope still refused to grant their kings the right to be crowned and anointed – an unassailable recognition of full sovereignty – because Henry of England stubbornly maintained that he was Alexander's overlord.

This fundamental difference of opinion came to a head two years later when it was finally time for the ten-year old Scottish king to marry his eleven-year-old English fiancée, an arrangement that had been made by their fathers almost as soon as they were born to finally settle the question of the Anglo-Scottish border that had long been a cause for war between the two kingdoms. The nobles and senior clergy of Scotland headed en masse for York, where the Minster was in the final throes of a major rebuilding programme in the latest, extravagant Gothic style. Here King

Henry III of England and a great gathering of English, Scots and French – friends and family of Alexander's mother, Marie de Coucy – put on a splendid show over the course of three days of celebration intermixed with a little necessary business.

On Christmas day, the boy king and twenty other young men put on their finery to receive the belt of knighthood from Henry himself. The following day, the feast of St Stephen, was dedicated to the wedding, the nobility vying with each other and 'glorying in their silk and variegated ornaments, that the worldly and wanton vanity of the scene, if it were to be described in full, would produce wonder and weariness in those who heard it.' The king and queen of England were of course the most glorious of all, dressed in heavy silk trimmed with gold braid, with mantles [*long, loose, sleeve-less coats*] furred with ermine, while their eldest son, twelve-year old Prince Edward, and his entourage shone in 'tabards of cloth of gold embroidered with the royal leopards.'[34]

The next day, the glorious company reassembled in yet another set of new outfits. The business of this day was rather more serious, of the kind that, from a Scottish point of view, was best done quickly. And so King Alexander placed his smooth little hands between those of his new father-in-law and swore to become Henry's man for life for his lands in England, estates that included the Liberty of Tyndale in Northumberland and the Honour of Penrith less than forty miles to the south-west in Cumberland. And that, so far as the Scots were concerned, was that.

But, much to their surprise, Henry was not finished, demanding that Alexander perform the same act of homage, this time for his kingdom. Not only that, but the Scottish king was to acknowledge, by placing his hand on a book and swearing a solemn oath, that he would be faithful to 'his lord, the king of the English', to whom he owed this allegiance, 'as his predecessors had done, as is plainly written in the Chronicles in many parts.'

If Alexander was intimidated, then he did not show it, presumably because his advisers had primed him for just such a possibility. In his high, unbroken voice, he piped up firmly that 'he had come there peacefully and for the honour of the king of England, and by his command, that by means of the marriage-tie he might ally himself to him, and not to give him an answer on such a difficult question. For he had not, he said, held full deliberation on this matter with his nobles, or taken proper counsel, as so difficult a question required.' Henry, no doubt taken aback that he had failed to win out over so youthful an opponent, nonetheless thought twice about allowing this disagreement to 'throw a cloud over such a calm and peaceful festival, or to trouble so young a king and his still more youthful wife', passing over the awkward moment in silence.[35] But the point had been made and taking careful note nearby was Henry's son, Prince Edward, who certainly never forgot it.

Henry and his wife were loath to part with their daughter and their affection and concern for their son-in-law, whom they seem to have regarded as an innocent lamb among Scottish wolves, was no doubt genuine. But the English king was also an incorrigible meddler and he now combined natural inclination with political expediency, using any and every opportunity to interfere in Scottish politics on behalf of the royal children. At the same time, the Comyn and Durward factions within Scotland were happy to appeal to him as an ally, though Henry accused them both of causing havoc and mayhem at different times. Three years after the celebrations at York, he decided he'd had enough of the Comyns, who then had control of the young king. Alexander and Margaret were spirited away from Edinburgh castle in September 1255 on behalf of a coalition of Scottish nobles prepared to back a coup-d'etat.

Robert (5) was one of them. He was even prepared to join the bishops of Dunkeld and Aberdeen, the earls of Fife, Dunbar, Strathearn and Carrick and eight other barons who now became Alexander's 'Council, Regents of the kingdom, and Guardians of himself and his Queen' for a term of seven years, by which time the Scottish king would be twenty-one and quite old enough to govern by himself.[36] However, the Comyns were far from beaten and two years later they got their hands on Alexander yet again.

But by now they realised that the boy-king was growing up and likely to take a dim view of being tossed between his warring nobles; it was time to settle their differences and run the country with their rivals for the five years that remained of the minority. And as the Scottish king began to assume the reins of government himself, Robert (5) and John Comyn of Badenoch decided to hedge their bets, both men joining the English king's household in 1262 for an annual fee of £50 (over £40,000 today).[37]

By this time, it was Henry who found himself at the mercy of fractious nobles, who had had enough of his arbitrary approach to government. Their leader was Simon de Montfort, an Anglo-French nobleman who had once been very close to the king, who was also his brother-in-law. In June 1258 de Montfort and Robert (5)'s nephew, the earl of Gloucester, led a group of nobility to parliament and forced Henry to hand over power to them. Six years later, this uneasy arrangement deteriorated into outright civil war.

Now it was the English king's turn to seek help and 'a host of Scots', including his two household knights, Robert (5) and 'the illustrious' John Comyn, as well as Dervorguilla of Galloway's husband, John Balliol, fought alongside Henry and Prince Edward at the battle of Lewes in May 1264. Henry lost that battle and both Bruce and Comyn found themselves locked up in Dover castle. Languishing in prison, Robert (5) was forced to rely on the diplomatic skills of his twenty-one year old son, who nonetheless managed to negotiate the ransom for his release within five months – probably with the help of his mother, Isabella of Gloucester - with two supporters of de Monfort, his cousin, the earl of Gloucester, and his father's younger brother Bernard.[38]

Less than a year later, the Bruce fortunes were once more on the up. Prince Edward, who had been kept as a hostage in Hereford castle near the Welsh border after Lewes, managed to escape and on 4 August 1265 his army defeated and killed de Montfort at the battle of Evesham.[39] As members of the winning side but with the costs of a ransom to recoup, Robert (5) and his son were eager to take revenge on the losers in what was pretty much a land-grab.[40] At the same time, King Henry made Robert (5) his keeper of Carlisle castle,[41] which lay only nineteen miles from Annandale, the first indication that Bruce may have been trying to create what was in effect a mini cross-border empire. It had been a rocky few years, but the family had once more emerged relatively unscathed, ready to take full advantage of the years of peace and strong family ties between the Scottish and English crowns.

****

Robert (5) was now approaching his fifties, but gave no hint of slowing down. Indeed, he was about to embark on the most risky and adventurous period of his life. His son, Robert (6), was now a man and more than ready for marriage, but such domestic matters were eclipsed by a far greater concern – the Eighth Crusade, called by King Louis IX of France in 1270 in what proved to be his last attempt to try to breathe new life into the enfeebled Christian kingdom of Jerusalem.

Prince Edward took the cross in 1268 and, though he would not leave England until August 1270, there was nothing half-hearted or cynical about his commitment to this great medieval obsession at a time when

England could scarcely afford either his absence, with his father, King Henry, now in his sixties, or the cost of his adventure so soon after the civil war.[42] But his example proved a potent one, attracting nobles from both sides of the Anglo-Scottish border to join up with him.

It was Robert (6) who initially jumped at the chance, receiving a safe conduct to travel with the prince, who was only four years his elder, in 1270. However, he seems to have decided – or had his father decide for him – to stay put on the family's southern English estates, basing himself at his favourite manor of Writtle in Essex. And so Robert (5) was free to make the arduous trip to the Holy Land himself, along with a retinue that may have included his faithful physician, Master Adam of Kirkcudbright, his steward, Sir Robert Herries, his clerk, William of Ayr, and another Annandale knight, Sir Adam Torthorwald.[43]

It was never destined to be a glorious affair; King Louis died of disease, which was rife in his army, at Tunis in North Africa on 25 August 1270, five days after Prince Edward's fleet left England. The rest of the crusading armies turned back, but the prince was not for giving up, pushing on to Acre in the Levant. Realistically, though, he had little or no chance of success without a much bigger army and by the autumn of 1272 he began the long journey home. By the time he reached Italy, he learned first of the death of his eldest son John and then of Henry himself. Edward returned home a grieving father and son as well as England's new king, the first for nearly sixty years.

Robert (5) may have felt that he achieved rather more from his travels, using the opportunity to expiate the sins of his great-grandfather, Robert (2), who had so offended Malachy, bishop of Down over 130 years earlier. The saint was buried at Clairvaux, the great monastery in north-eastern France where he had died en route to Rome. Robert (5) paid his respects at Malachy's tomb, promising to fund candles to be lit around it for all eternity. And then, finally, he came home to find that his wife, Isabella of Gloucester, was dead too.

To be honest, this presented him with an opportunity, as had the marriage of his son. The plan to secure a most desirable bride for Robert (6) probably occurred to Robert (5) while he was at Acre, where he learned of the death of a fellow crusading Scot, Adam of Kilconquhar. Adam was a junior member of the family of the earls of Fife who had done well for himself by marrying Marjory, only child of Neil, earl of Carrick. But now the young countess was back on the marriage market, with the prospect of an earldom coming with her to her prospective husband. It is tempting to believe the story that it was the physical charms of Robert (6), sent to tell Marjory of the death of her first husband, who so captivated her that she kept him in her castle of Turnberry until he agreed to marry her. While presenting the twenty-nine year old Bruce heir in a less than forceful light (unlike Marjory), the whole episode does put a nicely romantic spin on the marriage that produced Robert (7), the future king.

But really, this was the Bruces making a smart strategic move and quickly, even before Robert (5) reached home, in case anyone else got to the girl first. But the old crusader seems to have overreached himself in his enthusiasm for the match, for he neglected to send for permission from Alexander III, the marriage of any heiress to lands held directly of the crown being the king's to dole out to those whom he wished to reward or favour. When Alexander found out, he immediately took Turnberry castle and Marjory's other lands and property into his hands, but thankfully 'By means of the prayers of friends ... and' – far more to the point – 'by a certain sum of money agreed upon, this Robert gained the king's goodwill, and the whole domain.'[44] The Bruces finally had an earldom.

And it was a bonny one too, where, according to a later description, 'The land ... rises into gentle hills, well adapted for pasture, and not unfavourable for grain. The whole country not only abounds in the riches of the earth, and of the ocean, sufficient for the supply of its own inhabitants, but they have also large quantities to spare for their neighbours.'[45] Carrick looks west across the Irish Sea to Ireland where its earls had been given lands stretching from Olderfleet to Upper Glenarm, with other small properties near Coleraine and Port Stewart by King John of England.[46] Although at home in the Norman French world that so shaped the culture of western Europe, Marjory's ancestors had been just as at ease with the native Irish aristocracy and their west Highland and Hebridean cousins whose language and customs they shared too. This all represented a satisfyingly new landscape of opportunity for the Bruces.

*****

At first glance, the woman on whom Robert (5)'s eye alighted for himself was far less obviously appealing than his son's countess, not to mention his own exalted first wife. The widow of the sheriff of Northumberland, Christina hailed from Cumberland, bringing her new husband a suite of lands in both counties, including her family estate of Ireby eighteen miles south-west of Carlisle and some fifty miles south of the Bruce port of Annan. The attraction for Robert (5) was no doubt the excellent Cumbrian hill country that was at least as alluring as illustrious family connections, the only downside being that Robert (6) didn't share his father's enthusiasm for the match, later alleging (unsuccessfully) that the marriage was improper.[47] Over the following decades, Robert (5) and Christina dedicated themselves to protecting and expanding their property in the area, taking on other Cumbrian families in the English courts rather than on the battlefield.[48]

He probably needed the money. As well as trying to recoup the cost of his ransom, crusading did not come cheap when there were no spoils of war to compensate. And though English lands were profitable, the Crown took its cut every time a new heir entered the property and could use debts to the royal treasury as a means of applying pressure. In 1275 Robert (5) was told to stump up £238 11 shillings 7 ½ pence (around £172,400 today) for ongoing debts to the English king or have his livestock and other goods seized, though Edward showed sufficient gratitude towards a fellow crusader to split the payment and give him more time to make it.[49] The Bruces were a wealthy family, but as they rose through the ranks of the English aristocracy, their costs soared too.

On the other hand, there were potential rewards to be had from the English king's wars, of which there would prove to be no end during the reign of Edward I. As relations between England and Wales deteriorated in the 1270s, thanks in no small part to Edward's provocative disregard for Welsh law and custom and the abuses of his own officials, both Robert (5) and (6) went on campaign there.

Robert (6) served in the 1280s too,[50] which clearly impressed the English king. In September 1281, as Edward's 'bachelor' – the lowest rank of knighthood – he was loaned £40 (c.£34,000) because he was 'in want of money at present;' in April 1283 he was given custody of the castle and county of Carlisle like his father before him, though he would lose it only two years later for failing to present his accounts.[51] Robert (6) certainly could not be described as the most dedicated and reliable of royal servants, but he was very good at spending money.

At the same time, the younger Bruce was also trusted by Alexander III, even if he did not spend much time at the Scottish court. In July 1277 he was one of four Scottish envoys sent to Edward, Alexander's brother-in-law, to respond to the latter's 'request' that the Scottish king finally come south to endure the gentle palaver that was the offering of his homage and fealty.[52] Both men must have had strong recollections of the awkward moment twenty-five years earlier when Henry III had sought to pressurise ten-year old Alexander into adding his kingdom to the list of possessions he held of the king of England.

The Scottish king finally set off on the long ride to London in the autumn of 1278. Unlike his trip south to Edward's coronation four years earlier, this time he waived any right to his expenses, having once again extracted an assurance that his trip should not be viewed as implying inferior status, that he came because he wished to. This ceremony was not all glamour and feasting as both kings sought to defend their rights as they saw them without falling out. The question raised by King Henry back in 1252 about the status of the kingdom of Scotland had not gone away, but with such a fundamental difference of opinion on the subject, it was no nearer a resolution.

In the end, King Edward claimed that he and his heirs could, if they wished, bring up a demand for homage for the kingdom of Scotland in the future, while King Alexander stoutly asserted in response that 'no-one has the right except God alone, nor do I hold it except of God alone.' And certainly he was allowed, as a mark of his royal status, to have someone else perform the act of fealty – the oath of loyalty – in his stead, just as Henry III had used a proxy in 1259 for that particular bit of the ceremony after he had done homage for his lands of Aquitaine and Gascony to the French king, Louis IX, 'to avoid the derogation from his majesty which swearing in person would have implied.'[53] These were 'interesting' times for notions of what it meant to be a king, especially if that king happened to hold land in somebody else's kingdom.

The person Alexander chose to stand in his stead was Robert (6). Speaking in Norman French, the language of the aristocratic elite of western Europe, the thirty-five year old earl of Carrick swore 'upon his soul in these words:—"So may God help me, and these holy things: my lord the king of Scotland, who is here, will be faithful to you in life and limb and earthly honour; and will keep secret your counsels.'[54]

Robert (6)'s usefulness on this particular occasion probably stemmed from his familiarity with the language and culture of the English court, but he did his duty by Alexander on enough high-profile occasions to suggest that his relationship with the Scottish king went further than that. He may not have turned up to the Scottish court very often, but before he and the king headed south they were both at Roxburgh with more regular courtiers, working out a strategy to rebuff any potential English attempts to insert weasel French words into the homage ceremony that might compromise Scotland's status. Robert (5), as the senior member of the family and equally at home in England, not to mention allegedly, if briefly, heir to the throne forty years earlier, might have wondered why he was not chosen for this high-profile role. However, his son had one important attribute that his father did not; Robert (6) was an earl, and status was everything when standing in for a king.[55]

This time Alexander went to England without his wife, Edward's sister Margaret. The queen – predictably reputed to have been 'a woman of great beauty, chastity, and humility – three [qualities] seldom united in one individual' – died at Cupar in Fife in February 1275 at the age of only thirty-five and was buried in Dunfermline Abbey, which was already acting as the Scottish royal family's mausoleum.[56] At least there was comfort to be taken from the fact that she had done her duty in producing a daughter and two sons, and so Alexander did not feel under pressure to remarry immediately, supposedly enjoying his new-found bachelor status.[57]

Alas, in 1281 the king's younger son, Prince David, died at Stirling aged only nine. Later Scottish chroniclers, knowing what would follow, saw the boy's death as 'the beginning of Scotland's sorrows to come. Alas! Woe worth the day, Scotland! For, even though you had known that so many days of mourning and tears were in store for you, evils so great are hastening upon you without fail, That, if you knew, you never could think to bear them.'[58]

Two years later David's sister Margaret, wife of the Norwegian king, did not long survive the birth of her daughter, another Margaret. But most calamitous was the death in January 1284 of Prince Alexander, only four days shy of his twentieth birthday. Though he had been married to the daughter of the Count of Flanders for over a year, the couple had no children. King Edward, whose eleven-year old son Alphonso would soon become the third of his sons to die, leaving him with only new-born Prince Edward and a clutch of daughters, wrote from his heart when he assured his brother-in-law Alexander that, despite this terrible loss, 'we are united together perpetually, God willing, by a link of indissolvable love.'[59] The line of David I, which had ruled Scotland for over 150 years, was looking most precarious.

Chapter Three

Two funerals and a (potential) wedding

In which the unexpected death of Alexander III without a male heir persuades Robert (5) to try for the throne by fair means and foul, unleashing a short-lived civil war on Scotland. To avoid any repetition of this, Scotland's leaders enlist the help of Edward I of England to persuade King Eric of Norway to send over his daughter, King Alexander's granddaughter and now his heir. Eric and Edward agree that the little Maid should marry the English king's only son, a prospect that promises peace and stability for the Scots. Meanwhile, the youngest Robert Bruce – number 7 – grows up in obscurity in Scotland, southern England and possibly either Ireland or the north-west Highlands.

The island of Ailsa Craig with the ruins of Turnberry Castle in the foreground.

According to a chronicler writing many years later, those reckless lovebirds, Robert (6) and Marjory, countess of Carrick, soon produced a son 'who was to be the saviour, champion, and king of the distressed Scottish people, as the course of history will show forth, and his father's name, Robert, was given to him.' But even this brief, ecstatic eulogy was not enough for the writer, who, safe in the knowledge of the extraordinary career that the baby would one day embark upon and eager to explain to the world that his birth was all part of God's plan, added:

> In twelve hundred and seventy four years
> since Christ our manhood wore,
> And at the feast when Benedict died,
> That noble knight, King Robert, saw the light,
> Called from the womb by Heaven's almighty judgement.[60]

But an awful lot of water had to flow under the bridge before anyone could imagine that the seventh Robert Bruce should be trusted with Scotland's destiny.

It would, however, be in keeping with the supposedly romantic origins of his parents' marriage to imagine that the future king was born on 11 July 1274 in his mother's windswept castle of Turnberry on the Carrick coast. The truth may be unpalatable for some, for a chronicler from southern England states categorically that Robert belonged to 'the English nation' and, more specifically, that he came into this world surrounded by the pleasant meadows, vineyards, grass and grain of Essex at the manor of Writtle so beloved of his father.[61] He was probably the third child of ten – though we don't even know that for sure - at least two elder sisters arriving before him.

Robert's upbringing, about which we know almost nothing directly, was bound to have been a conventional one in many ways, designed to mould him into an Anglo-Scottish nobleman capable of serving effectively in the armies of two kings and managing his landed interests across Scotland, England and Ireland. The skills involved – from knightly pursuits to overseeing the administration of properties ranging from upland sheep runs through prime arable land and much in between – required many years of training. Preparations for knighthood alone, which a young nobleman might generally expect to achieve after the age of twenty-one, began at an early age to allow muscles and habits of service and loyalty to be honed into an instinctive way of life.

One of the first things that the future king would have learned to do was ride a horse, an expensive piece of kit which, according to one thirteenth-century commentator, was the most obvious way in which

'...princes, magnates and knights are separated from lesser people and ... a lord cannot fittingly be seen amongst private citizens except through the mediation of a horse.'[62] But this was not just for show. In the heat and noise of battle or tournament, a knight had to move quickly and carefully, turning if necessary in a confined space and providing enough reassurance to the animal beneath him so as to allow both to hang on to the discipline required to bring victory.

Training, first with the *pell* – a stake set into the ground – and then, when mounted, with the *quintain* – a target on a post that sometimes swung if struck – was the kind of practice that a young man would go out and do again and again so that he might become strong and agile, capable of judging distance and of protecting himself even in the flush of a victorious strike (since the quintain might bash his retreating head if he wasn't quick enough). He would also playfight with his companions, using wooden sticks, just as youngsters do today, or blunt weapons, and it is not difficult to imagine Robert (7) sparring with his younger brothers, especially Neil, who was probably closest to him in age. We might also imagine him as a young squire serving his father at dinner, for such menial tasks were part and parcel of a knight's training to serve and in no way detracted from his noble status.[63]

And yet we find no record of him participating in any of the military exploits that his father and grandfather were certainly involved in during the later 1280s and even the early 1290s, during which time he himself became a knight. Indeed, it is hard to point to any battle or even skirmish prior to his inauguration as king in 1306 and be absolutely sure that he fought in it, that he put into action the training instilled in him as a youth.

This stands in stark contrast to another, rather more unexpected, aspect of his childhood and upbringing, which *is* alluded to in stories of his life and shared somewhat more certainly with his brothers. It was traditional among the old families of the Celtic parts of Scotland and Ireland to which the earldom of Carrick belonged to send their sons away to be fostered with another family of suitable status to which they were allied, or wished to be. The bond between the young man and his foster parents and siblings was supposed to be as close as if they shared the same blood and Robert's foster-brother would reputedly give his life at his side during the dark and terrible days when he sought to recover his throne several decades later.[64]

Though we have nothing to help us to identify the family, Robert's familiarity with, and even – if the choice of the custom-built home created in the last years of his life is anything to go by – love for, the Irish Sea world makes it highly likely that he spent at least part of his youth immersed in the language, the music and poetry, and the very different military culture of the Gaelic West Highlands. Or he may have been sent to Ireland itself, given that his mother's mother was probably an O'Neill princess of Tyrone and his second wife was the daughter of the Anglo-Irish de Burgh earl of Ulster. Certainly it was said that Bruce's younger brother Edward was fostered in Ireland.[65]

Nor should we presume that this novel aspect of the upbringing of a new generation of young Bruces can be solely attributed to the influence of their 'Celtic' mother, Countess Marjory, who has left us nothing to help us confirm or deny such an assumption. But we do know that her husband, Robert (6), had begun to immerse himself in the opportunities offered by the Irish west, sending his men regularly to Ireland to purchase wine (no doubt imported, as it had been for centuries), grain and other foodstuffs, presumably to be transported back to Carrick.[66]

But there was one vital element of noble life that was relished by aristocrats of all backgrounds. Hunting was not just a sociable pursuit that made it so much more pleasant to do deals, make friends and influence people in a similar way to playing golf today; it was first and foremost an enjoyable way of keeping up those skills of weaponry and horsemanship so essential to the knightly class. Robert liked to hunt as much as anyone else – his manor at Cardross was kitted out with all the necessary accoutrements in the years before he died.[67]

The medieval nobility relied on men and dogs to flush out their prey and drive it to wherever they were waiting on horseback, a practice that would not have proved of much use when the future king was reduced to skulking in the hills as an outlaw in 1306-7. But it is tempting to imagine that he did learn how to track and kill a deer himself, as well as how to fish from local streams and when nuts and berries would be in season.[68] Nobles, whether brought up in the Anglo-Norman tradition or the Gaelic one, were trained to be tough; even though they might go on campaign with tents and a team of domestic staff, they could rough it if need be, as even Edward I did in 1298 when he bedded down on the ground next to his horse.[69] But growing up in both traditions may well have given the future king an even greater array of skills, a more inventive and resourceful outlook and a wider band of friends and allies than a more conventional Bruce upbringing.

And it is fitting, perhaps, that we meet him for the first time in the company of men who also made light of the divide between the Gaelic and the Anglo-Norman worlds that had so appalled the first Robert Bruce and his compatriots 150 years earlier. Aged around 10, the future king accompanied his father to an important meeting with the powerful Hebridean lord, Alasdair Óg Macdonald of Islay, around 1283/4. Alasdair Óg wished to confirm a charter granting the church of Kilkerran in Kintyre to Paisley Abbey recently gifted by his father. Given that the islands off western Scotland had been acquired by the Scottish crown from Norway only in 1266 and Alasdair Óg himself had been sent to Alexander III as a hostage for the good behaviour of the independent-minded lords of the region, he was not terribly well-known in Scottish society. And so, in order to give his words greater credibility, he asked for the help of both the bishop of Argyll and Robert (6), earl of Carrick, whose seals were far more easily recognisable.[70]

Unfortunately we have no idea where this meeting took place, whether young Robert sailed with his father in one of their galleys, the short crossing from Carrick to Kintyre or even to Islay itself a mere hop and a jump by sea than the route by road even today, or whether they had to make the tortuous fifty-mile journey on horseback north to Paisley. Or perhaps they did not go anywhere at all and Alasdair Óg, along with the bishop of Argyll and the other witnesses, came to them at Turnberry. Though the relationship between the Macdonalds and the Bruces did not always run smoothly, in the next few years both families were keen to work together.

****

As Robert and his sisters and brothers negotiated their almost entirely undocumented way through childhood, the storm clouds began to gather over Scotland. King Alexander may have thought that the succession was safe with three children to console him after the death of his wife in 1275, but by 1284 they had all followed her to the grave and he and his kingdom found themselves perched on the edge of a dynastic catastrophe. Forty-three year old Alexander may have reminded himself that his own father had reached the same grand age and been on to his second marriage when his heir was conceived, but there was now no more time to waste.

Figure 4: the Scottish royal family and its relationship with the English royal family to 1290

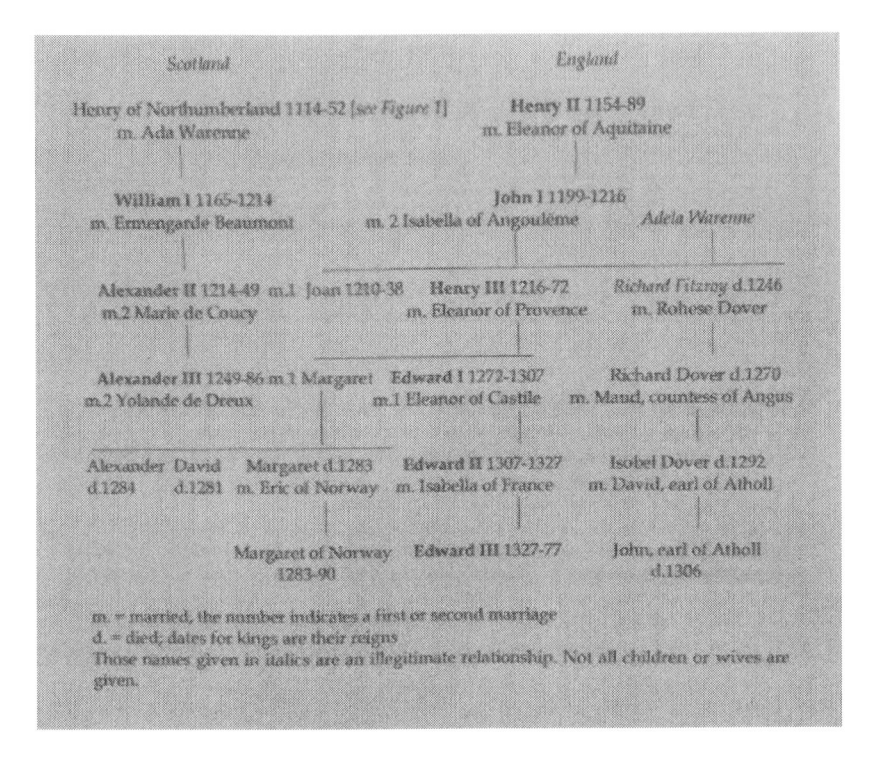

```
                        Scotland                                    England

        Henry of Northumberland 1114-52 [see Figure 1]        Henry II 1154-89
              m. Ada Warenne                                  m. Eleanor of Aquitaine
                      |                                              |
          William I 1165-1214                    John I 1199-1216
         m. Ermengarde Beaumont              m. 2 Isabella of Angoulême      Adela Warenne
                      |                                    |                        |
        Alexander II 1214-49 m.1 Joan 1210-38   Henry III 1216-72         Richard Fitzroy d.1246
        m.2 Marie de Coucy                      m. Eleanor of Provence    m. Rohese Dover
                      |                                    |                        |
        Alexander III 1249-86 m.1 Margaret   Edward I 1272-1307          Richard Dover d.1270
        m.2 Yolande de Dreux                 m.1 Eleanor of Castile      m. Maud, countess of Angus
                      |                                    |                        |
       Alexander  David    Margaret d.1283   Edward II 1307-1327        Isobel Dover d.1292
       d.1284    d.1281   m. Eric of Norway  m. Isabella of France      m. David, earl of Atholl
                                |                          |                        |
                    Margaret of Norway           Edward III 1327-77      John, earl of Atholl
                        1283-90                                              d.1306
```

m. = married, the number indicates a first or second marriage
d. = died; dates for kings are their reigns
Those names given in italics are an illegitimate relationship. Not all children or wives are given.

The next step was to secure that second marriage. The king settled on Yolande – a daughter of the count de Dreux in northern France and kinswoman of his French mother, Marie de Coucy – whom he married in Jedburgh Abbey in the autumn of 1285. Alas, it was Yolande who proved Alexander's undoing, though it was scarcely her fault. 18 March 1286 began conventionally enough, with the king and his advisers meeting in Edinburgh to discuss an important matter that King Edward had asked his brother-in-law to look into. But after dining, the king – ignoring his courtiers' entreaties – rode off into the dark and stormy night, determined to reach Kinghorn, where the queen was staying. He was found the next morning within sight of his destination, his neck broken.

Scottish chroniclers, writing many years later, were united in their misery – 'How worthy of tears, and how hurtful, his death was to the kingdom of Scotland, is plainly shown forth by the evils of after times.'[71] In truth, Alexander's death was a calamity, but it was not yet a disaster. Within the forty days required for summoning a parliament,[72] the great men of Scotland met at Scone and, 'adopting sound counsel for themselves, elected from the prelates as well as the nobles, Guardians of the Peace for the community.' There were six of these Guardians – Bishop William Fraser of St Andrews, Bishop Robert Wishart of Glasgow, Duncan, earl of Fife, Alexander Comyn, earl of Buchan, James the Steward and John Comyn of Badenoch.[73]

It is immediately striking that fully one third were members of the powerful Comyn family who had been so influential during the minority of Alexander III and who continued to occupy positions of power and influence when he reached adulthood. Despite the formal pre-eminence of men like the earls of Fife and Strathearn and even the vaguely royal Bruce earl of Carrick, Comyn of Buchan and his cousin of Badenoch [see *Figure 5*] had, along with their extensive network of friends and followers, effectively run large parts of the country for decades. On the other hand, three of the Guardians – Fife, Wishart of Glasgow and James the Steward – by no means danced to their tune.

Nevertheless, this surfeit of Comyns seems to have caused Robert (5) considerable anxiety as he took stock of the magnitude of the opportunity now, most unexpectedly, presented to him in his twilight years, an opportunity that he decided to pursue with every ounce of strength, cash and influence in his possession. Though his actions after 1286 seem outrageously self-interested to us now, he was viewed as a good man at the time. A canon of Lanercost, a priory lying less than thirty miles from Annan across the English border, wrote him a glowing eulogy when he died in 1295, surely based on personal experience:

> He was of handsome appearance, a gifted speaker, remarkable for his influence, and, what is more important, most devoted to God and the clergy …It was his custom to entertain and feast more liberally than all the other courtiers, and was most hospitable to all his guests, nor used the pilgrim to remain outside his gates, for his door was open to the wayfarer.[74]

And yet, however silver his tongue, even Robert (5) must have been painfully aware of just how much of a longshot it was to persuade the Scottish political community that he had the best claim to sit on the throne so calamitously vacated. In the first place, there was still the possibility that even those few months of wedded bliss might have resulted in the queen's pregnancy and this was soon confirmed by Yolande. Secondly, many of those now gathered at Scone, including Robert (5) and his son, had only two years before sworn to accept Margaret of Norway as heir if Alexander were to die without any more children of his own.

But leaving aside both these scenarios, which would involve another long minority, why would the nation pin its hopes on a man approaching his seventies, the son of David, earl of Huntingdon's *second* daughter, when there was now an adult male candidate descended from his *first*? Dervorguilla's fourth and only surviving son, John Balliol, was still in his thirties, added to which – and this would have crossed Robert (5)'s mind – Balliol's sister Eleanor was married to one of the most powerful of the new Guardians, John Comyn, 2nd lord of Badenoch.

Robert (5) clung to the fact that he was Earl David of Huntingdon's grandson rather than his great-grandson, as John Balliol was, and that John's mother Dervorguilla was still alive in the same generation as himself – a woman to his man [see *Figure 3*]. He was, however, well aware that this held little sway with the Comyns. Roused at last to action after decades of semi-detachment from Scottish politics, the venerable lord of Annandale accosted the Scone gathering, which seems to have been considering adult male alternatives to Margaret of Norway, 'keenly contesting' that anyone but himself had a right to the Scottish throne:

The nobles of the said kingdom with its above-named Guardians kept discussing among themselves who should be made their king, but they did not presume to express what they felt about the right of succession, partly because it was a difficult and troublesome case, partly because different people felt differently about that right and vacillated repeatedly, partly because they were justifiably afraid of the power of the parties which was great and much to be feared, and partly because they had no superior who by the strength of this power could demand the execution of their decision or compel the parties to observe it.[75]

They now knew that only the child that the queen was carrying and a three-year old girl lay between Scotland and the distinct possibility of civil war. Although a Scottish deputation had been sent south, as a matter of courtesy, immediately after Alexander's funeral on 29 March, the Guardians decided that it might be prudent to seek Edward I of England's active support, since they now had reason to believe that the Bruces, at least, were keen to challenge the rights of any daughter born to the queen, as well as those of the Maid. A Scottish deputation led by Bishop Fraser of

St Andrews and despatched in August 1286 caught up with Edward in Bordeaux while he was visiting his duchy of Gascony, 'urgently beseeching him that he would deign to assist them in their leaderless condition ... until they should succeed in getting a prince regularly elected.'[76]

The Guardians' nervousness at Scotland's predicament rings true. So does the expectation on both sides of the border that any involvement Edward might have in Scotland would be time limited, just as his father's had been during the minority of Alexander III. This was a difficult moment for the northern kingdom, but everyone expected that it would pass and one day things would go back to normal.

Having been snubbed at Scone, Robert (5) seems to have realised that his years spent carefully accumulating wealth and influence in England had left him without enough important friends in Scotland. As everyone waited with bated breath for the outcome of the queen's pregnancy, he began to remedy that. Though the full extent of his machinations is lost to us now, Robert (5) gathered together a high-powered group of nobles from Scotland and Ireland at his son's castle of Turnberry on 20 September 1286. Numbering four earls (Dunbar, Menteith, his son Carrick and the Anglo-Irish Ulster), as well as his neighbour and Guardian James the Steward, his new allies Angus and Alasdair Macdonald of Islay, and his first wife's nephew Thomas de Clare, the so-called Turnberry band was, on the surface at least, an agreement binding those who sealed it to help the two Anglo-Irishmen, Ulster and de Clare, to keep the peace in the western Irish kingdom of Thomond ruled by Turlough O'Brian, a Gaelic-Irish lord, but also claimed by de Clare.[77]

If we had been a fly on Turnberry's stone walls, however, I wonder what we would have heard, for all the Scots present had good reason to be smarting at the thought of yet another long period of Comyn dominance over any government chosen to support a newborn child of Alexander's, the Maid, or – God forbid! – John Balliol. And so, while Robert (5) and his guests were careful to put in the standard caveat that any military action taken in support of the Irishmen would not be at the expense of their allegiance, as English or Irish landowners, to Edward I, considerable discussion must have preceded the same caveat afforded 'to whoever will inherit and obtain the kingdom of Scotland by reason of the blood of his predecessor, lord Alexander, king of Scotland, who recently died, according to the ancient customs allowed and commonly practised up till now in the kingdom of Scotland.'[78]

Given how complex and often contradictory the rules governing the Scottish succession actually were – a veritable maze of past precedents and royal expositions on the subject – deciding on exactly which 'ancient customs' should be used in determining the new ruler was something that Robert (5) was surely already giving his close attention. From now on he would be known as 'the Competitor.'

Robert (7), the future king, was twelve years old at this point, a formative, impressionable age. He did not seal the band, despite having witnessed Alasdair Óg Macdonald's charter two or three years earlier and even though all the Scottish lords brought sons or brothers with them in order to reinforce their family's commitment to the agreement. This strongly suggests that he was not there, perhaps because he had already been sent away to live with his foster family.

Nevertheless, two vital issues that were already consuming his grandfather and must certainly have formed at least a part of the discussions at this gathering clearly made an enduring impression on the youngest Bruce. The first was Robert (5)'s unshakeable belief in the justness of his claim to the throne. The second was the conviction, no doubt shared by all the Scots present at Turnberry, that the Comyns would, if necessary, use their dominance of Scottish politics to skew the allocation of patronage and even interfere with others' rights and property, up to and including preventing the Bruces from claiming their inheritance by catapulting Balliol on to the throne. This was, of course, a very partisan view, but it was one that would deeply divide Scottish politics for decades to come. And always lurking at the back of these fevered discussions was Edward I, still not much interested in Scotland, but a very valuable potential ally for anyone wishing to strong-arm the rest of the Scottish political community. Both Robert (5) and (6) kept in touch, sending messengers out to Gascony in late 1286 and early 1287.[79] They had no intention of leaving any stone unturned in their quest for a throne.

****

Despite the nation's prayers, in November 1286 – only two months after the meeting at Turnberry – Queen Yolande gave birth to a stillborn child.[80] Now the implications of Alexander's untimely death truly pressed down upon the Scottish political community, and with good reason. And this time Robert (5) did not wait for any gatherings where he might argue his case, but summoned the men of Annandale to follow him on a pre-emptive strike to try to forestall any attempt to establish the Maid of Norway as queen or, God forbid again!, Balliol as king.

His first target was Dumfries with its royal castle – currently held by a close ally of the Comyns, Sir William Sinclair[81] - which lay only eight miles from his own seat at Lochmaben. He followed that up swiftly by taking his cousin Dervorguilla Balliol's castle of Buittle fifteen miles further south-west. His son, Robert (6), took another force to Wigtown whose royal castle and sheriffdom was probably held by the Guardian, Alexander Comyn, earl of Buchan. Galloway had been secured in one fell swoop, the devastation wreaked by the insurgent Bruces, which left fields uncultivated and flocks scattered, causing a loss of revenues for the next two years. But the Guardians did not expect them to stop there, strengthening the defences of royal castles as far apart as Edinburgh and Ayr and raising men to defend 'the peace and tranquillity of the realm.'[82]

But it was the Bruces who blinked first. In part, it was surely their tactics – even James the Steward, who had sealed the Turnberry band and would otherwise have supported them against the Comyns, baulked at such an outright defiance of the authority of the Guardians, of which he was one. By late spring 1287, Robert (5) and his son, the earl of Carrick, had dutifully handed back Dumfries and Wigtown to the Guardians and Buittle to Dervorguilla. Order was restored, though even the Comyns thought it prudent to leave the Bruces unpunished for the chaos they had unleashed. Indeed, in some ways Robert (5)'s sword-rattling in 1286-7 paid off; everyone knew just how far he was prepared to go to further a claim that he clearly, ferociously, believed was a just one. He would not be overlooked.

But even though normal government under the Guardians was quickly resumed, the Maid's father, King Eric of Norway, was openly nervous about sending his little daughter to Scotland if there was even a whiff of civil war. On the other hand, there may have been a degree of spin in his, and Edward's, protestations of concern – emphasising the instability of the northern kingdom enhanced the English king's role as mediator, trusted by the Scots and a source of reassurance to Eric. Margaret was, after all, Edward's great-niece.[83] The Guardians – now reduced by death to four (Bishops Fraser and Wishart, John Comyn of Badenoch and James the Steward) were nonetheless eager for the English king's intervention, seeing it as key to extracting definite promises that their 'lady' would cross the North Sea to put an end to any lingering uncertainty over the succession. It was Eric they seem not to have trusted.[84]

Edward returned from Gascony in August 1289 already in the depths of his own discussions with the Norwegian king, who owed him a lot of money that Eric hoped to get back from the Scots in arrears of his late wife's dowry.[85] Two months later, three Guardians – Bishops Fraser and Wishart and John Comyn of Badenoch – with the surprise addition of Robert (5), were finally invited to travel south to Salisbury to meet with envoys from England and Norway. Their brief, according to Edward, was to discuss what needed to be done to make the kingdom safe – a stipulation that the Guardians may have felt was unnecessary and which had perhaps prompted them to take Bruce with them, to prove that point and, no doubt, to keep him out of mischief. They were also very keen to address Margaret's 'state.'

This meant dealing with the thorny subject of the little girl's marriage, something that was of considerable financial, as well as political, interest to her father. And it was perhaps this that made the Scots suspicious of Eric's intentions and eager for Edward's help, for they can have had no wish to be bounced into accepting a suitor – the man who would rule Scotland by virtue of his wife's inheritance – from wherever in Europe the Norwegians might extract the best price. Both the Scots and their neighbour in England would want to give careful consideration as to who might fill that role.

On the other hand, the issue would prove just as tricky if the Maid married into a Scottish family. Indeed, it may have occurred to Robert (5) that an alternative to acquiring a crown for himself lay in uniting Margaret with his grandson, Robert (7), but he cannot have been the only Scottish noble to dream of such a possibility and the Comyns would have had a word or two to say on the subject anyway.[86] From the Guardians' point-of-view, settling on a home-grown husband would do nothing to lessen the internal tensions they had so recently been forced to confront and which divided even them.

As the great discussions and debates at Salisbury swept on past the end of October 1289, the Scottish envoys were probably rather relieved that on 6 November they managed to nail down their main demand in a formal treaty, a solemn promise from Eric's envoys that Margaret would be sent to Scotland or England within a year free of any contract of marriage. The price was agreeing to take steps to improve their own government and to sack any royal official the Norwegians didn't like, ostensibly in order to make the kingdom safe for the Maid, her inheritance intact.[87]

Behind these negotiations, Edward lurked with avuncular attentiveness, promising to smooth over any differences between the Norwegians and the Scots. He had, by this agreement – as well as his earlier dealings with Eric – manoeuvred himself into a position of ultimate authority over Margaret's future, and so, to some extent, over Scotland itself. But this was a reassurance to the Scots, not a source of anxiety. Nevertheless, Edward was being somewhat disingenuous, for what he and Eric knew, but the Scots didn't, was that he had already applied for papal permission for his five-year old son and heir to marry his little Norwegian cousin [see *Figure 4*] – a match suggested by Alexander III back in 1284. Only ten days after the agreement was sealed at Salisbury, the pope granted the dispensation.

Four months later the Scots were still in the dark. On 14 March 1290, an impressive 106 of them – bishops, abbots, priors, earls and barons – gathered at Birgham within sight of the border, formally approving what their negotiators had agreed at Salisbury. Edward's envoys waited on the other side of the River Tweed to come and check that the Scots had fulfilled that part of the treaty touching 'the amendment of the kingdom of Scotland.'[88] Almost immediately, rumours of a papal dispensation crossed the border, presumably with the English envoys.[89]

This put an entirely different complexion on matters. The Scots reaction was swift – three days later (17 March), the gathering produced a letter for Edward, one that reveals something of their astonishment and their desire to put themselves, if not in the driving seat, at least back into what was clearly a juggernaut with the potential to move at some speed. Not that they were aghast at the notion that Margaret should wed the English king's son – indeed, they were at pains to stress just how full of 'gladness and joy' [leez et joyus] they were at the rumours, for such a match would put to bed the threat of civil war.[90]

The Guardians continued to worry about Eric, though, dashing off a much shorter, far more pointed letter to Norway on the same day, pressing him to keep his promise to despatch Margaret to England by All Saints (1 November) but preferably as soon as possible. If he did not, they would 'take the best counsel that God gives us for the state of the realm and the good people of the land,' perhaps hinting that they might pass over the Maid's rights to succeed in favour of someone else.[91] Such a threat was extremely high-risk and unlikely to be followed through, but it was one of the few cards the Scots held. Once she was in England and well on her way to becoming Prince Edward's wife, so the Scots imagined, Eric would find it extremely difficult to marry her off anywhere else.

But however much they found his involvement reassuring, the Guardians and other Scottish notables gathered at Birgham were not so naïve as to imagine that King Edward had only their interests at heart. They knew perfectly well that, however much an Anglo-Scottish union might solve their most pressing worries, the marriage posed its own potential problems, not least because Prince Edward would, God willing and in the fullness of time, became king of both realms. What they needed were safeguards, and quickly; they therefore sent envoys – Robert, bishop of Glasgow and John Comyn, two of the Guardians, and Alan, bishop of Caithness – with 'reasonable' proposals to Edward in time for an English parliament due to begin the following month.

Robert (5) and his son were both at Birgham, the lord of Annandale topping the list of barons in whose names both the approval of the original Treaty of Salisbury and the excited letter to Edward about the possibility of a papal dispensation were sent. The pair had been spending far more time than usual in Scotland – indeed, in Robert (5)'s case, actually living there[92] – which tells us all we need to know about the importance they attached to this difficult, but potentially rewarding, period of political opportunity.

Nevertheless, as everyone waited to see if Margaret really would be despatched from Norway, Robert (5) must have been painfully aware that the crown was now more or less out of his reach. He was seventy, the last of his generation – even his cousin Dervorguilla Balliol had died at the beginning of 1290, leaving the claim to the throne of the eldest line of descent from David, earl of Huntingdon in the hands of her son John [see *Figure 3*].

But the game was far from finished. Only a month after the Scots heard of the dispensation, Robert (5) was at Lochmaben and looking to the future. He might now have little chance of a throne, but he could still add to his already considerable portfolio of lands through a complicated and underhand arrangement to acquire the whole of the Garioch. He already held a third of these lands as part of his inheritance from Earl David of Huntingdon, but now he wanted all of it and was prepared to use almost any means, up to and including outright forgery.[93] It was a typically energetic and devious strategy, but still only the tip of the iceberg in terms of what he was capable of. And surely this too proved a valuable lesson to his grandson, the future king.

Meanwhile, Scottish negotiations with Edward were going well for, by July 1290, 'it was decided to agree to the requests of the envoys, in such a way, however, that the kingdom of Scotland would be as free and quit of all subjection of service as had satisfactorily and freely been the case with regard to customs and rights, both ecclesiastical and secular, in the time of the aforesaid King Alexander ...'[94] The English king would also put pressure on his Norwegian counterpart to release his daughter.

But what the Scots could not agree to was Edward's unexpected and novel proposal for how Scotland should be governed until Margaret and Prince Edward came of age that included handing over control of Scottish royal castles to the English king. He tried to push the point, and, meeting with equal stubbornness on the Scottish side, even contemplated imposing his friend, the hard-boiled bishop of Durham, Anthony Bek, as a kind of super-Guardian for the two royal children to whom the other Guardians must defer. The impasse dragged on throughout August until, on the 27th, Edward got wind of the news that everyone was waiting for: Margaret was either on her way or about to leave.[95] The government of Scotland would just have to stay the way it was in the meantime.

The Scots, too, had heard the rumours. By 1 October they were sufficiently assured of the Maid's imminent arrival to start gathering at Perth, where they were joined by Edward's envoy, Bishop Bek. But by then it was too late; Margaret was already dead, probably of food poisoning contracted from the provisions sent with her from Norway. After four years without a ruler, now Scotland really did have a problem.

Chapter Four

Thwarted ambition

In which Robert (5) and John Balliol tussle for the throne of Scotland even as King Edward of England transforms himself step-by-step from a friendly ally and guarantor of peace into overlord of the northern kingdom.

St Margaret's Hope on Orkney, where the Maid is reputed to have died [Sylvia Duckworth].

According to Bishop Fraser of St Andrews on 7 October 1290, rumours of the Maid's death had an immediate effect, bringing turmoil to the kingdom and fracturing the political community. Most worryingly, Fraser had heard that Robert (5), who hadn't joined the welcome committee congregating at Perth a week earlier, was pulling together an army that included the earls of Mar and Atholl and other great lords in order to gate-crash the gathering. The bishop admitted that he wasn't sure what Bruce intended to do or how he intended to do it, but given that Perth was less than three miles from Scone, the site of royal inaugurations, he probably had a fair idea.

The man he was confiding in was, realistically, the only one who could maintain peace and order in the northern kingdom, the only one who could help such a fundamentally divided political community find a way out of this dangerous predicament. For only Edward I had the clout to persuade whichever side lost the battle for the throne to accept the result peacefully. In the depths of despair, Fraser urged the English king to come to the border immediately, 'to staunch the spilling of blood' so that 'the faithful men of the kingdom can keep their oath intact and put in charge of the kingdom the one who by law should inherit it ...' Though the bishop politely envisaged that the new Scottish king – whoever he might be - would welcome Edward's advice, he had no doubt that it would be the Scottish political community which would decide who had the best claim, as they had promised Alexander III by oath to do in 1284, should the direct line fail.[96] The English king was being asked to facilitate that process; what the Scots needed and wanted – but ultimately did not get – was 'a friendly umpire.'[97] That might seem naïve in hindsight, but Edward had not, so far, given any hint of the bombshell he would soon drop on Scotland, for the very simple reason that he had probably not, so far, thought of it.

Bishop Fraser, as a friend of the Comyns, expected the rights of their candidate – John Balliol – to be upheld by 'the faithful men of the kingdom,' an expectation based not only on the principle of primogeniture that stood Balliol in good stead as a member of the senior line of descent from David, earl of Huntingdon [see *Figure 3*] but perhaps also on the dominance of his allies over many of the men who would do the choosing. As a fourth son, John Balliol had not, for the first three decades of his life, expected to inherit anything at all, never mind a throne, and was originally en route to becoming a member of the clergy via the cathedral school at Durham before joining Edward I's service, perhaps as a clerk, in the late 1270s.[98]

He was certainly much under the influence of the bishop of Durham, Anthony Bek, who claimed overlordship of the Balliol estate at Barnard Castle in the north-east of England, which John inherited in 1278. In 1290, Balliol finally became master of his mother's estates in Galloway and eleven months later was calling himself 'heir of Scotland,' audaciously anticipating the outcome of the kingship contest by granting Bek 500 marks revenue from the manor of Wark, part of the lands of the kings of

Scots in Northumberland.[99] Given that Balliol does not come across as one of history's more forceful characters, the impetus behind this presumptuous award was unlikely to have been his.

John's pliancy stands in sharp contrast to Robert (5)'s obdurateness, though in the end Bruce's very stubbornness could look like craven subservience. Naturally he strenuously disagreed with any notion that Balliol was the rightful heir, but he was, as ever, profoundly aware of the weakness in his own position, which, up until now, he had attempted to overcome with brute force. But when, after Margaret's death was confirmed, the English king indicated that he would indeed come north to help the Scots, Robert (5) put his sword away in favour of more Machiavellian[100] methods. He and his friends now lobbied Edward, seeking to persuade him of the 'ancient' role of the so-called seven Earls of Scotland[101] in choosing the king, the Bruces having worked hard in the last few years to wield more influence than the Comyns over this senior group of nobles of which Robert (6) was one. Making it clear just how much they distrusted two out of the four surviving Guardians – Comyn of Badenoch and Bishop Fraser, whom they accused of various abuses of power – Robert (5) and his close ally, Donald, earl of Mar placed themselves under Edward's protection. And now, over fifty years after the (supposed) event, Bruce first asserted that Alexander II had designated him as his heir.[102]

Even as winter began to bite, the English king ordered his entire court, including his wife, Eleanor of Castile, and his only son, seven-year old Prince Edward, to set out for northern England 'so that he might more readily communicate with the council of Scots'.[103] They did not move fast, since Eleanor was suffering from a fever, reaching Harby in Leicestershire on 20 November. By then Edward's beloved queen was very sick indeed and eight days later she died.

The distraught king immediately abandoned his plans, turning back towards London. Eleanor's funeral took place in Westminster Abbey on 17 December and Edward then took himself off to the monastery founded by his cousin, Edmund of Cornwell at Ashridge, north-west of London, where he spent Christmas before meeting with his parliament from 6 January 1291.[104] This was where he revealed to at least some of his closest advisers that he had undergone a major rethink on Anglo-Scottish relations, announcing '…that he intended to bring Scotland under his control, just as he had subjugated Wales'.[105] It would soon become entirely clear to everyone else that his attitude to his defenceless northern neighbour had become rather more hawkish.

So far as the king of England was concerned, the question of who should inherit the Scottish crown had now become the means to a rather different end. In March 1291 he sent royal messengers to various monasteries throughout England ordering the monks to check through their archives to find any references to kings of Scots paying homage to his predecessors. This historical exercise was intended to furnish Edward with the evidence he needed to justify a rather different relationship with his northern neighbours than the avuncular role he had played up until the point when his plans to wield power in Scotland through his son and the Maid were entirely scuppered by the little girl's death.

In April the English king finally headed north again, making for Norham castle right on the border where he had summoned the Scots to meet him. They initially refused on principle to cross the Tweed into England to discuss the future of their kingdom, settling instead within shouting distance at Upsetlington on the other side of the river. The summons to Norham had certainly set the alarm bells ringing, but they did not yet know just how far Edward intended to go; nor, perhaps, was the king himself sure what this opportunity might bring him. But he, like Robert (5), would leave few stones unturned in the trying.

Persuaded to come south to a parliament on 10 May,[106] the Scots finally discovered the new price of Edward's help and were entirely dismayed. For now the English king not only insisted that he, rather than they, should decide who was the rightful king, but also that he should be acknowledged as Lord Paramount of Scotland. Bishop Wishart of Glasgow led the chorus of Scottish protests – 'from long ago the kingdom of Scotland was free to the extent that it owed tribute or homage to no-one save God alone and his agent on earth [*the pope*].' In any case, it was up to Edward to prove such an outrageous claim, which it was not within the power or competence of the Scots gathered at Norham to comment upon.[107] But in reality they had little choice but to resort to a delaying tactic; only a king could respond to claims upon his royal dignity.

Edward, needless to say, was well ahead of them. In the first place, he had his carefully selected histories culled from various monastic archives to justify English overlordship.[108] But just in case this was not utterly convincing, he declared that an acknowledgement of his rights as Lord Paramount would be required before anyone would be allowed to compete for the kingship. By now fourteen candidates – mostly Scots or

English, but including the king of Norway, the Count of Holland and Edward himself – were beginning to throw their hats into the ring. Most of them were only really putting in a marker, in case something might come of it in the future or to extract other, lesser prizes.

However, the fact that he had engineered more than two to choose from gave the English king the right to sit as judge, rather than arbiter, implying that he had power over the matter that he was judging, the future of the Scottish crown and therefore of the kingdom itself. This was the technicality that had persuaded the Scots to cross the River Tweed in the first place, perhaps against their better judgement, but with little room for manoeuvre; they had been assured that he intended for this power over Scotland to last only as long as the judicial process to choose a new Scottish king, now known as the Great Cause.[109] They would nonetheless have been right if they suspected that Edward had every intention of making it permanent.

Given his ardent belief in his own claim and his awareness that time was pressing on, Robert (5) was first to bend his knee to the Lord Paramount of Scotland. Indeed he, perhaps alone among the Scots, had known of Edward's plans to push his claims of overlordship since February 1291, thanks to Bishop Bek, who had canvassed his opinion in the weeks after the Ashridge parliament of January. Bruce had no qualms about telling Edward that 'whenever he wishes to make his lawful request, I will obey him and will help him by myself and by all my friends …' in return 'for grace for my right and for my truth which I wish to show before you…' He would even ask around among 'the old folk' to see what he could find out about the humiliating treaty agreed by King William after his capture in Northumberland in 1174, which, for the one and only time, gave the English king, Henry II, a degree of authority within Scotland itself, however briefly.[110]

Given his own close relationship with Bishop Bek, John Balliol may also have been sounded out. But if so, his Comyn backers, with their long experience of Scottish government and dealing with English kings, stiffened his backbone and put a swift end to any such compromising discussions, another sign of their confidence in his right to rule – they did not want to be the power behind a throne that was also being manipulated from England. Balliol was therefore the very last to throw his hat formally into the kingship ring, perhaps only doing so reluctantly when it was pointed out to him that acknowledging the English king as Scotland's overlord was the only way into the competition.[111]

Edward was now in the mood to be magnanimous, promising to move quickly and to maintain Scottish laws and customs for the duration of proceedings. The main stage for the Great Cause was the great Scottish trading port of Berwick. On 3 June 1291 he put in place arrangements to tackle the thorniest issue – the competing claims of Robert (5) and John Balliol, who were ordered to choose forty commissioners to prepare their cases, while he set about appointing twenty-four of his own. On 12 August in the great hall of Berwick castle, the king heard the petitions of all the various claimants, before having them sewn up into a bag and carefully stowed in the castle's treasury where they were soon joined by the Scottish government's archive from Edinburgh castle. And then, after all that excitement and despite Edward's promises to be quick, there was a lull in proceedings for the best part of a year while the Count of Holland – whose great-great-grandmother had been a sister of King William of Scotland [see *Figure 1*] – looked for some missing paperwork.[112]

While it could be argued that proceedings up until this point stuck to the letter of the law, Edward was also being wily. He wanted to use this extensive hiatus when he had ultimate control over the northern kingdom to try to woo Scotland's nobles, to present himself as a reasonable, generous dispenser of patronage who would look after their interests and protect the Scottish kingdom's traditional laws and customs. Earlier in the summer, he may even have sounded out the Comyns to see if they might, with the right inducements, have stomached doing away with Scotland's kingship altogether so that he could keep the kingdom under his own direct rule.[113] Around the same time – and presumably as part of the same charm offensive – the English king agreed to give his cousin, Joanna de Valence, in marriage to Comyn of Badenoch's son and heir, another John. This union was to prove of coincidental, but intense, personal significance to Robert (7), the future king, for this John Comyn was to become his greatest enemy while Joanna was sister of Aymer de Valence, who would lead armies against King Robert in the first years of his reign.[114]

Though the Comyns were not persuaded by Edward's plan to do away with Scotland's ancient kingship, it was by no means a ridiculous strategy, given how interlinked the two kingdoms were at the highest levels. Many of those involved on the Scottish side knew Edward well, had fought with him or already looked to him for lands and jobs. But in the end, knowing him meant that many did not trust him – they had seen what he was capable of doing during his conquest of Wales and it must have crossed at least some minds that Edward saw little difference between the Welsh principality and the Scottish kingdom; both had been ripe for the plucking. By now many Scots were beginning to realize that they had no-one to protect them but themselves. Only the Bruces and their allies still wholeheartedly viewed the English king as a solution to getting what they wanted and not a major headache in his own right.

****

On 1 June 1292 King Edward returned to Berwick. In contrast to the rather relaxed proceedings of the previous year, he was now in something of a hurry, urging his own council and the 104 auditors to get to grips with the fiendishly difficult legal question that had brought the Scots to seek his help in the first place: did Robert (5) or John Balliol have the better claim?

For five days, the two competitors set forth detailed legal arguments, pointing to historical precedent and the 'common law' (Balliol) versus imperial or Roman law or even a kind of 'natural law' 'by which kings reign' (Bruce). Finally, on 21 June, Edward asked the two competitors if they were finished, which they agreed they were, though they might add to their submissions in the future, should anything relevant come to light. The king then turned to the auditors and asked them if there was sufficient on the table, so to speak, for him to come to a decision. They – no doubt to everyone's relief – agreed that there was.[115]

Having paused for the Midsummer feast of St John, the court reconvened on 25 June, presumably in the expectation that this whole convoluted affair would come to an end at last. But Edward now found himself, somewhat inevitably, back where the whole process had started – trying to decide which body of law to follow on an issue that would, not so long ago, have been decided at the point of a sword. Indeed, it would already have been sorted out by the sword if Robert (5) had had his way six years earlier and would be fourteen years later when his grandson – who surely witnessed all this legal wrangling and absorbed his grandfather's absolute conviction that he was Alexander III's rightful heir – finally made good on the Bruce claim to the Scottish throne.

But in 1292, King Edward turned, somewhat perplexed, to the Scottish auditors for help, but found none forthcoming 'for they were in such disagreement about the laws and customs of Scotland in relation to so difficult and unheard-of a case that they dared not advise the king without greater counsel and fuller deliberation.'[116] His own auditors proved equally disobliging and by 3 July Edward reluctantly decided that he needed more expert advice, postponing proceedings until 14 October 1292 so that he could consult the scholars of Paris on inheritance law. They largely found in favour of following Scottish custom, with Roman law on nearness of degree coming second, whilst almost all denied that the kingdom of Scotland should be treated like any other lesser form of landholding as Balliol had argued.[117] So far, so good for Bruce.

However, Edward's council – and therefore the king – was against Roman law, which was not used in England, and on 29 October the council formally rejected that position in favour of Scottish *or English* custom.[118] Given the lack of any clear and proven guidance on the question from Scottish custom, it was but a short step to begin to seek answers in English law, but not as it related to England itself. Rather, Scotland was to be treated like any lesser form of English landholding. It is not difficult to imagine why Edward wished to place Scotland below England as a legal entity. The fact that this happened to echo the arguments of John Balliol was probably coincidental.

But using English custom brought another potential hazard into view, because, unlike usual practice in Scotland where the eldest of co-heiresses to earldoms took the whole inheritance, in England the oldest took the title, but shared the lands and property with her sisters.[119] Unsurprisingly both Bruce and Balliol were quite adamant – at this point at least – that Scotland should remain undivided. Edward was content to agree, perhaps for the simple reason that he might one day wish to swallow the kingdom whole.

By 3 November 1292, the council could finally venture an answer to the original question – which of Bruce and Balliol had the rightful claim? Despite the conclusions of the Parisian lawyers, the writing had been on the wall for Robert (5) since 25 October and on 6 November he was tersely informed that he had lost.[120] He had played every possible card at his disposal over the best part of two years, making John Balliol – some thirty years his junior – look positively half-hearted in comparison. But he had a whole new pack of cards up his sleeve, having covertly made deals with four other candidates whose claims – based on very different arguments – might yet trump Balliol's, whose victory over Bruce was only the first step in John's progress towards the throne. The most important of these were Count Florence of Holland and Eric of Norway, as the Maid's nearest living relative. Neither was remotely interested in actually sitting on the Scottish throne. Should Florence win, Robert (5) had agreed, in effect, to buy it from him for the price of his valuable English lands. King Eric had also agreed to pass the crown to Bruce in return for the long-standing arrears of his dead wife's dowry.[121]

And now, in what might otherwise have been one of his lowest moments, Robert (5) could thank providence for his own farsightedness. Only four days after he was told that Balliol had beaten him, Bruce bounced back into the competition claiming new arguments. Eric's claim was given short shrift, even if sympathetic noises were made about the debt, but Robert (5) had already managed to squeeze one last advantageous agreement out of him. Two months earlier, in September 1292 his granddaughter Isobel and his son, Robert (6), were given permission to sail to Norway. A year later Isobel Bruce took possession of a ship-load of luxurious tunics, capes and hoods, many of them trimmed with fur against the Norwegian cold, as well as bedspreads and hangings, 24 silver plates, 24 salt cellars, 12 cups, 4 pitchers, 4 basins and a thurible for holding incense sent by her family to Bergen, where she married King Eric.[122]

Count Florence's claim took somewhat longer, armed as he now was with not one but two forged documents, courtesy of Robert (5). The first was Earl David's resignation of his rights to the throne in return for the Garioch, concocted for Bruce in 1290. But the second was a new fabrication, designed to take that resignation a step further in order to show that Florence's great-great-grandmother Ada had been recognised as King William's heir presumptive. In the end, though, Robert (5) chickened out of giving the Count of Holland the 'originals' and the copies were not good enough. King Edward, too, had had more than enough of this infernal Scottish wrangling.

But still Robert (5) wasn't done. This time he had no qualms about performing a remarkable volte-face, agreeing in a new petition on 14 November with what his more distant cousin, John Hastings – grandson of David, earl of Huntingdon's third daughter [see *Figure 3*] – had always argued; that Scotland should be split among Earl David's descendants. Unlike Hastings, however, Robert (5) admitted that Balliol should become king – he could scarcely do otherwise, given that he himself had sought the crown – but through this logical extension of Balliol's own arguments, the kingdom would have shrunk to an almost derisory size.[123] So far as Bruce was concerned, something was always better than nothing. Scotland doesn't seem to have meant much to him except as a potential acquisition, in whole or in part, the diminution of its ancient kingship of no moment when it came to expanding his own possessions.

And yet back in June, when he and Balliol were first outlining their arguments, Robert (5) had stood up for the more mysterious attributes of the role he hoped to win, asserting that kingship and kings were beyond the laws of property and inheritance that governed their subjects. Now, five months later, it was Balliol – only a hair's breadth from taking the throne but facing the threat of a kingdom butchered among Earl David's descendants – who argued that tangible things 'do not make the king, nor confer the royal dignity, but it is the royal dignity which makes the king ... this dignity is a whole and the highest lordship where kings reign.'[124]

Such fine words, unconnected as yet with any clear-cut body of law, had done Bruce no good at all, but now, finally, they bagged John Balliol a crown and an undivided kingdom. But in truth, the result – formally handed down by Edward and his council on 17 November 1292 – was the one that most suited the English king, and not just because it agreed with the way he envisaged the thorny issue of a future lack of male heirs to be dealt with in England.[125] In establishing himself as Lord Paramount, it made sense to Edward to view Scotland as a piece of property slotted into a hierarchy that placed England and its kings at the very top. He did not believe for one minute Balliol's arguments about Scottish kingship being 'the highest lordship' given that, so far as Edward was concerned, Scotland's ultimate lord was now himself. That, far more than establishing the rightful heir after the death of the Maid, was the most far-reaching result of the two-year deliberations of the Great Cause.[126]

The new King John was quickly inaugurated at Scone, as was traditional, on St Andrews Day, 30 November 1292. Edward graciously spared the Scots his presence, though Sir John de St John of Hampshire was his choice to stand in for the infant Earl of Fife who would otherwise have led the inauguration ceremony; Bishop Bek also attended. Ten days earlier, Balliol had sworn fealty for the kingdom of Scotland at Norham in England in terms immediately written down to confirm that this was a personal oath of exclusive loyalty to the English king from his own lips, there no longer being any need for the earl of Carrick to do it for him to save the majesty of Scotland's ancient crown. On Christmas Day, the two kings dined together at Newcastle, the company consuming seven barrels of wine from the royal store; the following day John did homage to Edward for his kingdom and all that belonged to it, just in case anyone had misunderstood the situation the first time round. On 2 January 1293 the nobility of Scotland sealed a document releasing their superior lord of all his previous promises on the constitutional position of the northern kingdom.[127] Scotland now had its own monarch, but one whose kingdom was, in theory, reduced to an appendage of England. Only time would reveal whether Edward intended that it should also be one in practice.

Chapter Five

Dealing with defeat

In which Robert (7) – the future king – makes his political debut as earl of Carrick, only to be humiliated at a Scottish parliament after which the Bruces end up with nothing in Scotland. Meanwhile King John is tied up in knots by King Edward's intrusive demands, but the prospect of war between England and France gives the Scots an opportunity to wiggle free of English overlordship. The stage is set for war.

King John of Scotland.

The winter of 1292-3 was a harsh one in both Scotland and England; 'Much snow fell; the north wind came and pulled up the forests and withered the plants which it found; it unroofed houses causing much loss, and violently threw some to the ground, thus accomplishing much devastation.'[128] The Bruces must have felt equally gloomy, their hopes as crushed as the vegetation.

Though it's hard to feel sorry for Robert (5), there's no denying his absolute conviction that he had been robbed of his rightful inheritance. And he had put so much effort into trying to make his dream come true, not just in the last two years, but almost from the very moment of Alexander III's death six years before. His lawyers' bills alone must have been astronomical, not least because, even as the Great Cause was entering its final phases, he and his wife were also defending themselves in a number of property disputes in England.[129] But he had added not one acre to his holdings to make up for all this trouble and expense.

Not surprisingly, he and his son gave Balliol's inauguration at Scone a miss, though a number of his allies, including Robert, bishop of Glasgow and the earl of Atholl, did go to Newcastle at Christmas to watch the new king swear away Scotland's ancient liberty. There is no need to impute a particular spinelessness to King John, though plenty have in the centuries since; King Edward had made it impossible for any of the candidates to avoid accepting him as overlord of Scotland and Robert (5)'s behaviour throughout this period gives us every reason to imagine that he would have sworn the same oaths had he become king, presumably in the firm belief that they were a price worth paying.

And yet this is not how history has seen the matter. Less than twenty years later, the Scots – or at least those who supported Robert (5)'s grandson as king – argued that 'the faithful people without doubt always held, as it had understood and believed to be true from their ancestors and forefathers, that the said Lord Robert, the grandfather, was the true heir after the death of King Alexander [III] and his granddaughter, [Margaret,] daughter of the king of Norway, and [was] to be given preference before all others for the government of the kingdom.'[130] In the aftermath of King Robert's highly controversial seizure of the throne in 1306, he and his propagandists needed to present a rather different version of the past in order to justify it, but their success in doing so is still extraordinary.

Within a century, the Competitor was entering the pages of the history books smelling entirely of roses, while Balliol positively stank. This was not put down merely to genealogical superiority, but moral character. It was supposedly Anthony Bek of Durham who first alerted King Edward to the likelihood that Robert (5) would scupper his devious plans because:

> If Robert of Bruce were king of Scotland, where would Edward, king of England, be? For this Robert is of the noblest stock of all England, and, with him, the kingdom of Scotland is very strong in itself; and, in times gone by, a great deal of mischief has been wrought to the kings of

England by those of Scotland.' At this, the king, patting him on the head – as it were – answered in the French tongue, saying : – 'Par le sank Dieu, vous aves bun chante;' which is to say, 'By Christ's blood! You have sung well. I will change my plans.'

The plot thickened as Edward decided to test the two candidates for the Scottish throne. He sent:

... for the elder Robert of Bruce, and asked him whether he would hold the aforesaid kingdom of him in chief, so that he – Edward – might make and appoint him king thereof. Robert answered straightforwardly, and said: – "If I can get the aforesaid kingdom by means of my right and a faithful assize (court), well and good; but if not, I shall never, in gaining that kingdom for myself, reduce it to thraldom (slavery) – a kingdom which all the kings thereof have hitherto, with great toil and trouble, kept free from thraldom, in security of peace." When he heard this, and Robert had moved away, Edward called John of Balliol, and plied him in like manner with the same question as before; but Balliol, after having quickly deliberated with his council, which had been quite bought over, fell in with the aforesaid king's wishes, that he should hold the kingdom of Scotland of him, and do him homage for the same.'[131]

A fabulous story, but, as we know, utter twaddle, damning not only John, but 'his council' – presumably meaning the Comyns – and deliberately so.

In reality, the Bruces spent a quiet Christmas, presumably licking their wounds. But they soon had to face reality. It was probably rumours of John's first parliament, due to begin on 9 February at Scone, that proved the catalyst for yet another attempted sleight of hand, which ultimately fared no better than the rest. The parliament's last item of business concerned those who had not yet turned up to swear homage to the new king. These included Robert (6), earl of Carrick and his friend, Angus Mor Macdonald.[132]

It was decided that they should be summoned again with the added threat that the king would pass judgement on their failure to turn up the first time. But this was deemed insufficient, as the entry was quickly amended to include a specific date – the day after the close of Easter (17 May 1293[133]) – and an injunction to local sheriffs to take six men with them to deliver the summonses.[134] This ultimatum posed a considerable dilemma for the Bruces, since King John would be entirely within his rights to seize the earldom of Carrick if Robert (6) continued to ignore his summonses.

What is sadly impossible to tell is when the Competitor bent the knee to his rival for the lordship of Annandale, which he certainly must have done or else he too would have been on the list. Perhaps he got it over with quickly, so that he need not show his face in the very public arena of a parliament. At 73(ish), Robert (5) realised that his own race was finally run; but that certainly didn't mean he had given up. Instead he gathered his family to him and attempted to undertake an extraordinary series of legal cartwheels designed to invest his son, Robert (6), with the Bruce claim to the throne, whilst at the same time relieving him of any lands in Scotland and therefore freeing him of the need to pay homage to King John to whom he would otherwise have been honour-bound to be loyal.

This plan called for the involvement of the Competitor's grandson, Robert (7), who was now eighteen. Unfortunately for the young man, his first foray into public life was to be a humiliating one, though on paper it looked as if that humiliation was the price he had to pay for an earldom. The arrangement was supposed to be a simple, but effective, transfer of rights and property: Robert (5) would keep Annandale, but resign his claim to the throne to Robert (6), who would in turn resign his earldom of Carrick to Robert (7). And, in an attempt to place this beyond King John's jurisdiction, the formal transfer of the earldom was backdated to 9 November 1292, just before Balliol was formally judged to be Alexander III's heir.

Though there is nothing to tell us one way or another whether the Bruces responded to the 17 May deadline, young Robert did dutifully turn up to the next parliament at Stirling on 2 August 1293. Flanked by Donald, earl of Mar, James the Steward, Sir John Soules (the Steward's brother-in-law), Malcolm, earl of Lennox, and Gilbert of Carrick, he handed over a letter from his father, who was conveniently out of the country en route to visit his daughter in Norway.[135] Robert (6) wrote in suitably contrite (or was it ironic?) style, addressing John as 'the magnificent and serene prince' and requesting 'your highness affectionately' that the king should accept his son's homage 'as the true and legitimate lord of the said earldom.'

King John smelled a rat. For a start, it was not for his subjects to pass on lands that were ultimately the sovereign's, or at least not without paying for the privilege. Having taken advice, he asserted, quite rightly, that 'it is the usual practice by the laws of the kingdom of Scotland that the lord king have sasine of the same lands before he takes homage.' He demanded that young Robert (7) release 'such sasine [*see glossary*] as he had of the lands' – the best he could do, given Robert (6)'s absence – and ordered the sheriff of Ayr[136] to take control of the earldom.

Fearing that the Bruces would react badly to this, the king stipulated that Robert (7) would only get it back if and when he produced the original letter of resignation and another letter from the sheriff certifying that the earldom had been peacefully handed over. Mar and the Steward, 'each of whom bound himself in entirety,' then formally guaranteed that the fee to get the earldom back would be paid to the crown, while Lennox, John Soules and Gilbert of Carrick also agreed to ensure that, within six weeks of Robert (6)'s return to either Scotland or England, the king would receive the letter of resignation. Only then would he take young Robert (7)'s homage.[137] The ball was back in the Bruces' court and they needed to move quickly if they were not to lose a significant amount of revenue to their rival, the king of Scotland.

Young Robert (7) had no choice but to capitulate to King John's demands and he cannot have enjoyed the experience one jot. To make matters worse, in the end he was made to look a fool since it seems that, on his return by the end of September 1293, Robert (6) decided that he had not, in fact, resigned his earldom to his son.[138] To make matters much, much worse, he also seems to have decided not to go through with the homage and fealty either, meaning that the earldom of Carrick remained in King John's hands, its revenues lining royal pockets rather than those of the Bruces. For the best part of three years, Robert (6) endured a somewhat nomadic existence, spending some of his time in Ireland and later on campaign with Edward I in Wales and presumably living on the limited revenue of his Irish lands and handouts from his father. By the time of the Competitor's death in the spring of 1295, the former earl of Carrick had almost no money left at all.

This painful charade cannot have done much to sweeten his relationship with his eldest son, the future king. In the meantime, however, Robert (7)'s job was to do as he was told and bring advantage to the family, for they certainly needed it. Around this time he married Isabella, daughter of Robert (5)'s close friend and ally, Donald, earl of Mar, following in the footsteps of an older sister, who had married Gartnait, Isabella's brother and Donald's heir, a few years earlier.

But, while King John could – and clearly did – exert his authority over even subjects as uncooperative as the Bruces, he was finding it increasingly impossible to resist King Edward's authority over his own kingship. In this, Edward – as Duke of Gascony – was well-schooled by his own feudal superior, Philip IV, the young king of France, who was attempting to emphasise *his* pre-eminence by stressing the superiority of the French parliament in Paris over Edward's Gascon courts.

Formalising feudal relationships in this way was part of an ongoing process that had been gathering pace throughout the thirteenth century; intentionally or otherwise, such developments helped to transform a particular set of feudal lordships into national monarchies where the king's jurisdiction – his sovereignty - extended across the entirety of his domains, often cutting across the power wielded by those beneath him, however powerful, but offering royal justice to all subjects. However, when that jurisdiction transcended national boundaries or challenged the sovereignty of one king through his relationship with another – circumstances that, as we have already seen on a number of occasions, had generally proved negotiable with care in the past when it was more loosely defined and exercised – there was bound to be trouble.

To begin with, Edward niggled away at his vassal king John with a series of 'requests', mostly on behalf of 'foreigners and malcontents,' but also two of Robert (5)'s allies, James the Steward and Alasdair Macdonald of Islay.[139] These were either sorted out or ignored. The Scottish king even had to remind Edward that they had agreed that he was to be excused from appearing before royal justices (in this case, of Yorkshire), as he had been summoned to do as if he were merely and only another English lord.[140]

But it was John's undoubted need to reward his own supporters now that he had the wherewithal to do so that ultimately set him on a collision course with an English king with characteristically intrusive notions of what it meant to be a superior lord. The cause célèbre that underlined the new relationship between Scotland and England involved Macduff, great-uncle of the current, underage earl of Fife, who claimed that he had been wrongfully deprived of property given to him by his father, first by the Guardians – a decision reversed by Edward when he had personal charge of Scotland in 1292 – and now the Scottish king. Whatever the rights or wrongs of the case, the upshot was a peremptory demand that John appear at Westminster in London at the end of September 1293 to justify his actions. He tried to resist, arguing in person – oh, the irony! – that Edward had no right to demand his presence. But he soon backed down when threatened with the confiscation of three Scottish castles, promising to return the following year to answer the case against him.[141] That too was postponed until 1295, but by then Edward had well and truly made his point, not least by putting in his own official to administer Fife while Duncan, the current earl, grew to manhood.[142]

The Bruces had little choice but to try to keep out of trouble, to weather this storm as best they could. They needed to keep in with Edward I, since clearly they could expect nothing at the hands of King John, but they were now only receiving scraps from the table compared to the magnificence to which they had once aspired. Robert (6) spent the summer and early autumn of 1294 in Ireland and was allowed to postpone payment of unspecified debts to Edward's exchequer until a year after his return, a favour then extended for another year.[143] Robert (5) and his wife seem to have remained largely in Scotland, presiding over their little cross-border empire.[144] Nevertheless, the old man still had stamina enough to travel south to Essex occasionally, where he enjoyed a spot of hunting.[145]

But now the final chapter in the ten-year drama of Anglo-Scottish relations since the death of Alexander III rushed upon the participants with some speed. The catalyst was the increasingly fraught relationship between Edward, as Duke of Gascony, and his superior lord, Philip IV of France. In March 1294 Philip confiscated Gascony, demanding that the English king answer charges against him in Paris. When this summons reached him, Edward formally renounced his homage. The stage was set for war between England and France.[146]

This was a conflict that the Scots would now be dragged into whether they liked it or not, for Edward presumed that the northern kingdom's men and resources were his to command as much as those of England, Wales and Ireland. But this was a mistake for two reasons. Firstly, while Scotland's political community cannot have relished their king's abject appearances at Westminster to answer for the decisions of his courts, it was scarcely an issue that troubled them directly. But a demand from south of the border to serve overseas in an English army was unprecedented (unless they also happened to be English landowners) and potentially very expensive, the costs also being borne by a lord's tenants, the so-called 'middling sort,' who would need to serve with them. It was intolerable.

Ironically, however, Edward's impending showdown with Philip gave the Scots their best chance of recovering their autonomy, for they were now very useful to the French king. If they were able to ally with such a major power, it would surely be possible to force Edward out of Scottish affairs once and for all. The only worry was whether their own king would be prepared to do what was necessary.

In the spring of 1294, presumably when news of Philip's seizure of Gascony reached Britain, King John wrote to Edward wondering what was expected of him in the impending 'foreign expedition.' To be fair, this was probably because the Scottish king was also a major English landowner, whose father and brothers had all served in English armies.[147] But the implications of a Scottish king serving personally in an English army were far more problematic. Edward wrote back on 20 April, thanking Balliol 'for his friendship' but telling him that 'at present the expedition is not taking place.' Meanwhile, King John was expected to attend the English parliament in June when a day was set aside for Scottish business.[148]

He was en route back to Scotland from this parliament at Westminster when the letters – dated 29 June - finally summoning him and twenty-six Scottish nobles to fight in France were sent out.[149] By the time he crossed the border, his Comyn relatives and the rest of Scotland's leaders were in no mood for compromises even if, to begin with, they fobbed Edward off with 'trivial' excuses as to why they could not fulfil their promises.[150] What they needed was time in which to prepare and they could not yet afford to alert Edward to their designs, even if it was later said that King John himself 'set forth openly the injustices, insults, slights and shame which he had endured, and strove to the best of his manly ability for a remedy to be applied by all means against the wickedness of the aforesaid king [*of England*].'

One of these injustices was surely the ban on travelling overseas already imposed on English ports that Edward asked John to enforce on Scottish ones, cutting off the kingdom's valuable overseas trade at a stroke.[151] In truth, these alarming developments probably earned the Scottish king a stern talking-to by his own nobles who in effect now took government into their own hands. Their first step on the road to revolution was to send an embassy to the pope, seeking to be free of the oaths of homage and fealty they had sworn to the English king, which they now claimed were extracted by force.[152]

This was a nightmare scenario for John, with his deep-rooted ties to Edward I, not to mention his vast family estates in England, but yet again he was given little or no choice. It did not help that the Scottish king owed his English master for numerous debts, including a whopping £3290 [over £2 million today] for the **relief** of his mother's lands, and though Edward excused him of £3000 of it, such a blurring of the lines between a subject and a fellow monarch gave the English king yet another way to turn the screws on his Scottish inferior.[153]

Both Robert (5) and his son, the earl of Carrick, were summoned to fight as Scottish nobles, though the Competitor was also included in the call-up of major English landowners, because, of course, he was one.[154] But Edward's plans were soon put in jeopardy by the outbreak of war in Wales in September 1294. Robert (6) almost certainly repeated his service of the 1280s in helping the English king to put down Madog ap Llewellyn's uprising and was rewarded with respites of 'all the debts of whatever nature' that he owed to the English treasury by Edward's 'special grace.'[155] The year ended as it began, with terrible weather and a lack of any obvious way for the Bruces to rescue their ambitions.

****

A few months later, at the very end of March 1295, Robert (5), the Competitor, died at Annan, though he too chose to be buried among his ancestors in Guisborough Priory. For many, including his son and grandson, it must have been hard to imagine life without the old man's indefatigable scheming, his endless determination to wrestle any scrap of advantage out of even the most apparently hopeless situation.

For his son and heir, Robert (6), the most immediate problem was money – he needed to sort out his own affairs as quickly as possible so that he could rejoin the royal army once more campaigning in Wales. Early in April, he wrote rather frantically to Edward, complaining that he had been both to London and Essex "where his lands lie, and is still there, endeavouring in every possible way to procure horses and armour for himself and his people, but 'on the faith and loyalty which he owes to God and the King,' assures him he has been quite unsuccessful in his attempts to borrow for the purpose, or get a penny of his rents. Wherefore he prays the King's pleasure in this emergency.'"[156]

Five days later he was still at Hatfield begging Edward's chancellor to speed up the inquisition into his father's lands, a necessary prelude to deciding how much they were worth and therefore how much Robert (6) would have to pay to redeem them. Speed was still of the essence – he urged the Chancellor: 'For his love to do this quickly, as he wishes to go to the King with the inquisitions and do homage.'157 Finally, on 17 April, the fifth lord of Annandale was laid to rest among his ancestors in

Guisborough Priory, some 230 miles north of Hatfield. Robert (6) had clearly inherited something of his father's energy, when it suited him.

By 4 July, he had finally done homage to King Edward, then at Aberconwy in North Wales, for his extensive English lands, which would help to restore at least some of his own personal fortune – the income from Writtle alone was valued at £100 17 shillings 5 pence annually (c.£67,500 today), while Hatfield came in at £63 13 shillings 4 ½ pence (c.£42,500). The two together brought in only slightly less than the income from Annandale at £194 2 shillings 6 ¾ pence (£152,600).[158] But so far as the family's ancient Scottish lordship was concerned, Robert (6) faced the same dilemma as he had over Carrick and once again he seems to have decided to forgo the agony of swearing homage and fealty to King John.[159] Now, after over 180 years, the Bruces had no Scottish lands at all.

Who knows how his son, Robert (7), felt about the loss of his birth right, the painful repercussions of his father and grandfather's obsession with their claim to the throne? His mother was dead by now, leaving in limbo the status of the earldom of Carrick, which he had, only two years before, so nearly called his own, for his father had only held it through his wife and it was never guaranteed that he would keep it once she died. Such things had always been in the gift of the king of Scots, which obviously did not help the Bruces now. Living in England was scarcely exile, but it must have galled young Robert that so much of his inheritance was now denied to him; and that his father had all the stubbornness of the Competitor, but none of the bold ideas with which to buttress his ambitions.

However, Robert (6) certainly had the Competitor's debts to pay – all £99 9 shillings and 6 pence of them (over £67,000 today) – with considerably fewer resources to pay them with. On 10 August 1295 he agreed to settle with Robert (5)'s executor, half to be handed over on 2 February 1296 and the other half on 22 May.[160] Around the same time, he negotiated with King Edward for the marriage of Maud Burnell, a splendidly rich widow. The income from her dower lands came to a most helpful annual £147 (c.£103,600) from properties spread across Surrey, Shropshire, Wiltshire, Somerset and Essex.[161] Given that Maud's manor of Boreham lay only seven miles from Writtle, we can presume that the newly-weds had met socially in the preceding years, but the fact that they actually knew each other was no doubt only an added bonus compared with her other, more tangible assets. Both Robert (6) and his son seem to have been spending quite a bit of time in London, presumably in order to cultivate Edward's favour as much as possible. In truth, they mostly managed to run up a number of substantial debts.

Nevertheless, it certainly helped from a financial point-of-view that on 6 October 1295 Edward agreed to give Robert (6) another stab at keeping Carlisle Castle. That this decision was connected to the potential – uncertain as yet – for military action between Scotland and England is given considerable weight by the fact that, ten days later, the English king ordered the seizure of lands in England held by Scots and any wool that might be found there.[162] Edward was reacting to the Scottish king's refusal to come south to answer, yet again, for his judgement on the Macduff case. He had no idea what John and the Scots were really planning.

As late as March 1295, King Philip of France believed that the northern kingdom was still under Edward's control, including it, along with England and Ireland, in a list of enemies that he wanted his ally, the Count of Flanders, to stop trading with.[163] Even with the outbreak of sheep scab – a new and terrible disease caused by mites that King John had to deal with in only his second parliament of August 1293[164] – any threat to Scotland's wool trade was taken very seriously indeed and in May 1296, Philip was now pleased to countenance a lifting of the Flemish embargo for Scotland and to call the Scots his friends. At a parliament at Stirling in early July 1295, King John and his council – which now effectively ran the kingdom – agreed to send an embassy comprising Bishop Wishart of Glasgow and Bishop Crambeth of Dunkeld, along with Sir John Soules and Sir Ingram d'Umfraville, to negotiate a formal treaty with France.[165]

In truth, the Scots were not in nearly such a position of strength as the remarkable confidence that they showed throughout this period suggests. They may have been flattered by the promise of the French king's niece in marriage to their own king's son, but the rest of the treaty's terms committed Philip to little more than making comforting noises if Scotland were invaded, while John promised direct action should the English cross into France. At the same time, and despite their long-standing differences with King Eric over money and any influence that Isobel Bruce might have exerted as his queen, Balliol's government agreed with the Norwegians not to attack each other so long as France was at war with England.[166]

On 16 December 1295, Edward ordered his nobles to muster at Newcastle on 1 March 1296, but this was first and foremost an ultimatum, since the Scottish king and many of his nobles were summoned too.[167] The English king had some grounds for hope that John could be brought back into line – Balliol had, after all, dutifully agreed to hand over three of his border castles for the duration of the impending war with France only two months before.[168] Around the turn of 1295-6, the English king planned to send north a powerful embassy that included John's former father-in-law, the earl of Surrey,[169] the bishop of Durham and Robert (6), presumably in order to give Balliol yet another stern talking-to.[170] Bruce's inclusion was perhaps intended to remind the Scottish king that he could be replaced if necessary.

According to one English chronicler, the Scottish government 'insultingly refused audience to my lord the Earl of Warenne, father-in-law of the King of Scotland, and to the other envoys of my lord the King of England.'[171] The Scots, armed with the pope's absolution of their oaths given under duress, were now intent on war, refusing Edward's every demand whether or not their king was inclined to accept them.

CHAPTER SIX

Bitter disappointment

In which Scotland and England go to war. The Bruces side with Edward I, expecting that Robert (6) will be made king in John Balliol's place. But after the Scots are defeated, Edward shockingly reveals that he intends to rule Scotland directly.

Site of the shrine of St Margaret, Dunfermline Abbey, Fife [Kim Traynor].

On 23 February 1296, the Scots ratified the treaty with France at a parliament held in Dunfermline, whose Benedictine abbey housed the royal mausoleum and shrine to St Margaret, grand-daughter, wife and mother of kings.[172] Around the same time, King John handed over Annandale to John Comyn, earl of Buchan – son and heir of the dead Guardian, Alexander, and cousin of John Comyn of Badenoch [see *Figure 5*] – a necessary prelude to war, given the lordship's strategic importance just across the border from Carlisle. Meanwhile, the men of Fife, who had been living under Edward's direct rule, were keen to take charge at Berwick, directly on the front line; Englishmen living in Scotland were expelled and their goods seized; the three border castles that John had agreed to hand over remained in Scottish hands.[173]

By 11 March, the Scottish army – led by the earls of Buchan, Menteith, Strathearn, Lennox, Ross, Atholl and Mar and including John Comyn of Badenoch's son, John – was mustering at Caddonlee near Selkirk. But this army did not cross the border yet. Instead, Buchan took a part of it south towards Annandale and on Easter Monday (26 March), they rode on towards Carlisle, which was held against them by Robert (6), or, perhaps more specifically, a member of his retinue, Sir William Carlisle. Pursued by 'snow, rain and easterly winds,' the Scots set fire to a swathe of countryside from Nichol Forest through Arthuret to the gates of the town itself. Despite managing to set a large part of it ablaze, they were in no position to breach its castle's stalwart defences without siege engines and had re-crossed the border by 1 April.[174] This was a hit-and-run operation and it was surely no coincidence that Carlisle was the target – Buchan was wreaking revenge on the head of one of Scotland's most important families for choosing loyalty to England.[175]

He cannot have expected to find Robert (6) in Carlisle – keepers of castles usually delegated their responsibilities to others. In any case, there was surely now only one thing on Bruce's mind and staying close to Edward was essential if his ambition was to be fulfilled. Though loyalty to English kings in showdowns with Scottish kings had been something of a family tradition in the twelfth century, what was no doubt driving Robert (6) over a century later was his firm belief that Scotland's overlord would belatedly recognise the Bruce claim to the Scottish throne as the right and sensible option. Not that Edward I had necessarily said as much, but it must have been the understanding. There was really no other contender if – or should we say, when – Balliol was stripped of his kingship for rebellion.

Robert (6) seems to have been on semi-permanent alert in the first months of 1296, ready to spring into action at any moment. He joined the king at Ketton in Lincolnshire on 11 February 1296, where he was granted yet another respite of his copious debts until 24 June, suggesting that Edward expected this whole sorry Scottish episode to be over by then.[176]

Bruce's entourage – which was to ride with Anthony Bek, bishop of Durham, Edward's great friend and fixer - numbered six knights, Simon

Lindsay, William Bruce, Robert Bardolf, William Rothing, Archibald le Breton and William Carlisle, along with two esquires, Edmund and William Baddow, his clerk, Ralph Durham, and his cook, Walter Cryps.[177] Lindsay and Carlisle were both from Cumbria, suggesting that Robert (6) had been able to maintain the links so strenuously cultivated there by his father and no doubt helped by his own recent appointment as keeper of Carlisle castle. The rest, including his cousin William, were southerners, Rothing, le Breton, and the two Baddows closely linked to the Bruces in Essex.[178] There was no safe-conduct for Robert (6)'s twenty-two year old son, but the future King Robert was there, ready for his first taste of warfare and, perhaps more importantly, to recover his family's fortunes and hopefully improve them.

On Easter Sunday (25 March), the English king and his army lay at Wark castle right on the border, solemnly observing this most important of Christian festivals. But, despite the solemnity of the occasion, there was still official business to be done. As a prelude to his invasion of Scotland, Edward made four major Scottish noblemen swear homage and fealty to him again, just to make sure that they knew without a doubt where their loyalties should lie and presumably as a message to others. The earl of Angus was to all intents and purposes an Englishman with a large estate based on Prudhoe in Northumberland as well as a Scottish earldom; Dunbar's earldom lay in south-east Scotland, which had once been English territory and he too had lands in Northumberland. It should come as no surprise that these men remained in the English camp, even if, in Angus's case, his family had been close to the Balliols at Castle Barnard and Dunbar's wife was sister to John Comyn, earl of Buchan. Both – and their successors – were generally consistent in their loyalties, unlike many others.

Joining them in confirming Edward I as their one true lord were Robert (6) and his son, who was at last called earl of Carrick.[179] Since the Bruces did not yet possess either the earldom or the lordship of Annandale, it was perhaps a moot point. But that was surely only a matter of time, though getting them back couldn't come a moment too soon, for the family was still routinely in debt.

On the same day both men acknowledged that they owed £120 (around £83,000 today) to a London merchant, which was now overdue. Despite the respite from debts issued to Robert (6) back in February, the sheriff of Essex was ordered to collect it from Bruce revenues in the county. A week later, the sheriff was told to extract another £60 (c.£40,000 today) to be paid to three merchants of Winchester who had clearly been subsidising the everyday living expenses of both father and son, including their poultry bills.[180] Edward could have organised a postponement, so it is hard not to see this as deliberate on the king's part, perhaps to underline just how beholden they were to their English lord and master.

But even if the English king currently wished to keep the Bruces at arm's length, Robert (6)'s loyalty, in contrast to the 'madness' attributed to King John and the rest of the Scots, was viewed as entirely sensible, even honourable by English commentators – 'Sir Robert de Brus, with all his followers, held always his faith towards king Edward, has shown him love in his wars against the Scots.'[181] Funnily enough, the Scots viewed it rather differently, with accusations of treachery against Robert (6) vociferously put about at the time and surviving even the complete retelling of King John's reign to suit his son once he became king. As a later writer put it:

> And, just as afterwards when King Robert Bruce was making war, all the supporters of Balliol were suspected of treason in his war, so also in this Balliol's war … all the supporters of Bruce's party were generally considered traitors to the king and kingdom. But alas! Through discord of this kind, the innocent masses were exposed to the frenzied bits of these wolves and lay lacerate throughout the length and breadth of the land.[182]

But in 1296, the future king shared his father's loyalty to Edward I.

The English army finally crossed into the northern kingdom on 28 March 1296, heading for Coldstream priory fifteen miles inland. There they camped in the priory's fields and orchard and helped themselves to the monks' livestock, knocking down courtyards, shattering carts and ploughs and utterly destroying the orchard to the tune of £118 (over £71,000 today).[183]

The next day Edward moved to Hutton, only seven miles west of Berwick. The gates of the great trading port, which only a few years before had welcomed him during the Great Cause, were now firmly shut and many of its inhabitants were up on the walls shouting abuse. The keeper of its castle, Sir William Douglas, standing on the castle ramparts on the western edge of the town with its walls spreading down towards the River Tweed to the south, must have felt invincible.

Meanwhile, the English fleet was moored just off the coast and several smaller boats moved up into the river Tweed as the English army advanced towards the town on Friday 31 March. The taunting from those baring their bottoms on the walls cannot have improved Edward's mood but it was the setting on fire of a number of English boats on the Tweed that finally caused him to snap. After that, the English made short work of taking the town. Its walls – which were mostly made of timber and mud – were quickly breached and many, though certainly not all, of its citizens massacred in an orgy of bloodshed. One of Edward's clerks dismissed the whole affair in a few short words, saying that it was done 'without tarrying.' It was everyone for themselves, both the victors and the defeated, for the English king had promised his soldiers that they could keep whatever they could take.[184]

Safe in the castle, Sir William Douglas might have decided to hold out, but he decided to capitulate on terms. Edward appreciated this speedy submission and was prepared to be generous. The English king spent the night in his newly-acquired fortress, 'his people in the town, each person in his house which he had taken'. Having seen the deficiencies in Berwick's defences at first-hand, Edward ordered that ditchers, bricklayers, carpenters and smiths should be sent immediately from Northumberland to start patching things up.[185] This was, however, only the first step in conquering Scotland, though the king tarried at Berwick for almost all of April.

King John, meanwhile, cannot have been too far away for, less than a week later, on 5 April 1296, his two emissaries – monks from Roxburgh – sought an audience with King Edward. Their message was straightforward – because of English aggression, including the seizure of castles, lands and possessions, the killing of merchants and others, and the violent abduction and imprisonment of those living in England, as well as the recent invasion, the Scottish king now renounced his homage and fealty. Edward was astonished and incensed, supposedly responding: 'I tell you, foolish felon, you commit a great folly, because if the man who sent you does not wish to come to us, we shall come to him.'[186] Robert (6) – who was now 'with the king' rather than the bishop of Durham – was probably there to witness King John formally become a rebel in Edward's eyes and must have rejoiced, for surely such defiance meant there was no way back for Balliol now.[187]

With the homage formally revoked, the main Scottish army – led by the earls of Ross, Menteith and Atholl and Comyn of Badenoch's son, John

– finally crossed the border into Northumberland, devastating Carham priory and the surrounding villages before plunging as far south as Hexham, over forty miles beyond. That it was as destructive as most invading armies is not to be doubted, though there was also considerable propaganda value to be gained – on both sides – from exaggerating the barbaric acts of the enemy couched in the most heinous terms imaginable. On this occasion, it was said that the Scots at Hexham 'with barbarous ferocity committed the consecrated buildings to the flames, plundering the church property stored therein, even violating the women in that very place and afterwards butchering them, sparing neither age, rank nor sex.' But this kind of rhetoric was levied just as strenuously against Edward I and his men in Berwick.[188]

The Scottish army returned from devastating Northumberland in the last week of April and now, at last, the two sides finally confronted each other. A group of Scots had occupied the castle of Dunbar, held by its countess – John Comyn of Buchan's sister – against her own husband. The English king dispatched the earl of Surrey, King John's former father-in-law, to besiege them, and on 27 April 1296 Surrey inflicted a full-scale defeat on the Scottish army that turned up to try to save them. The castle surrendered the following day to Edward himself, who had hot-footed it from Berwick for the occasion.[189]

Scottish chroniclers gave the Bruces – or at least Robert (6) – an entirely dishonourable role in Edward's early successes in Scotland, even suggesting that he provided counterfeit banners to dupe the Scots at Berwick into thinking they were being relieved by a Scottish army and thereby persuading them to open the gates. This is probably a garbled version of the more plausible cunning plan adopted by Surrey to use banners abandoned by the defeated Scottish army to similarly trick the garrison at Dunbar.[190]

A more believable accusation against Robert (6) is that he used his influence with old allies such as the earls of Mar (Robert (7)'s father-in-law) and Atholl to persuade them to act as double agents. But much of this can be put down to malicious gossip fuelled by assumptions made about Scottish loyalties by those writing in the years after the feud between the Bruces and the Comyns degenerated into civil war in 1306. Atholl was imprisoned in the Tower of London for his part in holding Dunbar castle, so he certainly wasn't nobbled, while Earl Donald of Mar stayed with Balliol and the Comyns over the coming months.

On the other hand, William Douglas in Berwick castle certainly didn't put up much of a fight once the town had fallen and was given remarkably good terms on which to submit. He and some of the men who were with him even supposedly agreed to stay with Edward for the duration of the conflict. And it is plausible – though impossible to prove – that James the Steward's equally sudden submission on 13 May came at the prompting of his Ayrshire neighbour, Robert (6). He was alleged to have 'come with dissimulation to king Edward, with all that belongs to him', which included Roxburgh castle, and not only swore fealty but promised 'especially to aid him [*King Edward*] against John de Balliol, late King of Scotland, and all his abettors in Scotland or elsewhere.' In the following weeks, the Steward was conspicuously active in bringing other Scots to Edward's peace.[191] But more fool the Scottish government for putting men with little love for Balliol in charge of the south-eastern frontline. At the very least, these stories tell us just how suspect the Bruces had become in the eyes of many influential Scots at the dawn of this unprecedented and traumatic breach in Anglo-Scottish relations, a distrust that echoed down through the centuries even into accounts of the period written long after Robert Bruce became king and changed the course of history.

But presumably, at the time, his father, Robert (6), couldn't have cared less what those he regarded as his enemies – Balliol, the Comyns and their allies – thought of him. So far as he was concerned, Scottish politics was simply a game of winners and losers and as long as King John was on the throne, the Bruces were decidedly in the latter camp. Only by becoming king himself could Robert (6) reverse the catastrophic eclipse of the family in Scotland, not least by winning back to his side those friends and allies who had had little choice but to accept Balliol's regime. Now surely – with John described as 'late' king of Scotland as early as 27 April,[192] the very day of the battle of Dunbar – it was time for Edward to raise up the rightful king of Scotland. And so, with military victory confirming the righteousness of the English cause:

Robert de Bruce the elder approached the king of England and begged him to fulfil faithfully what he had previously promised him as regards his getting the kingdom. That old master of guile with no little indignation answered him thus in French: 'N'avons-nous pas autres chose à faire qu'à gagner vos royaumes?,' that is to say: 'Have we nothing else to do than win kingdoms for you?' That noble man, discerning from such a response the treachery of the wily king, withdrew to his lands in England and put in no further appearance in Scotland.[193]

This was a staggering, shocking revelation. After ten years of hoping, dreaming and scheming, it was all over. It is not far from the truth to say that Robert (6), who pales in lacklustre comparison with his father and his son, just gave up in the face of Edward's crushing put-down. But for Robert (7), in the flush of youth and with his life ahead of him, the humiliation of witnessing not only the casting aside, once and for all, of his family's claim to the Scottish throne, but his father's craven response to this deliberate slight had a profound effect. Edward's cavalier disregard not only for the independence of Scotland's centuries-old kingship,[194] which had long been evident, but now for its very existence struck at the heart of young Robert Bruce's ambitions, the very person he desired to be.

****

After the defeat of the Scottish army at Dunbar, the campaign degenerated into a game of cat and mouse between the two kings. John, flanked by his Comyn relatives, was marched further and further north. Edward, true to his word to the monks of Roxburgh, went after him.[195] Castle after castle fell with little or no resistance – the janitor at Stirling, finding himself the only one left when the rest of its garrison vanished, vacated the premises himself, 'leaving the keys hanging above the open doors.'[196]

However shocked and upset the Bruces must have been, they still had a job to do to help cement the English king's control of what would no doubt be his newest acquisition. On 14 May 1296, while Edward and his entourage were at Roxburgh, Robert (6) was given powers to bring men – both English and Scots – from the borders of Annandale and the surrounding area to the king's peace. His son was given the same powers for Carrick. Two days earlier Robert (6)'s safe-conduct had been extended until the end of September – subduing Scotland was going to take a little longer than the Midsummer Edward had first hoped would mark his return south.[197]

So now, at last, the Bruces set off home to their Scottish estates, surely for the first time in nearly four years.[198] Edward, on the other hand, left Stirling on 20 June, striking out deep into the kingdom he now claimed as his own, trickles of Scottish notables coming to him to swear homage and fealty and to denounce King John as he progressed through Perthshire in leisurely pursuit of the retreating Comyns, Balliol in tow.

The English army spent Midsummer in Perth, prompting the Comyns to dolefully accept that Edward was not going away. John Comyn of

Buchan and his cousin of Badenoch approached the king, who told them bluntly that they and Balliol should go to Brechin castle within a fortnight to thrash out the terms of their submission. The task was, as ever, entrusted to Anthony Bek, bishop of Durham, the Scottish king's old mentor, and an agreement was reached. On 2 July, at the castle of Kincardine near Fettercairn, John – still described as 'king of Scotland, by God's grace' – abjectly confessed his sins, blamed his counsellors and renounced the French alliance, placing his kingdom and his subjects in Edward's hands, but clearly hoping for the best.[199]

But now Edward changed his mind, declaring that John should submit entirely to his will. Such a dramatic turn of events hints at a visceral sense of righteous anger emanating from a king who, though certainly high-handed, was not in the habit of sending out negotiators to make an agreement he had no intention of keeping. The most obvious reason for his rage was probably the realisation, by the Scottish king's own admission, that his government had dared to make a treaty with France. The cry went up in England that the Scots and the French were plotting 'To destroy England from Tweed into Kent'.[200] That this was almost entirely of Edward's own doing and that the Scots' actions were really rather predictable would have taken a brave man to point out.

On 7 July, in the churchyard at Stracathro, a trio of Englishmen led by Bishop Bek stood guard as King John, flanked by Balliol's brother-in-law Badenoch and the earl of Buchan, formally and expressly renounced the treaty with France. The following day at Brechin castle, five miles to the south, Balliol resigned his kingdom into Bek's hands on Edward's behalf. Only then, on 10 July at Montrose nine miles east, did the king suffer the former Scottish government to come before him and a much larger crowd of English notables. One by one, Comyn of Buchan, Donald of Mar, Comyn of Badenoch and the rest of those who had stayed with Balliol to the bitter end knelt before their 'dear lord', promising to 'serve him well and loyally against all persons who can live and die whenever we shall be required or warned by our lord, the king of England aforesaid, or by his heirs, and that we will never know of anything to their hurt without hindering it to the best of our power, and letting them know of it.'[201]

John, so it was said, was subject to a far more resolutely humiliating treatment, for Edward was master of the power of symbolism. There, in front of the entire company of Scots and English, he, 'stripped of his royal accoutrements and holding a white wand in his hand (prompted by force and fear for his life …), gave up with stave and rod all right which he had or could claim in the kingdom of Scotland.'[202]

The Bruces did not witness the utter humiliation of their rival, a process that also marked the end of their own hopes of securing a crown. Robert (6) had certainly been busy collecting homages and fealties in Galloway, as he had been charged with doing in May. At the beginning of July, however, he was at Turnberry, the main castle in Carrick, which technically was now the responsibility of his son. Desperate to ingratiate himself – presumably in order to extract at least some recompense for the thwarting of his ambitions – he wrote to Edward's chancellor offering to do anything he was ordered.[203]

Meanwhile, all the trappings of an independent Scottish monarchy – from royal records to the Stone of Destiny on which generations of kings had been made at Scone and believed to be the pillow mentioned in the book of Genesis - were taken down to London where, in the stone's case, it was made into 'the seat of the priest at the high altar' in Westminster Abbey.'[204] John Balliol and his son Edward followed on behind, stripped not only of their royal pretensions, but their vast estates in Scotland and England.[205] The English king continued his victory parade over the rest of the summer, reaching Elgin by the end of July before returning south. He was back in Berwick by 22 August 1296, job almost done.[206]

Though Edward had certainly not neglected the business of government during his Scottish progress, his return to Berwick marked a positive outpouring of administrative decisions and commands as he sought to settle his northern acquisition along lines acceptable to himself, but with occasional nods towards Scottish practice where it didn't seem too outlandish. The first piece of business that he insisted upon was yet another reminder of Scotland's new and altogether demoralised status, for at a parliament on 28 August an endless procession of Scottish landowners were forced, yet again, to swear homage and fealty to their 'dear lord.'

Just because Robert (6) and his son, as well as the earls of Angus and Dunbar, had served Edward loyally over these last, difficult years did not mean that they were exempt. The activities of Scottish troops – the brief siege of Carlisle, the equally brief occupation of Dunbar's castle and the devastation of his lordship of Annandale and Angus's lands in Northumberland, which lay in the path of the Scottish army rampaging down to Hexham – look remarkably like a deliberate targeting of these four 'treacherous' Scottish magnates. But, like those against whom they had so recently fought, the Bruces and the two earls were affected by the events of 1296, for now they held their Scottish estates directly of the king of England. And so, as Scottish landowners, they once more promised to serve Edward faithfully against all men and to protect him from harm, not least by letting him know if such harm was being plotted by others, a stipulation almost certainly inspired by the king's continuing anger towards the French treaty.[207]

This was all an object lesson in the new politics of Scotland, and, while it can have made little difference to Dunbar and Angus, the Bruces surely found the process disconcerting. This time there could be no land-shuffling so that Robert (6) might avoid paying homage and fealty for his Scottish estates; any attempt to breathe life into the Bruce claim to the throne would by definition mean outright rebellion against an infinitely more powerful king than John Balliol. For young Robert, the fact that he now really had acquired the earldom of Carrick[208] may have afforded him some comfort. But his actions within nine months of pledging his unconditional allegiance to Edward suggest that, even as he made his oaths of loyalty, he was prepared to contemplate what his father most emphatically would not.

The process of sorting out Scotland in general and giving back the Bruces their lands in particular, was now in full swing. On 4 September, orders were issued to the sheriffs of the Mearns (now Kincardineshire, centred on Stonehaven), Aberdeen, Perth and Angus, as well as the bailiff of the lands of Tyndale in Northumberland that used to belong to the Scottish kings, ordering them to restore lands and tenements recently occupied by the king's enemies, as well as grain, to Robert (6), since he had always been loyal. The following day he and his son, the earl of Carrick, were allowed to take possession of the lands of any of their sub-tenants who had rebelled, provided they weren't in prison.[209]

But this was surely the very least that the Bruces could have expected for their loyalty and the complete capitulation of Robert (6) in the face of Edward's determination to rule Scotland directly. They surely had grounds for feeling hard done by, as they were passed over for any offices of state, however insignificant, many of which were now going to Englishmen. On 8 September Galloway and Ayrshire, including Balliol's castles of Buittle and Cruggleton and the royal castles of Wigtown and Ayr, were given into the keeping of Sir Henry Percy. Edward's 'dear and faithful' earl of Carrick, James the Steward and the earl of Dunbar (who had lands in Ayrshire) were ordered to release any hostages they had seized to guarantee the good behaviour of those who had recently submitted to Percy, thereby losing any revenue they might have extracted for the hostages' release.[210]

Nephew of King John and grandson of the earl of Surrey who defeated the Scots at Dunbar and was now royal lieutenant in Scotland,[211] Henry Percy was only a year older than Robert (7). Indeed, both young men were probably knighted by Edward I during the 1296 campaign, perhaps as a prelude to the capture of Berwick. Though Henry was born in Surrey, the Percy's family seat at Topcliffe lay only some thirty miles from the original Bruce estates in North Yorkshire. He had seen action with his grandfather in Wales four years earlier, which, together with his relationship to Surrey, gave him excellent credentials to capture some of the patronage now available to Edward at the successful conclusion of his Scottish war.[212] Indeed, a few years later it was said of Percy that he 'seemed to have made a vow to humble the Scots.'[213] He and Robert (7) were to cross paths many times between 1296 and Percy's death in October 1314.

In 1296 Robert (7) was twenty-two. He had been married to Isabella of Mar for a few years and now, at last, became a father to his daughter Marjory, though at the cost of his wife, who died around the same time. This was not his only child born in these years, however, for he also had an illegitimate son – another Robert. It could be argued that Bruce had much to be cheerful about, not least his confirmation, at long last, as earl of Carrick, which placed him above his father in rank.

And yet, in many ways his career had stalled even before it got started, certainly compared to men like Henry Percy. The king clearly had no intention of rewarding either Bruce for a loyalty that had been as conspicuous as it might have appeared craven. For a man with ambition, this was surely intolerable, but at least a lack of responsibilities beyond those of a major landowner gave him time to consider his next moves. He certainly seems to have seen his future as lying in Scotland, unlike Robert (6) who went back south to give full attention to his ongoing debts.[214] 1296 had not proved to be the year of dazzling success that the Bruces had imagined at its outset. For Scotland, it had been disastrous, its four-hundred-year-old monarchy obliterated in a matter of weeks, its army and military leaders exposed as hopelessly unequal to the task of defending the realm.

Chapter Seven

Rebellion

In which William Wallace and Andrew Murray kickstart Scottish resistance to English rule and young Robert (7) finally decides to stand up for Scotland – or, at least, his own ambitions. Despite success at Stirling Bridge, the Scots are once more defeated by Edward I at Falkirk in 1298. Though he wasn't there, Robert (7) decides to continue the fight, against the English king and his own father.

Edward I of England with his neatly bobbed hair, as doodled by a very artistic royal clerk.

In the aftermath of his surprisingly easy conquest of Scotland, Edward I is supposed to have turned to the earl of Surrey – newly appointed as his lieutenant of the northern kingdom – and crudely joked that: 'It's a good thing to get rid of a turd [Bon bosoigne fait q'y de merde se deliver].'[215] Given that he urgently needed to attend to the far more important business of retrieving his forfeited duchy of Gascony from Philip IV of France – postponed because of the outbreak of hostilities in Scotland – his words may not have been spoken entirely in jest.

Now aged fifty-seven, the king of England was still a formidable ruler by any standards, as adept at the intricacies of law and administration as he was well-versed in military tactics. He was known for his long legs – his 'longshanks' – which made him 'elegant in appearance, being a head taller than average'. He also had an unspeakably violent temper – as a teenager he had ordered that a young man he happened to meet should have one of his ears cut off and one of his eyes pulled out 'without any pretext' – though he learned to control these violent rages and could even, on occasions, behave with restraint. His other obvious physical attributes were a drooping eyelid, a lisp – a symbol of masculinity shared with the great Trojan warrior, Hector – and memorable hair, which, as a child 'was silvery-blond in colour; in his youth, it began to turn from fair to dark, while in old age it became a magnificent swan-like white'.[216] Drawings, sometimes sketched by bored clerks on the side of official documents, suggest it was a long bob that curled beautifully at the ends.

Edward had good reason to feel pleased in September 1296 but in truth he just wanted Scotland settled so that he could get on with organising a continental campaign. Ordinary English footsoldiers were probably more satisfied with their exploits, composing jubilant songs that saw them through the long victory march round Scotland and back south again, and no doubt reprised on many occasions in the taverns once they got home. The battle of Dunbar proved a particularly fertile source of pride.

> The foot folk
> Put the Scots in a poke
> And bared their buttocks
> By way
> Never heard I say
> Of readier boys
> To rob
> The robes of the rich
> That fell in the field.
> They took of each man
> May the rough, ragged fiend
> Tear them in hell.[217]

More than half a century of resolute peace, of commerce and good neighbourliness, of marriage and investment on both sides of the border were cast aside in a matter of months as the English from the king down to the 'ready boys' of his army sought to bolster their national pride and material wealth at the expense of the Scots. That was the tragedy that Edward I inflicted on Anglo-Scottish relations for generations to come for little more reason than because he could.

****

The Scots were dumbfounded. 131 nobles, including their king and the earls of Ross, Atholl and Menteith, now languished in English prison. The rest of the Comyns – the mainstay of Scottish government and the economic, social and political networks that controlled large swathes of the country – had been ordered to take 'hunting leave' on their estates in England. Their military leadership had been tested and found to be grievously wanting.

Scotland was now governed by a trio of Englishmen: the chancellor, Walter Amersham, the treasurer, Hugh Cressingham, and the earl of Surrey as royal lieutenant. The earl had no interest in governing Scotland, despising the weather as bad for his health and venturing no further than his Yorkshire estates for the best part of a year. The real power in the northern kingdom was Cressingham, a notoriously fat and haughty royal clerk, who knew how to rake in money for his royal master and for himself. Within nine months of his appointment, he sent the astonishing sum of £5188 (over £4 million) from Scotland to the English treasury to bolster Edward's war chest for the upcoming conflict with France, an unprecedented sum from a nation that had, till now, paid comparatively little to its central government exacted by a ruler that many viewed as having no right to demand it.[218] The northern kingdom was, yet again, drifting along without effective, impartial leadership at a time when firm but fair English government might have gone some way to persuading the population at large that there were benefits to be had from the new regime. Instead the Scots were asked to give, and give again, on an unprecedented scale, without getting much more than contempt in return.

But for young Robert (7), the future king, restored to enjoyment of the rolling hills, wooded valleys and, perhaps, young women of Carrick,[219] this vacuum represented an opportunity, especially once it became clear in the first half of 1297 that Scotland was to stump up just as much as England in the run-up to war with France. Measures such as the compulsory purchase of wool at low cost by the Crown, to be sold at a profit, were detested south of the border,[220] never mind north of it, where the unprecedented demands of a heavily bureaucratic medieval state headed by a king with an almost limitless capacity to embroil himself in warfare were bound to cause dismay and outrage.

By May 1297 Sir Henry Percy was already complaining to Edward that he hadn't been paid the latest instalment of his annual fee of 1000 marks (£537,000) for keeping Galloway, which, given that he needed to pay his own men out of it, would become a serious problem if cash wasn't forthcoming soon. Soldier-lords like Percy expected to make money out of Scotland, not get themselves into serious debt for their service. The king ordered the exchequer in London to despatch £2000 (around £1 million) to Cressingham in Berwick as a temporary stop-gap to be paid back. But, as the Scots began to dig in their heels, refusing to hand over even the taxes they were used to paying, it was England that found itself shelling out for the administration of Edward's most recent conquest.[221]

But even as Percy was making his complaint, the first blows against the new regime were already being struck in various parts of the country. Most famously, legend has it that 'William Wallace was chosen by the commons of Scotland as leader to raise war against the English.'[222] On 3 May 1297 he launched a violent attack on Edward's sheriff of Lanark at the head of a band of men. They came at night, supposedly while the sheriff was holding a court, killing him outright and setting his house on fire. Laying hands on a royal official was a most serious crime because it was seen as an assault on Edward's own majesty. That Wallace decided to take such a violent and irrevocable step was momentous indeed. Whatever his emotions, he felt them passionately.

Legend would also have us believe – as anyone who's seen *Braveheart* will know – that his actions on 3 May were revenge for the sheriff's killing of his wife. But his movements after the murder at Lanark suggest a systematic targeting of English officials, particularly those involved in taking homage and fealty, symbol of the loss of Scottish sovereignty. It was surely hatred of the regime itself that moved him and it is not difficult to find evidence for its oppressiveness. Even the English had heard that, to add injury to insult, royal clerks charged with extracting homage from anyone over the age of fifteen 'took a penny [about £3.20] from each, whereby they became wealthy fellows.'[223]

As if the seizure of wool, ordered in mid-April 1297, was not enough, other rumours soon began to circulate in Scotland that played on the deep fears of the 'middling sort,' who now believed that 'the king would have seized [them] to send them beyond the Scottish Sea in his army, to their great damage and destruction.'[224] This was a completely alien concept to those who, though not members of the higher nobility, were very influential at a local level. For many, this was rapidly becoming a cause worth fighting for.

And it was exactly the kind of cause that young Robert (7) was keen to embrace, primarily in order to prove his leadership credentials, though we cannot entirely rule out the possibility that he felt some of the outrage at Scotland's plight at the hands of the English. An expensive foreign war that had nothing to do with a broad and locally-important section of the Scottish political community provided an ideal opportunity for the young man to play a leading role in national affairs while Balliol and the Comyns were in prison or exile.

On 4 June, a month after William Wallace killed the sheriff of Lanark, Henry Percy was ordered to arrest and imprison 'disturbers of the peace' from his base at Carlisle as the counties on the southern side of the border were put on red alert.[225] This was most probably a reaction to Wallace's attacks on Edward's men in south-western Scotland, bolstered by support from Sir William Douglas - the former keeper of Berwick castle - whose lands lay only twelve miles south-west of Lanark where the uprising began. Nine days later, three Dumfriesshire knights in the service of one of Percy's men were applauded by the king 'for their late ready and willing service in repelling disturbers of the peace and recapturing for the king castles which had been taken in those parts.'[226]

But the bishop of Carlisle already had his suspicions about the 'unfaithful and fickle' Robert (7) and decided to test his loyalty by summoning him to Carlisle, ostensibly to discuss royal business. The young man had no choice but to agree, arriving on the agreed day at the head of an entourage of his own men.[227] The bishop then revealed his true purpose, demanding that Robert swear on the sword of St Thomas that he would faithfully serve the king against his Scottish enemies and preserve Edward from harm with all his might. Once more, he had no choice but to do as he was commanded.

Given that oaths were solemn, divinely-observed promises, Robert (7) was allowed to go back to Scotland, though the fact that he had already sworn similar oaths not once but twice the previous year might have given the bishop pause. Indeed all the churchman seems to have achieved was to alert Bruce to the fact that a number of Scottish noblemen, including himself, were being watched. The minute he got back over the border, he rode straight to Sir William Douglas's lands, which lay north of his father's lordship of Annandale and east of his own earldom. He set fire to part of them and took Douglas's wife and children back to Annandale. This was a carefully calculated move, for at that moment Sir William was now some eighty miles away with Wallace, going after Edward's justiciar (chief law officer) at Scone. Robert was making it look as if he was fulfilling his oath – 'devising an outward show,' a chronicler says – but was actually spiriting away Douglas's family, presumably including William's eldest son, eight-year old James, safely out of reach of Edward's officials.

Bruce got a nasty shock when he arrived in Annandale, however. Summoning his father's chief tenants, he admitted to taking the oath at Carlisle, but swore it had been forced out of him and he was most upset about it, that no man hated his own flesh and blood and so he was determined to return to his people, beseeching 'his dear friends' to join him. It was a rousing speech, but it fell on stony ground. During the night, the lords of Annandale slipped away rather than break their oaths to King Edward, or at least to their lord, Robert (6), who now lived more or less permanently in the south of England.[228]

Despite the lack of support from his father's knights, Bruce did have friends prepared to take a stand. He now joined Robert Wishart, bishop of Glasgow and James the Steward in riding out against English officials in south-western Scotland. Despite the shocking nature of what had happened at Lanark and his success in taking Dumfriesshire castles, however briefly, William Wallace was not the kind of man to attract too much attention as yet, since no-one in Edward's government either in Scotland or England had the faintest idea who he was. But a rebellion led by Robert (7), earl of Carrick and two former Guardians certainly made the officials in Berwick sit up and take notice. Even more worryingly for Edward's men, while William Wallace's revolt probably started spontaneously, by now there was collusion between him and 'the great lords of Scotland' as Sir William Douglas left Wallace to join Bruce and the others.[229]

The rapidly deteriorating state of Scotland's government was still not serious enough for Edward to change his plans to go abroad, but he did decide to give some of those Scots currently forced to stay in England a chance to prove their loyalty. On 11 June Sir John Comyn of Badenoch and his cousin, the earl of Buchan, were given leave to go home to deal with another band of insurgents in the north of Scotland. These included Badenoch's own nephew, Andrew Murray, who had escaped from

Chester castle, where he'd been imprisoned after the battle of Dunbar. Murray headed back to the Black Isle just north of Inverness to raise his father's men against English garrisons in the area.[230] The Comyns, who had over the last century gained their broad northern estates precisely because of their ability to use hill and glen to their own advantage, proved quite unable to do so now, protesting feebly that Andrew and his men 'took themselves into a very great stronghold of bog and wood, where no horseman could be of service.' It wasn't long before the English began to suspect that they were with King Edward in body, but not in heart.[231]

Back in the south, the revolt grumbled on. On 24 June Henry Percy, still at Carlisle, was granted powers 'to arrest, imprison and otherwise do justice on persons making meetings, conventicles and conspiracies against the king's peace in various parts of Scotland,' though most of the action was clearly just across the border in Dumfries and Nithsdale. He was joined in this important task by Sir Robert Clifford, another young knight of Robert (7)'s age who had inherited a strategic string of lands and castles commanding the routes across the western Pennines south-east of Carlisle.

The pair then set out with a force gathered from Cumberland and Westmoreland, spending the night at Lochmaben, Robert (6)'s castle in Annandale, which – along with the rest of the elder Bruce's lands – had been confiscated, presumably for his son's rebellious activities. The lord of Annandale was himself supposed to be coming up to Scotland, having been granted a safe conduct for a year on 12 June 1297, presumably in order to try to talk sense into his rebellious offspring.[232]

Pushed back north and unwilling to test themselves in battle after the disastrous showing at Dunbar, Robert (7), Wishart and the Steward agreed to discuss terms at Irvine on the Ayrshire coast, reaching a formal agreement on 7 July that saw them spared imprisonment so long as they surrendered hostages. They had been careful to argue that they had taken action not against Edward's right to rule Scotland, which would have been asking for very real trouble, but the way in which that rule had been exercised. They made much of the terrible burden that serving overseas would place on the middling Scots they claimed to represent, a service that young Robert had himself been summoned to perform. At the same time, they demanded a return to the ancient laws and customs of Scotland that they believed Edward's officials either had no knowledge of, or interest in.[233]

But the English did not take long to find their behaviour disingenuous at best. It was even said that Bruce and the others deliberately prolonged negotiations at Irvine, 'discussing the concessions with frivolous points, so that Wallace could gather more people to him.'[234] Cressingham, the treasurer, certainly thought so, convinced that, whatever Percy and Clifford had agreed at Irvine, the man the treasurer viewed as robber-in-chief was now bedded down in south-east Scotland where he had begun to gather and train all those, as later Scottish writers fervently imagined, 'who were in bitterness of spirit, and weighed down beneath the burden of bondage under the unbearable domination of English despotism.'[235]

Meanwhile the treasurer had himself been busy raising 300 horsemen and 10,000 footsoldiers in Northumberland for an expedition due to ride out from Roxburgh on 17 July. However, Percy and Clifford arrived in the nick of time the night before, flushed from their diplomatic victory at Irvine nine days earlier. But still Cressingham was not happy, since, as he emphasised to the king on 23 July, for all this talk of successful agreements, Scotland north of the Forth was in an uproar, while William Wallace lay 'with a large company' in Selkirk Forest – an expanse of game-filled woodland and scattered communities less than fifty miles west of Berwick itself – 'like one who holds himself against your peace.' But there was a limit to what any of them could do without the royal lieutenant, the earl of Surrey, whose arrival was eagerly anticipated, so no expedition was planned. And thus, as the treasurer remarked with profound and desperate understatement, 'matters have gone to sleep.'[236]

The next day he went further, informing his royal master in no uncertain terms that 'by far the greater part of your counties of the realm of Scotland are unprovided with keepers, as well by death, sieges, or imprisonment; some have given up their bailiwicks, and others neither will or dare return; and in some counties the Scots have established and placed bailiffs and ministers, so that no county is in proper order except Roxburgh and Berwick and this only lately.'[237]

He was right to be concerned. Robert (7), for one, may have negotiated his way out of a military defeat at Irvine, but that did not mean he was reconciled with his and Scotland's fate, since the two were surely now inseparable in his mind. Indeed, it is to be wondered whether the youngest Bruce ever had any intention of fulfilling the main condition of the agreement made with Percy and Clifford – the handing over of his baby daughter Marjory as a hostage – or whether the whole thing was just a delaying tactic as the Scots waited for Edward to leave the country for the continent. To be fair, the English were still openly suspicious of him, which is no great surprise given that he had already broken a sacred oath taken only a month or so before. His word was no longer enough; at Irvine he was forced to ask Wishart of Glasgow, the Steward and Sir Alexander Lindsay to stand as pledges for his loyalty until he fulfilled the agreement's terms.[238]

By late July Percy and Clifford had gone south, intent on prising the earl of Surrey out of Yorkshire while Cressingham continued to warn the king that Scotland was far from settled. The treasurer also hinted on 24 July that he had his doubts about some of those 'who ought to come to your service, and about whom there had been a delay for certain reasons, as I have heretofore intimated to you, when the earl [*Surrey*] comes ... I will discover the good, and whether there are any bad...' He surely meant Robert (7) and his friends, remarking in a similar vein two weeks later that 'if they come [*to Berwick*], we hope it will be well; and if they do not come, we believe it will be necessary for every man to do his best.' He was equally cynical about what might be expected from the Comyns of Buchan and Badenoch and their friends who were supposed to be dealing with Andrew Murray and others in the far north.[239]

On 1 August, Surrey wrote to the king himself, having finally reached Scotland. He and the other officials there expected the bishop of Glasgow, Robert (7) and the Steward to arrive at Berwick on the 8th to fulfil the terms of the agreement with Sir Henry Percy. Once that was done, Surrey promised that 'we will advance into the country ... to establish the condition of the country in the best manner that we can.' He also mentioned that Sir William Douglas was safely locked up in irons in Berwick castle 'because he did not produce his hostages on the day appointed for him, as the others did.'[240]

Surrey was misinformed; Bruce certainly hadn't handed over his daughter or any other hostage, though English officials may have been reassured by the fact that Wishart and the Steward were guarantors for his compliance. Needless to say 8 August came and went without any sign of young Robert in Berwick. The bishop of Glasgow did turn up, however, and promptly found himself imprisoned in Roxburgh castle for Bruce's failure. This incensed William Wallace, who rode out of Selkirk Forest to the bishop's house – the palace at Ancrum, just north of Jedburgh and fourteen miles west of the Forest in which he lurked – taking away with him all of Wishart's furniture, arms and horses, even his sons (which, along with the arms, he really shouldn't have had as a churchman).[241] Wallace obviously knew the kind of treatment meted out by Edward's men to those with whom they were displeased and he wasn't about to let it happen to his mentor.

On 22 August the king was on board his ship, the *Cog Edward*, at Winchelsea ready to sail to Sluys in Flanders.[242] Despite the fact that many great lords had refused to serve personally on the continent because of the widespread antipathy towards the whole campaign, Robert (6) had originally signed up to go with him; his loyalty to Edward was unshakeable, certainly so long as he had debts that needed to be put off. It is difficult to tell whether he had actually gone to Scotland in June/July, but it seems most likely that the order to give him back his lands, issued on 31 July, was a reward for his son's capitulation and not necessarily for any part he might have played in it. Nevertheless, young Robert (7)'s continuing failure to abide by the terms of the Irvine agreement probably explains why, in the end, his father was left behind when Edward finally sailed.[243]

Almost all the Scots who went with the king were those who had been imprisoned after Dunbar and who were now promised their freedom in return for their service. The earls of England had pleaded with Edward not to go 'for his honour and the salvation of the people,' not least because 'the land of Scotland is beginning to rise up against him,' a state of affairs that was only going to get worse if he went abroad.[244] But there was no question of further delay. Now everyone, both Scots and English, waited to see what would happen next.

****

At some point in August, William Wallace left Selkirk Forest with his well-trained band of men and headed for Dundee at the mouth of the Tay estuary where he settled down to besiege the castle there.[245] An important east coast port, Dundee was vital to the nation's commercial interests and to keeping Scotland in contact with the continent, a lifeline that would be essential if the kingdom were to secure the international support it needed to resecure its independence.

But then news came that Surrey had left Berwick with a small English army – essentially the men recruited by Cressingham in Northumberland in mid-July – and was heading north. Wallace had already been put in touch with Andrew Murray, who was now making his way south to join him. Between the two of them, they had an army intent on challenging whatever might be sent against them.

There was no need for either the English or the Scots to worry about where to find each other for there was only one place for large numbers of men to cross the river Forth and that was via the bridge at Stirling. Wallace and Murray, their army ranged in the hills to the north of the Forth, were approached by James the Steward, the earl of Lennox and a number of other Scottish lords, who had told Surrey they could broker a peace with their insurgent countrymen. Murray and Wallace sent them packing. The next day, 11 September 1297, Surrey sent his own emissaries to speak with the Scottish commanders, but the result was the same. 'Tell your commander,' Wallace said,' that we are not here for a good peace, but are ready to fight to avenge our own people and free our kingdom.'[246]

The stage was set for battle, but the English entirely misunderstood the rules of the game as played by their unlikely opponents. In essence, Surrey 'was defeated by William Wallace [*and Andrew Murray, of course*], who, being at hand in order of battle, allowed so many of the English as he pleased to cross over the said bridge, and, at the right moment, attacked them, caused the bridge to be broken, where many of the English perished, with Hugh de Cressingham, the King's Treasurer; and it was said that the Scots caused him to be flayed, and in token of hatred made girths [*belts*] of his skin.'[247] Surrey seems to have expected the Scots to allow his army to cross the bridge and line up properly; he now learned the hard way that this new breed of commanders were looking for any advantage to make up for Scottish inferiority in numbers, equipment and – for many – experience.

Surrey, unlike Cressingham, survived the day, rushing off back to Berwick and on into England as fast as his horse could carry him. Behind him, English rule collapsed like a house of cards, most remaining English garrisons surrendering to the Scots. In October Murray and Wallace sent letters to the Baltic ports informing them, as 'commanders of the army of Scotland and the community of the same kingdom,' that Scotland was once more open for business. A month later they were calling themselves commanders in the name of 'the famous prince the lord John, by God's grace illustrious king of Scotland …'[248]

But by then young Andrew Murray was probably already dead of wounds sustained in the battle,[249] leaving the Scots with something of a constitutional headache. So long as Murray was alive, there was at least a nobleman who was also Comyn of Badenoch's nephew at the helm; without him, there was only an independent-minded son of (perhaps) a royal tenant and knight of Ayrshire[250] whose early activities suggested a degree of collusion with the Bruce faction. Nevertheless, the political community had no choice but to accept William Wallace's extraordinary rise to power, for the moment at least; over the winter of 1297-8 he became both a knight and sole Guardian of Scotland, even if the English – and no doubt quite a few Scottish nobles – likened this to the transformation of a raven into a swan.[251]

Young Robert (7)'s movements, let alone his intentions, are obscure in the months after his submission at Irvine in early July. His silence speaks volumes, however, along with tantalising hints of further resistance to English rule at the end of the year that may have been co-ordinated with Wallace. The new Guardian took his men on a bloody assault of the north of England in October and November 1297. Bad weather had ruined much of the harvest and Wallace saw the wisdom in taking his men 'to invade the country of their enemies ... and to spend the wintry part of the year there so as to spare their own very limited food supplies...' It was down to Sir Robert Clifford, as well as the formidable bishop of Carlisle, to organise the defence of the western border counties of England against the destruction of the Scottish army, which again set fire to large swathes of Cumberland.[252]

In mid-November Clifford and the bishop were still hoping (really, against hope) that Bruce and 'his friends' would finally fulfil the terms of their submission agreement, which suggests that young Robert (7) had not openly joined Wallace. But still his failure to produce his hostages kept the bishop of Glasgow in prison in Roxburgh.[253] Finally, in December, Robert (7) seems to have led his men out against the English once more, even if he was not yet ready to play anything more than a low-key local role. If we want to be cynical, then it was probably because the Comyns were now flexing their muscles in national affairs, even if they could not have things their own way so long as Sir William Wallace was Guardian.

Fearing that another Scottish force intended to cross the border only a few weeks after Wallace's army had returned home, Carlisle's defences were strengthened on 11 December 1297. At Christmas Clifford led his own retinue of seven knights and sixteen esquires at the head of nearly five hundred footsoldiers north into Annandale even as Robert (6) was despatched north, presumably in yet another attempt to influence his son.[254] Just as the Scots had sought to stave off the effects of a ruined harvest by pillaging northern England, so Clifford's men were encouraged to seize what they could 'like jackals', returning home a few weeks later with 'prisoners and great plunder.' Nevertheless, a hundred footsoldiers had been left north of the border 'as they believed the Scots were coming.'[255] No-one now expected Bruce to appear in Carlisle with his daughter.

Meanwhile, Edward's campaign against France proved not only eye-wateringly expensive but humiliating as his costly allies withdrew or did not even turn up in the face of French success. On 9 October – by which time he may have heard of the disaster at Stirling Bridge – the king agreed a truce with Philip IV and began the long and mortifying process of going home.[256] The very next day his government in London agreed to reissue the great charter (Magna Carta) extracted from King John of England in 1214 to limit excessive and arbitrary government and, lo and behold, the English were prepared to pay their taxes once more.[257]

Though Surrey had hoped to redeem himself by raising another army to go after Wallace over the winter,[258] Edward was of the firm opinion that, if he wanted something done, he should do it himself. The only silver lining was a sudden outbreak of unity in the face of defeat at the hands of the Scots in an England that had been close to civil war. Even the agreement to abide by the Magna Carta did not necessarily solve the financial problems that had led to such widespread discontent in the first place, however, and those officials trying desperately to save the few English garrisons left in Scotland or protect the north of England often found themselves without pay or supplies as the winter dragged on.[259]

In Scotland, Wallace's government not only established normal peacetime control over much of the country but reached out to potential European allies, primarily the French king and the pope. The new bishop of St Andrews, William Lamberton, visited both Rome and Paris in 1297-8, kick-starting the process of lobbying to have King John restored to his kingdom. But much still rested on what would happen when Edward himself marched north into Scotland once again.

The king was back on English soil by mid-March 1298 with plans to muster his next army by late May, postponed till 23 June. With his usual eye for legal niceties, he paved the way for military action with manoeuvrings played out at a council meeting held in York in April, to which Scottish representatives were scrupulously invited. When, as expected, they did not turn up, their slighted monarch felt himself entirely justified in ordering the forfeiture of their lands. Such an extreme measure, which he had applied to Wales but not en masse to Scotland except very briefly in 1296, turned the northern kingdom into a potential goldmine for anyone interested in the prospect of winning new lands and property.[260]

There was no need to summon the Scottish lords to join the royal army once their failure to come to York made their intentions clear. The exception that proved the rule was Robert (6), but he was now to all intents and purposes an Essex man.[261] He also had little choice but to toe Edward's line for the king had lost patience with his failure to pay back all manner of debts, including loans. On 4 June an exasperated Edward ordered the sheriff of Essex to seize Robert (6)'s goods to the tune of over £650 (nearly half a million) and have it sent to York by the middle of the month.[262] Given the king's desperate need for money, this is perfectly understandable, but he may also have felt a distinct lack of sympathy for a man who allowed his Scottish lands to be ravaged by 'rebels' that surely included his own son.

Three days later Robert (6) was granted safe-conducts for himself and his men to accompany the king to Scotland. The fact that these were to last until Christmas suggests that Edward intended to be absolutely sure this time that his northern province was fully under control before he went home.[263] The army he mustered in the early summer of 1298 was immense by medieval standards, numbering some 3000 horsemen and over 25,000 footsoldiers. This was a testament to how miraculously the previous year's troubles had evaporated in the aftermath of Stirling Bridge and Edward's tacit acknowledgement – through the reissuing of the Magna Carta – that he had treated his people badly.[264] The king was absolutely determined to make 1298 a much better year than 1297.

And it was not as if everything was sweetness and light in the Scottish camp. The Comyns were beginning to make their presence felt, coming out openly against the English once they knew that Comyn of Badenoch's son John was on his way home after being captured at Dunbar. Although the men and money they could lay their hands on was no doubt helpful, Wallace may have found the Comyns' and their friends' disdain for his authority over them somewhat wearing, even if this contempt did not necessarily extend to a 'secret plot against the guardian under the guise of expressions of virgin-innocence but with their tails tied together.'[265] Nevertheless, it is possible that the pressure put on Sir William by Scotland's natural leaders may have tempted him to seek to justify his unorthodox rise to power with a conventional military victory against the English king himself.

In its first phase, Wallace's plan was a simple, albeit scarcely chivalrous, one. Edward's army was exactly the kind of monstrous military machine that does indeed march on its stomach. The king was well aware of the need for provisions, and was even attempting to pay for them with hard cash rather than the usual far-fetched promises of money. But just because food was ordered, didn't mean it would arrive.[266]

As the English marched through south-eastern Scotland in the first week of July 1298, they found a desolate, stinking wilderness, the fertile plains and rolling hills blackened by fire, crops destroyed and animals removed so that there were neither provisions to be had, nor anyone to ask where the Scottish army might be lurking.[267] Wallace had determined to starve the English, either to force them straight back home again or to weaken them so effectively that he and his army might best them for a second time.

The strategy worked, to begin with at least, since most of Edward's ship-borne supplies couldn't reach him thanks to malicious 'contrary winds.'[268] The king put on a brave face to conceal his own anxiety since he had no idea where Wallace was, or what his intentions might be. By now (mid-July), as the English lay camped at Kirkliston ten miles west of Edinburgh, Edward was forced to consider the possibility that the Guardian intended to launch an attack on the unprotected northern counties of England, ordering spies to be sent out 'as secretly and circumspectly as possible' to find out. At the same time, he decided he had no choice but to fall back towards Edinburgh in the hope that supplies would finally arrive and someone somewhere might tell him in which wood or bog Wallace lurked.

The news came not a moment too soon from the pro-English earls of Dunbar and Angus, who had just received word from their spies. The pair rushed into Edward's presence. 'My lord king', they said, 'the Scottish army is at a distance of only six short leagues[269] from you, near Falkirk.' The Guardian apparently knew of Edward's intention to retreat to Edinburgh and meant to follow them and attack at night. The English set off immediately to cover the distance between the two armies. On a moor east of Linlithgow, roughly half-way, they camped for the night, rising early on Monday 22 July 1298. As Edward went to mount his charger, the great beast kicked out at him, breaking two ribs and sending a ripple of panic through his army. But the king calmly got on his horse and they all hastened on their way through the quiet streets of Linlithgow.[270]

At last, the weary English 'raised their eyes' and saw a multitude of spears on the slopes of a hill opposite. Thinking this was the Scottish army, they rushed across, but, when they crested the hill, the enemy had disappeared. Edward called a halt and bade the bishop of Durham say mass for St Mary Magdalene, whose feast day it was. God rewarded their piety; even before the sacrament was finished, they could see Wallace and his men getting ready to fight.

Sir William could have chosen not to give battle, could have allowed his men to slip away, a contingency that King Robert certainly factored into his own plans before the battle of Bannockburn sixteen years later. Perhaps Wallace was goaded into a fight by the Scottish nobles with him. But the Guardian was also perfectly well aware of the toll the previous weeks of hardship must have taken on Edward's army and presumably felt that his spearmen – many of them no doubt veterans of Stirling Bridge – were quite capable of seeing off the English cavalry from this strongly-defensive position towards the top of a small hill.

He divided them into four battalions of schiltroms – the classic Scottish 'hedgehog'-like formation – each man holding his spear out and up, standing shoulder to shoulder with his neighbour and facing outwards.' To protect them further, archers from Selkirk Forest under their commander, Sir John Stewart of Jedburgh – James the Steward's brother – were placed between each schiltrom. The Scottish cavalry, surely led by the Comyns, were either at the back or the sides.[271]

Despite a disastrous charge by two brigades of English cavalry and the corresponding flight of their Scottish counterparts – perhaps unconvinced that they had anything to contribute to Wallace's strategy – Edward managed to regain the initiative. He used his archers to pick holes in the schiltroms, the Scottish spearmen falling 'like blossoms in an orchard when the fruit has ripened.'[272] Those survivors who did not flee were finished off by the English cavalry and infantry in more conventional fashion.

Wallace, like the Comyns, did not wait to be slaughtered, riding off, probably into the safety of the Torwood to the north-west of Falkirk. His brief and extraordinary moment at the very pinnacle of Scottish government was over, though his work was far from done. For the time being Sir William largely disappears from view, though he occasionally resurfaces, still grimly intent on attacking the English.

Edward's soldiers were once more exultant, well pleased with themselves and their king, the difficulties of the previous year entirely forgotten.

> Berwick, Dunbar, and Falkirk too
> Show all that traitor Scots can do.
> England exult! Your Prince is peerless.

> Where you he leads, follow fearless.[273]

Victory must have tasted sweet to Edward too after the trials and tribulations of his war against France. But even though most Scottish castles were re-equipped with an English garrison, the battle of Falkirk did not bring Scotland to heel in the way that Dunbar had done two years earlier; while the English king controlled south-east Scotland as far as Stirling, with a toe-hold at Lochmaben in the south-west, he could not claim to rule the rest of the kingdom.

Falkirk also taught Scotland's leaders an important lesson. As they met in the coming months to squabble and bicker over who should become Guardian in Wallace's stead, there was one thing they could all agree on: fighting battles was no way to win the kingdom's freedom. Edward found that he had little time to celebrate before his enemies in Scotland were plotting once more to confound him.

Ironically, too, given that Falkirk was a Scottish defeat, it nonetheless persuaded Robert (7) to nail his colours once more to the Scottish mast for all to see. Edward discovered this for himself when he dashed across to Ayr in late August 1298, presumably having been alerted to trouble brewing in the west.[274] But he was too late – the town was deserted and in flames, Robert having already taken to the hills, a strategy that would stand him in good stead in the years to come. Though Edward wanted his men to pursue him into the difficult country to the south, their great war-horses were far too expensive to waste on such boggy, uneven terrain and, in any case, the army was running out of supplies. The king had to be satisfied with taking Robert (6)'s castle of Lochmaben on 3 September, underlining the fact that, until then, it must have been taken and held by Edward's enemies. Given that young Robert (7) granted a charter there in May 1298, we might surmise that the master of Annandale over the preceding year may well have been him and not his father.[275]

For the next six years, however, Lochmaben became Edward I's castle lost to both the ineffectual lord of Annandale – who may even have been in the English army during its brief siege – and his ambitious son. Even Robert (6)'s loyal knights who had rebuffed young Robert's impassioned speech in 1297 became royal servants, taking the king's pay to defend the border against those for whom Falkirk had settled nothing.[276]

Robert (7)'s calculation in choosing this moment to relaunch his career as a Scottish patriot in such a public manner was surely a simple one. He would know that Wallace couldn't survive for much longer as guardian, given that military success was the only reason Sir William had reached that lofty position in the first place. He would also know that, despite their less than glorious role at Falkirk, the Comyns were already manoeuvring themselves into position to take over. He was not about to let them do so without a fight, not when there was an empty throne glinting somewhere in the distance.

Chapter Eight

Difficult times

In which Robert (7) becomes Guardian of Scotland, but has to share power with his rival, John Comyn the younger of Badenoch. However, much to Robert's chagrin, King John is released into papal custody in the summer of 1299 thanks to successful Scottish lobbying. Robert gives up the guardianship, but stays on the Scottish side, trying to recover his castle of Turnberry in the autumn of 1301. But his loyalties are soon tested to breaking point when news arrives that Balliol has returned to his family lands in northern France. Would King John soon be coming back to Scotland at the head of a French army?

The Tay Bridge at Dundee with St Paul's cathedral in front of it, standing on the site of Dundee castle. [Paul McIlroy].

With Robert (7)'s return to active duty, the Scottish struggle against English rule was made all the harder by the political divisions that his presence naturally unleashed; for he clearly wished to lead resistance to Edward's regime, presumably with the ultimate goal of re-establishing an independent Scottish kingship with his name on it somewhere down the line. Seven hundred years later, the future king's reputation might tempt us to imagine that this wasn't particularly controversial, but if we're honest about his achievements up till now, then it should be clear that his leadership credentials rested not on proven military success, but the divisive spectre of his family's claim to the throne. This was further complicated by the fact that the Bruce claim was, of course, currently held by his father, who had little or no political sway in Scotland.

Nevertheless, Robert (7)'s confidence in his own destiny had clearly been given a boost in the previous year's uprising, but it is hard not to see something of his grandfather in the sheer bravado with which he approached the Comyns, Scotland's most powerful family, and made it clear that he was going to lead the kingdom in the ongoing war. Even though we have no real idea how he did it, what arguments he used, and how large a following he had among the nobles and the bishops, it is still remarkable. His own family had spent most of King John's reign in self-imposed exile, his father was a spendthrift lackey of Edward I, and Robert himself had scarcely covered himself in glory, coming out of nowhere to capitulate at Irvine and stopping short of open support for Wallace, even if there are hints of collusion.

Nevertheless, by the end of 1298 Robert (7), earl of Carrick had become Guardian of Scotland. But he certainly hadn't won the argument entirely, for he had to share power with the eldest son of Comyn of Badenoch, who was also nephew of the exiled King John. Like Bruce, this John Comyn was still in his twenties, but had considerably more experience under his belt to justify his elevation to the highest office in the kingdom.[277] He had been one of those who defended Dunbar castle in 1296, ending up in the Tower of London for his pains. Serving with Edward in Flanders in return for his freedom in 1297, he slipped away from the English army at Aardenburg as it made for the Belgian coast at the end of February 1298.[278] His credentials, in other words, were far more impressive and he now took on the mantle of leadership not only of Scotland, but his family, for we hear no more of his father until his death around 1302. Not surprisingly, this was a most uneasy relationship. Right from the word go, these two young men embarked upon a feud that would change the course of Scottish history, one that reflected the power-struggle between their two families, but also hints at a far more personal animosity.

Robert (7)'s first documented act as 'one of the Guardians of Scotland' was to confirm on 5 December 1298 the lands and office of constable of Dundee given to Alexander Scrymgeour 'by gift of Sir William Wallace, former Guardian.' But nowhere did this document mention King John, in whose name Wallace certainly claimed to be acting in the original charter.[279] This was the dilemma for Bruce and the Scots who supported him – pausing to refight the battle over the crown of Scotland would have done serious, if not permanent, damage to the war effort against Edward. But it must have galled them to imagine for a single second that Balliol might be the ultimate beneficiary of their dangerous enterprise.

Nevertheless, for those Scots traipsing around the courts of Europe, there could be no room for doubt if they wished to manoeuvre some heavyweight names on to their side. Certainly Bishop Lamberton – whose trip to the continent in 1298-9 did much for the Scottish cause – was not arguing for anything other than King John's return. The same was true for other Scots already abroad and, thanks to them, the pope and the French king had been arguing for Balliol's release from as early as January 1298. Then, presumably at Lamberton's express urging, King Philip of France wrote to King Edward again in June 1298, demanding that he set free the Scottish king and other Scottish prisoners. At the same time, the pope wrote to the king of Scotland himself, asking John to 'show favour' to Lamberton, who had just been made bishop in Rome – presumably because the appointment was made by Wallace as Guardian without the imprisoned Balliol's consent.[280]

Ten months later, on 6 April 1299, King Philip wrote to Bruce and Comyn as 'Guardians in the name of King John', apparently 'moved to his very marrow by the evils brought on their country through hostile malignity.' In a line that must have sent shivers down Robert's spine, the French king said that he admired 'their constancy to their King and their shining valour in defence of their native land against injustice,' urging them to keep up the good work. However, despite being 'not unmindful of the old league between their King, themselves, and him,' Philip wasn't so upset by their plight as to promise immediate aid. Nevertheless, he told them that he 'is carefully pondering ways and means of helping them,' but would not reveal more in the letter, in case it was intercepted, entrusting his words to Bishop Lamberton of St Andrews 'for whom he asks full credence.'[281] It was the bishop's return to Scotland in the summer of 1299 with this message, along with news of the pope's support on similar lines, that brought the canker at the heart of Scottish resistance to Edward I out into the open.

****

In the first half of 1299, the former king of Scotland was tucked up in England, enjoying a degree of freedom to hunt that implied that Edward believed Balliol had no interest whatsoever in regaining his throne. Indeed, John may, in the months after his humiliating abdication, have wished that the Scots would leave him alone, as he initially had high hopes that he might be restored to his English lands.[282] But that became an impossible dream once rebellion broke out in 1297 and Bishop Lamberton of St Andrews and other senior Scots began to press the northern kingdom's case in Europe.

The results of their efforts were dramatic; on 7 July 1299 Edward was presented with a letter from Pope Boniface VIII demanding the immediate release of any Scottish clerics in custody, which was good news for the bishop of Glasgow, still held in Roxburgh castle. Another letter asserted that the pope was also moved to 'praying and admonishing the King that he would leave John de Balliol, lately King of Scotland, in the keeping of the Holy Father, since he had surrendered to his mercy.' This demand was reiterated by Philip of France, who, making at least some effort to help the Scots, was equally insistent that Balliol should be released as part of an Anglo-French peace treaty that also paved the way for Edward's marriage to Philip's sister, Marguerite. Even more worryingly for the English king, the pope was now minded to insist that the whole issue of who should, or should not, rule Scotland be submitted for his judgement, though Edward wasn't actually sent that letter for another year.[283]

Balliol's release into the custody of the bishop of Vicenza, acting for Pope Boniface, followed swiftly on 18 July 1299. The fact that John was caught at Dover trying to smuggle out the gold crown and Great Seal of Scotland either means that he was sentimental about his brief years as king or that he hoped to use them again in the near future. He was soon enjoying a rather more promising exile in the bishop of Cambrai's castle of Malmaison in northern France, where he – like Edward and the Scots – awaited further developments.[284]

Even though the 'former king of Scotland' was far from free to do as he pleased, his removal from the custody of the English king was a major blow to Edward and a significant boost to many of those fighting to restore the northern kingdom's independence. But not all. It was certainly not good news for the Bruces – in that, both father and son could surely agree. In the first instance, as news of John's release spread across England, even Robert (6) – perhaps still hoping against hope that Edward might one day look favourably on his own claim to the Scottish throne – was spurred into action at this unexpected turn of events. He must have written in protest to the bishop of Vicenza, to whom the former king was initially entrusted, for he received a letter in return in the bishop's own hand, though whether this showed that the pope was in any way sympathetic to reopening the Great Cause is unknown.[285] There can be no doubt that Balliol's release put a completely different complexion on the former king's usefulness to those fighting against Edward, as both Robert (6) and his son – though on opposite sides in the war – would have been painfully aware.

Militarily, too, there was good news for the Scots as 1299 proved to be a year of respite. Edward decided to postpone another campaign in order to celebrate his marriage to Marguerite of France in fulfilment of the terms of the Anglo-French peace treaty, which would finally get him Gascony back. This left English garrisons – mostly in south-east Scotland – vulnerable to attack. Sir Robert Clifford's men in Lochmaben also felt the sharp end of more than one year's terrible harvests, unable to get provisions locally and paying dearly for them elsewhere.[286] At least some of the raids on Galloway over the summer were led by young Robert (7), who seems to have been determined to wrest Annandale out of Edward's hands, though presumably he had no intention of giving the lordship back to his father.[287]

News of Balliol's release was almost certainly brought to Scotland on the return of the embassy led by Bishop Lamberton, who was looking for a boat to take him home from the Flanders coast in early July 1299 after his diplomatic assault on France and the papacy.[288] It is not difficult to imagine that the news was just as shocking to young Robert as it was to his father. The internal conflict that he surely felt in reconciling his desire to advance his own family's credentials to rule with the growing momentum behind the restoration of Balliol as king was about to come to an explosive head.

Having made life difficult for the garrison at Lochmaben in early August 1299, Bruce headed north to Glasgow within the next week or so. With him was Sir Malcolm Wallace, though there was no sign of his brother, Sir William. At Glasgow Robert and his men joined his fellow Guardian, John Comyn, and an impressive array of Scottish nobles, including the earls of Buchan and Menteith and James the Steward to create a Scottish army that transcended, for the moment at least, the serious divisions within it. Comyn had already sent an advance party to Selkirk Forest to recce the strength of the English hold on south-east Scotland.

Edward's officials, despite an impressive network of spies, did not yet know exactly where the Scots intended to attack, so precautions were taken right across the border. Memories of Wallace's raids two years earlier were still raw and the order was given to bring in all unharvested crops immediately, for fear the Scots would come for them. Scottish raids, along with a more general lack of grain, had left these northern English communities in such a terrible state that 'our people cannot resist since they have nothing to eat.'[289]

On 20 August, the English constable at Roxburgh finally had more up-to-date information. A week earlier the advance party sent out by Comyn from Glasgow had swept into nearby Selkirk Forest; it was soon followed by the 'great lords of Scotland', including Bishop Lamberton of St Andrews, the earls of Carrick, Buchan, Atholl and Menteith, John Comyn and James the Steward, who intended to launch an attack on Roxburgh. The advance party advised them that the castle's defences were too strong, however – despite the bishop of Glasgow's attempts to undermine its defences from within.[290] The Scottish leaders did not know what to do with this news, keeping 'quiet', so far as the English garrisons were concerned, until 19 August.

By this time they were gathered at Peebles, where their united front collapsed in dramatic fashion. The underlying cause was surely the festering effect of the news of King John's release, but it was Sir William Wallace who started the fight, even if at that very moment the former Guardian was some sixty miles away trying to stop supplies from reaching the English garrison in Stirling castle.[291] As the Scots nobles kicked their heels at Peebles, Sir David Graham, a close ally of John Comyn, demanded the seizure of Wallace's lands and goods 'because he was leaving the kingdom without the permission or approval of the Guardians.' Sir William's brother, Sir Malcolm, retorted that nothing should be taken 'for they were protected by the peace in which Wallace had left the kingdom, since he was leaving to work for the good of the kingdom.' Both gentlemen then called the other a liar and 'drew their daggers.'

Someone rushed off to tell the earl of Buchan and John Comyn himself that a fight had kicked off. Comyn then 'leaped at the earl of Carrick [Robert (7)] and seized him by the throat, and the earl of Buchan turned on the bishop of St Andrews, declaring that treason and lésémajestie were being plotted.'[292] It is possible, in the current overheated state of Scottish politics, that the Comyns were worried that Wallace's imminent trip to the courts of Europe was intended to put a Bruce on the throne rather than bring about John Balliol's restoration. Certainly Sir William's early anti-English activities had taken place alongside, and were almost certainly co-ordinated with, Bruce, Wishart and the Steward's rebellion, while he had proved himself no friend to the Comyns.

But in fact the former guardian had no intention of upsetting the status quo by arguing for someone other than King John in the courts of Europe. In essence, Wallace probably had little time for the politics that inevitably went hand-in-hand with noble alliances and spheres of interest and were certainly not peculiar to Scotland. However, the fact that he travelled to the continent with men with Balliol connections and even visited John during the three and a half years he spent on the Continent[293] seriously undermines any suggestion that he was, like his brother, firmly in the Bruce camp. But this did not stop the Comyns from fearing the worst from a man who had certainly never paid them the attention that the family felt was their due. It wasn't necessarily what Wallace was doing that bothered them, but that he was doing it without asking them.

Nevertheless, the fact that John Comyn dared to lay hands on Robert (7) reveals a far more fundamental reason for the whole fracas – he did not trust his fellow Guardian one jot. It probably galled Comyn that Bruce, as an earl, preceded him in any formal documents. But he must have had well-founded suspicions that Robert's commitment to the cause of Scottish independence was indistinguishable from his family's claim to the throne. For Comyn, this flew in the face of Balliol's undoubted, if brief, reign as a properly inaugurated king of Scotland. Even if – and it was now a big if – King John was out of the picture, the heir to the throne must be his nearest living relative. Balliol's son Edward remained under the English king's control south of the border and was therefore of no use to the Scots. But John Comyn was himself Balliol's nephew and, even if he – like Bruce – did not view ruling in his own name as a realistic possibility at this point in time, he certainly had a fundamentally different view from his fellow Guardian as to what should happen to the vacant Scottish throne if his uncle failed to return.

So now the Scottish political community was forced to confront what had probably been obvious for some time – the two Guardians just could not work together. The need for a solution to this serious problem was made all the more urgent by a letter brought to them at Peebles describing trouble in northern Scotland caused by Scots loyal to Edward I. It was quickly agreed that William Lamberton, bishop of St Andrews should join Bruce and Comyn as a third and senior Guardian to try to keep the peace and get things done, a decision that can only mean that the Comyns did not believe that Lamberton was part of the Bruce faction. A very serious crisis had been averted, for the moment at least.

As everyone headed for home, Sir Ingram d'Umfraville, a friend of Comyn's, was made sheriff of Roxburgh with 100 men-at-arms and 1500 footsoldiers from each lordly retinue to harass English garrisons in the south-east and even take the war into northern England.[294] Robert (7) returned to the south-west to continue his exertions against the garrison of Lochmaben.[295] It had been a tumultuous few weeks that had brought him face-to-face with the realities of Comyn power and Comyn antipathy to his own aspirations. In the north of Scotland, they ruled more or less as kings,[296] while his own influence was limited to parts of the south-west. It was John Comyn who had sent the advance party to spy out English positions in the south-east earlier in August and he had therefore presumably already decided what the strategy of the Scottish army gathering at Glasgow should be before Robert got there. Indeed, it was probably Bruce's presence at Peebles that resulted in the hiatus in Scottish activity once the advance party reported on the strength of the English garrison at Roxburgh, a hiatus that hints at profound disagreement as to what they should do next.

Nevertheless, Robert's position as Guardian remained secure; the only issue had been how to make his relationship with Comyn work, a problem solved by the addition of Bishop Lamberton. His ability to win friends and influence people may have been compromised by the English foothold in his father's lordship, but he does seem to have been able to exert some pressure on the Comyns to ensure that his allies received a share of the patronage pie. His friend, John, earl of Atholl, for one, was described as sheriff of Aberdeen in March 1299, attending a court held by John Comyn, earl of Buchan and justiciar of Scotland.[297]

At the same time, the English in south-west Scotland faced considerable difficulties after Edward's return south after Falkirk. For a start, there was no-one in overall charge of English-held Scotland, Surrey having proved in spades that he was neither willing nor able to do the job. Now there were two royal lieutenants, one based at Berwick and the other at Carlisle or Lochmaben. Even then, it was proving difficult to keep men in post, particularly in the vulnerable south-west. Sir Robert Clifford, who had been responsible for the defence of the western border since 1297, bowed out in August 1299. However, his replacement lasted only a few months and doesn't seem to have made any of the planned expeditions against Bruce to retaliate for Robert's attempts to poach Lochmaben's supplies from south of the border in early autumn.

The Scottish garrison at Caerlaverock castle was also a thorn in the side of the English at Lochmaben. Only fifteen miles to the south-west, Caerlaverock was owned by the Maxwells, who were close allies of the Comyns,[298] so the fact that the castle was commanded in 1299 by Robert Cunningham, a nephew of James the Steward, suggests that the Bruce faction were also having some success in carving up south-west Scotland among themselves, albeit in dangerous war conditions. Nevertheless, the fact that Cunningham was killed by men from Lochmaben at the beginning of October (much to the Steward's distress), as well as Bruce's own inability to make any headway against his father's castle despite the food shortages within its walls, highlights Robert (7)'s failure to prove himself as an effective war leader.[299] He could certainly have argued that he had a far more difficult job than John Comyn, but, as William Wallace had already learned to his cost, it was results that counted in these difficult times.

With little to show for his personal military endeavours, Robert (7) returned east in November 1299 to join the great lords of Scotland in another united effort against the English. The Scots were now focusing their efforts on a siege of Stirling castle, which was always vulnerable to attacks on its food supplies, situated as it was in the very middle of the country and over forty miles – by land or river – from the nearest English garrison at Edinburgh. Wallace had begun the process of trying to prevent Edward's men inside Stirling castle from receiving sustenance from outside in August 1299, but he had finally left Scotland by October at the latest since we know that he was in Paris on 2 November.[300]

Less than two weeks later, Bruce, Lamberton and Comyn were in the Torwood, another great forest only eight miles south-east of Stirling, picking up where the former Guardian had left off. There they would be reasonably safe, but could confront any attempt to resupply the castle via the nearby Roman road and keep an eye out for ships sailing up the Forth a few miles to the north-east. But there was other business to attend to, for on 13 November they sent a letter to King Edward, agreeing to a truce between Scotland and England that Philip of France was trying to arrange. They probably didn't spend all that much longer besieging Stirling, leaving it to fall to local men a month or so later, around the turn of 1299/1300.[301]

****

The letter sent by Lamberton, Bruce and Comyn to Edward I in November 1299 clarified what had been the underlying bone of contention at Peebles in August, for it was sent in the names of the 'guardians of the kingdom of Scotland in the name of the renowned prince, the lord John, illustrious king of Scotland, chosen by the community of the said kingdom ...'[302] Robert had well and truly lost that argument; Scottish resistance to English rule was now entirely focused on the restoration of the king that Edward had so emphatically cast off the Scottish throne three years earlier, helped by the Bruces.

Some of this new-found confidence may, despite the Comyns' doubts on the matter, have been down to Wallace. At the same time as the Guardians sent their letter to Edward – and therefore only a few months after Balliol's arrival in northern France – King John had to be sent a severe reminder that he had promised not to try to remove himself from papal custody. He was also told that 'no one, of whatsoever state, order or dignity he be, dare under pain of excommunication in any way hinder or attempt anything in the contrary.'

Something had clearly happened to give the pope a fright and the most likely explanation is that Sir William Wallace and his embassy had stopped off to see Balliol at Malmaison on their way from Scotland to Paris a few weeks before. To ease his mind further, the pope ordered that John be moved first to Châtillon-sur-Marne near Reims and then, in December 1299, to Gevrey-Chambertin near Dijon, safely out of the path of any Scots coming from the ports of the Low Countries.[303]

Back in Scotland, Robert (7) therefore found himself leader of a cause that was, in one vital respect, the opposite of the one for which he would have given his life and he surely wondered what exactly he was fighting for. It will come as no real surprise, then, that between November 1299 and May 1300, he went some way to answering that question by stepping down as Guardian, even if he was still prepared to call out his men to serve in his earldom of Carrick's contingent of any army summoned to defend the realm.[304] But his decision surely dismayed those friends and allies who viewed his presence among the leaders of Scotland's government as offering at least a partial counterbalance to the power of the Comyns.

These powerful divisions, which Robert's resignation did little to heal, came to a head yet again when Scotland's great lords met at a parliament held in Rutherglen near Glasgow in May 1300. This time John Comyn turned on Bishop Lamberton, who was supported by Bruce's friends, the earl of Atholl and James the Steward. Having only two guardians was still clearly impossible, with Comyn announcing melodramatically that he didn't want to stay in office with the bishop. The only solution was to appoint another guardian and in the end – surely to no-one's real surprise – the Comyns prevailed. Their friend, Sir Ingram d'Umfraville – a relation of the Balliols as well as sheriff of Roxburgh since August 1299 – was chosen as Robert (7)'s replacement.[305] The Bruce star was now in danger of being eclipsed altogether.

But from the point of view of the war with England, it was perhaps just as well that John Comyn was powerful enough to force unity on the rest of the political community, for Edward was intent on leading yet another army north in this year's campaigning season. This time the focus was on south-west Scotland and the parliament at Rutherglen had to be postponed until 24 June because the earl of Buchan was currently away negotiating with the men of Galloway, whose instincts to remain as independent of the Scottish crown as possible had been only slightly tempered by the fact that John Balliol used to be lord of the region. Buchan, who held the lands of Cruggleton deep in Galloway, was perhaps also attempting to prove – deliberately or otherwise – that the Scots could get along perfectly well without Robert (7) in the south-west too.

The Scots probably knew that Edward intended to muster at Carlisle on the same date as their postponed parliament. The English king recrossed the border once more on 5 July 1300, reaching Caerlaverock castle – still held by the Scots, despite the loss of their constable the previous year – five days later. The siege did not last long, whereupon Edward headed north-east to inspect the castle at Dumfries, recaptured by his men earlier in the year.[306] English control of south-western Scotland had just become considerably more convincing.

The Scots had learned their lesson since Falkirk; there would be no repeat attempt to engage a vastly superior English army led by the king himself, a decision that can surely be credited to the Comyns. Instead the motto was 'harry and harass,' but even that was dangerous. Between 6 and 8 August, as Edward continued west into Galloway, the Scottish army attacked a party of English out foraging at the mouth of the Water of Fleet. Though a number of English horses were killed, Edward's men ultimately came out on top, capturing some of Edward's 'worst enemies' – including the Scottish warden of Selkirk Forest, Sir Robert Keith – who were then sent south to English prisons.[307] Even so, the king had to leave Scotland yet again before he was ready as autumn and the harvest approached and money and supplies both became scarce. He had hoped to traverse through Galloway and then turn north as far as Ayr, to bring the war right to the doorstep of Robert (7), earl of Carrick.

On the plus side, it probably afforded Edward some satisfaction that Annandale was proving a model Anglo-Scottish lordship, now paying at least some taxes to the exchequer in Berwick (and not, therefore, to Robert (6)). He also had reason to be pleased that the threat from Caerlaverock had been dealt with; that Dumfries castle was in the process of acquiring a brand new 'pele' just like the one newly built at Lochmaben; and that royal officials in the south-east were making expeditions to try to make Selkirk Forest less accessible to the Scots. On the downside, Galloway was still largely a no-go area, suggesting that the earl of Buchan had been successful in his discussions with its lords.[308] There had been progress, but Edward may have felt he was taking one or two steps forward, only to have to retreat at least one back.

To add to his woes, in August 1300 – as his campaign began to grind to a halt in the wilds of Galloway – the English king finally received the letter from Pope Boniface drafted the previous year, questioning his right to intervene in Scotland and demanding that the whole contentious issue be submitted to Rome for judgement.[309] This was not a command that Edward could ignore, but he was certainly not going to submit to it without a fight. To be brutally honest, Scotland just happened to be the issue that these great men were currently sparring over, but it was part of a much longer history of confrontation between popes and the kings of England and France in particular over their respective powers and jurisdictions, and – as ever – their desire to extend them.

Before he left, the king agreed a truce with the Scots to last until 31 May 1301.[310] Although this gave everyone a breathing space, a formal cessation of hostilities probably suited Edward best, since it prevented the Scots from attempting to undo the gains of the summer's campaign, giving him time to prepare for the next one in comparative peace. He decided on a two-pronged attack – he himself would command an army marching into Scotland from the east, while his son – 17-year old Edward, recently made

Prince of Wales – would have nominal charge of a force attacking from the west. It was his father's dearest wish that the young man might have 'the chief honour of taming the pride of the Scots.'[311]

The king arrived at Berwick on 5 July 1301, the rest of his army gathering over the following week. Their target was the immense state-of the art castle at Bothwell, south-east of Glasgow, taken by the Scots in 1299/1300 without siege equipment but using the starvation tactics they had successfully adopted at Stirling. Edward and his men slowly made their way to Glasgow, plagued all the way by Scottish raiding parties and finally arriving on 21 August.[312] At least the king could take comfort from the 'good rumours' that reached him there of his son's activities in the west.[313]

The Prince of Wales was at Ayr around the same time, quickly and easily taking whatever remained of the town and castle after Robert set them on fire in 1298. The prince then turned his attention on Bruce's castle of Turnberry, thirteen miles along the coast to the south. After a short siege, it fell, though Robert himself was already gone. John Comyn was targeted too, his castle of Dalswinton also falling to the English in early September. However, it was soon snatched back, allowing the Scots to continue to move relatively freely, despite the presence of two English armies not so far away and a number of English garrisons close by.

The leadership of the Scottish army brought out to shadow the two English ones reflected another shift in Scottish politics, for by now Sir John Soules had become Guardian, though probably alongside John Comyn.[314] Soules had family connections to the Comyns, but was also close to the Bruces, having gone with Robert (7) to King John's court in 1293 to sort out the whole messy business of which Bruce held the earldom of Carrick and who should therefore pay homage for it. Soules had also gone with Bishop Lamberton to the continent in 1297-8 and was supposedly appointed as Guardian by none other than John Balliol himself. Like Lamberton, he was clearly trusted by the Scottish king and was perhaps viewed as a more 'neutral' figure – that is, not firmly tied to the interests of the Comyns – back in Scotland.[315]

So the new Guardian, along with John Comyn, earl of Buchan, led out a Scottish army into the south-west, initially stationing himself at Loudoun. Another Scottish force lay thirteen miles further east at Stonehouse. This allowed the Scots to keep an eye on Ayr to the west, where the Prince of Wales was based, and King Edward's army in Glasgow to the north. But watching was one thing; acting was another.

Meanwhile, the king settled into the siege of Bothwell castle, which belonged to Andrew Murray, the four-year old son of Wallace's colleague at Stirling Bridge who was being brought up in the far north of Scotland 'among the king's enemies.'[316] Edward had promised this considerable prize to his cousin, Sir Aymer de Valence, and by 22 September, the mighty castle was his.

With the English making gains in central and western Scotland, Soules and the former Guardian, Ingram d'Umfraville, headed south with a force that supposedly numbered 'forty bannerets, twelve score [240] men-at-arms [and] seven thousand footmen or more' to see if they could succeed at Lochmaben where Bruce had failed. Attacking English garrisons, which were often reduced to a skeleton staff due to Edward's own need for men, was a sensible strategy, but that didn't make it easy. Despite a number of English casualties, the new pele at Lochmaben stood firm and the Scots withdrew to Dalswinton. But they were expected to return in greater numbers, which may well have persuaded Edward to send his son back down into Galloway from Turnberry. By the end of September Soules and his army had moved on, though the king was well aware that the Scots might now set their sights on his over-stretched and undermanned garrisons in the south-east.[317]

By this time Edward had already made a major decision, having set his creaking war machine into overdrive in August to find – from God knows where – the men, money, provisions and equipment that would allow him to spend the winter in Scotland. He had certainly not forgotten about the continuing diplomatic face-off with the pope that had intensified over the summer, replying to Boniface's letter with some of the material carefully selected from monastic sources gathered to back his claim to overlordship before he came north in 1291. This prompted the Scots and their envoys in turn to marshal their arguments via their own carefully collated historical examples to show that the English king had no right to intervene in the affairs of an independent Scottish kingdom.[318] Edward may well have felt that he was in a race against time to finish off his reconquest of the northern kingdom in case he was told categorically to stop what he was doing while Boniface looked into the issue, a process that might well drag on for months, if not years.

At the beginning of October, when he should have been flushed with his recent success at Bothwell, the king was desperately trying to keep his armies and garrisons together from his new headquarters at Dunipace just south of Stirling. His own men needed money to stop them heading for home, the prince needed money, the south-eastern garrisons were on the point of deserting for lack of money and it was the same story in the south-west. His immediate plan, given his demands for siege equipment, was to retake Stirling castle, but that was not the extent of his ambitions for this year's campaign. It was still his fervent hope to complete 'the bridge across the Forth' so that he could make 'such exploit against his enemies that his business' would quickly reach 'a satisfactory and honourable conclusion.' But by the middle of October it was patently clear, much to Edward's great distress and ire, that none of this was going to happen in 1301. It would take all his officials' ingenuity and far too much of England's dwindling resources to keep him in Scotland until the next campaigning season.[319]

In fact Soules and the Scottish army never did go east. Instead they moved north and west to fill the vacuum left when the Prince of Wales and his men headed down into Galloway before finally heading towards Stirling to join his father. Riding out from Dalswinton north-west through Ayrshire, the Guardian reached Turnberry around 3 October, besieging the castle 'with four hundred men-at-arms and petail [infantry] enough to damage it as much as they could.'[320] Even so, they did not succeed and Soules headed further north towards Renfrewshire through districts that had only recently submitted to King Edward.[321] On 25 October the English paid 'a certain boy' to go towards Glasgow 'to find out the rumours there about the Scots.'[322]

Robert (7) was surely with Soules in trying to retake his own castle. Indeed, it is striking that the Scottish army in this last phase of the campaign of 1301 seemed intent on recovering territory lost to both Bruce and his neighbour and friend, James the Steward. The alternative was unthinkable. A hunted man in his own earldom and his father's lordship, Robert's only other option would have been to cross the water to his Irish lands, though given that they sat within the boundaries of the Anglo-Irish earldom of Ulster, they were scarcely risk-free. Nor were they a long-term solution to the fact that he was, to all intents and purposes, homeless.

****

At the very beginning of October 1301, news reached Scotland from the continent that only served to darken King Edward's mood. It had a similar effect on Robert (7). At some point over the summer, so a letter sent to Edward on 1 October revealed, John Balliol was 'acquired' by Philip IV of France and allowed to go and live in his ancestral castle of Bailleul in

Picardy, 120 miles north of Paris, though whether this was thanks to a formal agreement with the pope or some sort of kidnapping is unclear. Not only that, but it was commonly believed that the king of France was ready to send Balliol back to Scotland 'with a great force.'[323]

Edward probably knew that his desire to winter in Scotland was already doomed, but this news must have made it difficult to know what to do. Certainly the fact that he appointed negotiators in mid-October to arrange a truce with the Scots – something that King Philip's ambassadors had been trying to broker since late August – suggests he was now determined to ensure that the gains he had made in south-west Scotland remained intact until he could mobilise a proper army once again or at least see what Philip's intentions towards Balliol might be.[324] He had certainly given up on Stirling, moving off towards more comfortable quarters at the royal manor at Linlithgow on 21 October. He remained there for the next two months before finally admitting defeat and heading for home on 1 February 1302.[325]

Six days earlier, on 26 January, Edward concluded the Treaty of Asnières with Philip of France that included the granting of a truce to the Scots until 1 November 1302, well beyond this year's campaigning season. Not only that, but he had been forced to accept that the French king would take possession of all lands, castles and revenues captured 'from John Balliol or from the Scots since the messengers of the king of France came to the king of England' – around 24 August, when Edward appointed his own envoys to treat for peace – to be handed over by 16 February 1302 until the end of the truce.326 Since the 1301 campaign had started rather late in the season, this affected much of what had been captured, including Turnberry and Bothwell. At one fell swoop Edward, and the loyal servants to whom he had granted many of these castles and lands, were to lose them again, though hopefully only temporarily. What had seemed almost within his grasp was now drifting further away. And he wasn't getting any younger.

CHAPTER NINE

New beginnings and old endings

In which Robert (7) submits to King Edward who sort of, maybe, suggests that he can claim the Scottish throne if King John were to come back. But only a few months later the Scots are dumped by their continental allies and the English king begins to plan for what he hopes will be a final campaign in 1303. Robert (7) plays a key role in bringing an end to Scottish resistance as the Scots, led by the Guardian, John Comyn, finally capitulate.

The battle of Courtrai was one of medieval Europe's most revolutionary battles where footsoldiers carrying spears used and adapted the terrain to put mounted knights at a disadvantage.

For Robert (7) 1301 was, if anything, even more disastrous than it had been for King Edward. He can have had little appetite for a life on the run, surrounded by enemies on all sides and with the odds heavily stacked against him regaining control of his earldom, never mind establishing himself as a credible Scottish leader. The thought of Turnberry being handed over to the French and John Balliol returning triumphantly to his kingdom must have been unbearable. So he decided not to bear it.

First of all he sent out feelers to Edward's keeper of Galloway, Sir John de St John, at Lochmaben. Presumably after seeking guidance from the king at Linlithgow as to acceptable terms, St John accepted Robert's submission, probably around the turn of 1301/2, in the presence of 'many good people', which almost certainly included his father's knights of Annandale.[327] Bruce and his tenants were guaranteed that they would be neither harmed nor imprisoned and that they could keep their lands and property. But the English king was prepared to go further, agreeing that if Robert lost out by the terms of any papal ordinance or treaty or peace in the war with Scotland or France, then Edward would compensate him, probably a subtle reference to the handing over of Turnberry to the French under the Treaty of Asnières. Robert was also promised control of his nephew, the young earl of Mar – and therefore of the revenues of his earldom - and even some of the lands in Carrick of Sir Ingram d'Umfraville, who had replaced him as Guardian.

But that was not all, though the precise meaning of one crucial element of Robert's submission remains frustratingly elusive. It must certainly have required careful consideration – and drafting – by the king and his lawyers, for it envisaged both the possibility of the kingdom being taken out of Edward's hands and given back to John Balliol and that 'the right' [Edward's claim to overlordship] might be 'disputed or reversed or repealed in a new judgement' – presumably by the pope. In that case, Robert was allowed to pursue *his* right in the king's court or, if it was to be heard in another jurisdiction (presumably the pope again), then Edward would give him all help and support. Finally, the king guaranteed that, should the kingdom of Scotland remain peacefully in his hand, he would protect Robert from anyone who sought to harm him 'as a lord should for his man.'[328]

This extraordinary document lays bare Edward's deepest fears as the harsh winds of winter mocked him and his dwindling, starving army, but it is hard to imagine that such a complex and delicate matter was negotiated over the ninety miles that supposedly separated the two men. Surely, having received the basic guarantees that he would not be harmed or lose his lands, Robert went to Edward for the first time in at least five years on the understanding that they each had something that might prove useful to the other. Bruce must have been contrite, of course, for the king had been grievously offended by his foolish and reckless behaviour. But the unique terms offered to him are proof – were it still needed – of just how vulnerable Edward felt himself to be as Pope Boniface and Philip of France ran diplomatic rings round him.

The English king knew that his claim to overlordship over Scotland might look unconvincing to a papal court, despite his best efforts, whether on strict points of law or for Boniface's own political considerations, or both. And then there was the other possibility that Philip of France might intervene militarily on Balliol's behalf. In either of these worst-case scenarios, young Robert was being encouraged to throw a spanner in the works by putting forward his own right – that-which-should-not-be-named-out-loud but without doubt his claim to the Scottish throne, which Balliol's return would also jeopardise – either in an English court or, if necessary, somewhere else.[329]

Of course, he would have to claim the throne as King Edward's man, but, like his grandfather, this was something he could presumably swallow, for now at least. With his submission, the future king's mind can finally be read and the ambition that lay behind his actions over the past six years laid bare. For all his fine patriotic words to his father's knights of Annandale, Robert could only contemplate an independent Scotland if it had a Bruce king. And he also surely had it in his head that that king should be himself, rather than the man who really had the Bruce 'right' to the Scottish throne.

For what is also remarkable is the fact that both Robert (7) and the king had no qualms about ignoring the shadowy figure of Robert (6), now approaching seventy but still alive and, occasionally, kicking. Indeed, it was probably in the aftermath of his son's return to Edward's peace that the old man dared to complain, somewhat querulously, 'that he has been kept out of his lands of Annandale and Lochmaben castle for four years, and still is, to his loss and great grievance and undeservedly. He begs that he may have them that he may serve the king and hold of him on this march as his neighbours do. If not better treated than hitherto, he can neither borrow nor live without making great mischief.' The king – who had long experience of Robert (6)'s money woes – swept away his complaint, replying dismissively that when he 'is free to make judgement on Scottish affairs then he will hear the reasons of said Robert and do justice to him.'[330]

Meanwhile, while young Robert (7) may have gone with the king to Roxburgh in mid-February as Edward began his long journey home, he was certainly back at Linlithgow at the beginning of March along with the lords who now ruled English-held Scotland, including Sir Robert Clifford, proud possessor of Caerlaverock castle since 1300, and Sir John de St John, who looked after the western border and had received Bruce's submission. But they soon went their separate ways.[331]

At least Robert could now head for home, his earldom newly restored to him. A week later, at the grange of Maybole, he acknowledged that he would no longer ask the tenants of Melrose Abbey [in Roxburghshire] living in his earldom of Carrick to serve with him in a Scottish army going 'abroad [*forinsec*]' – perhaps south of the border or some considerable distance from home – but only for the defence of the realm.[332] With his return to Edward's peace, some sort of normality would hopefully now descend on his lands, after the fraught campaigning wherever and whenever Robert had thought it necessary over the last few years.

He was now, seemingly overnight, a part of the English establishment, with access to money and supplies which, however scarce when Edward brought an army north, somehow always just managed to feed the king's men staying in Scotland permanently.[333] That Edward may never have trusted Robert entirely would not be a great surprise, but, as we will see, he was well enough rewarded over the next few years. He was also given a most useful marriage, to Elizabeth de Burgh, daughter of Edward's ally, the powerful earl of Ulster who had come to Turnberry in 1289 and within whose earldom Bruce's Irish lands lay.

But however generous Edward chose to be, it would never be enough, for within seven or eight months of Robert's submission, the merry-go-round of western European politics abruptly swung 180°. And that meant there was now no question of the English king supporting Bruce's royal ambitions. Instead Robert (7)'s role was to play a conspicuous part in winning Scotland back at last for his royal master. Whether he liked it or not.

****

Scotland's fate hung in the balance, relying, at least in part, on the deeds and decisions of others. Ironically, however, it was the desire of another nation – the Flemings of the Low Countries – to resist their absorption into France that seriously jeopardised Scottish attempts to regain their own independence. In July 1302 – only nine months after the Scots and the English heard that John Balliol might be coming home at the head of a French army – Flemish militias drawn largely from the great cloth-making towns of Bruges, Ghent and Ypres rose up against French occupation, marching to meet Philip IV's knights outside the walls of Courtrai

(Kortrijk in Flemish) only a few miles from the border between Flanders and France. Though some of the French were concerned that the boggy ground would make a mounted charge difficult, they were overruled by the majority, who could not imagine being bested by a bunch of farmers, merchants and craftsmen.

More fool them, for, just like Andrew Murray and William Wallace at Stirling Bridge, the Flemings were well-disciplined and prepared to fight to the death in defence of their freedom. For them, this war was no game, no power-play between rival lords; it was all or nothing. Indeed, even before a blow was struck, their leaders had changed the rules of engagement, insisting that no-one should take either prisoners (for ransom) or booty so as to keep their battle lines intact. This was an extraordinary decision. Nobles following the code of chivalry did not expect to be killed except through bad luck, simply because they were so valuable, unlike footsoldiers who were fair game. But after Courtrai, it was something they had no choice but to accept as part of the landscape of war.

There were a number of elements to Flemish success. One was the pits and ditches they dug so as to ensure that the French cavalry was forced to attack where the Flemings wanted them to. A second was the extreme stupidity of the French commander, who would not let his crossbowmen pick holes in the Flemish lines before the cavalry were let loose on them. Another was the three metres of stream that lay between the two sides. When the French cavalry began to charge, they inevitably had to slow down to cross, taking the sting out of their terrible momentum; at the same time, the Flemish lines were close enough to the stream to make it impossible for the knights to regain the speed they needed to terrify the opposing spearmen into breaking ranks.

All the same, it took great nerve and restraint to stand firm. But even where the French did break through, they were quickly dealt with by the rows of spearmen waiting behind. In close combat, weighed down by heavy armour, their horses terrified by the lethal goedendags (spiked clubs ironically called 'good days') as well as the long spears, the flower of King Philip's chivalry proved no match for these well-organised, determined footsoldiers. In the end, it was a bloodbath; around 40% of the French men-at-arms were killed. At Agincourt 113 years later, when King Henry V of England defeated another French army, the figure was 55%.[334] It was the dawn, however gradual and uncertain, of a new age.

Courtrai is one of the most important battles that most people have never heard of. And it is vital to our story not only because of the dramatic shift in Scotland's fortunes that came in its wake, but also because the warrior king that Robert (7) would one day become picked up the challenge thrown down by the Flemings a few years earlier. There can be little doubt that he studied the details of that startling, shocking victory, whether in a written account or verbal report, so similar are the tactics he would eventually employ.

But all that lay several years in the future. Now he probably rued the day he decided to sue for peace from King Edward in the belief that King John would soon be back to disinherit him yet again. After Courtrai, Philip of France had a very different foreign policy: he was intent on crushing the Flemings, just as King Edward had wanted to crush the Scots after Stirling Bridge. And to do that, he needed no other distractions, which meant peace with England as quickly as possible, which in turn meant ditching his allies, the Scots. To add to Scotland's woes, the pope and the French king now fell out irrevocably and Boniface also found that he needed Edward I as a friend.

All of this created a very different political landscape for the English king and the Scots by the time the truce between them expired on 1 November 1302. On 13 August, for example, Boniface wrote to the Bishop of Glasgow in strident tones, ordering Wishart to pay attention to the letters the pope was writing to the Scottish clergy 'concerning the discord between Edward I and the Scots of which the bishop is chief instigator.'[335] Though the aged Wishart had not been in the thick of the action since his imprisonment at Roxburgh in 1297, he was still a hugely influential figure behind the scenes. But, as Edward had realised two years earlier, the pope's commands could not be ignored forever, especially by a member of the clergy. The best that Wishart and the rest of the Scots could hope for was to delay any action in the hope that the political landscape would change once more.

But it was the noises coming from France that perturbed the Scots most. On 8 September the Guardians held a parliament in Aberdeen and a month later Sir John Soules, the bishops of St Andrews and Dunkeld, the earl of Buchan, James the Steward, Sir Ingram d'Umfraville and Sir William Balliol, a distant cousin of the Scottish king, were all appointed as ambassadors to Paris. All but Balliol and Matthew Crambeth of Dunkeld had been guardians of Scotland, but Crambeth had been, and probably still was, stationed in France, receiving a stipend from King Philip every six months between September 1298 and November 1301.[336] This, then, was as high-powered a delegation as the Scots could muster. Their brief was a simple one – to ensure that France only made peace with England if the agreement included the Scots.[337] Given that Soules was leaving the country, Sir John Comyn – now lord of Badenoch on his father's death – became sole Guardian.[338]

Though Philip IV was not above stringing them along with encouraging words, the Scots in France had very little to bargain with by the time they arrived, though they may never have known that the man they were fighting for now had no interest in returning to his kingdom. On 17 November 1302, John Balliol, King of Scotland wrote to his 'very dear lord and good friend,' King Philip. In it, John acknowledged that 'you have been to us, and still are, a good lord and helpful, and that you have had, and still have, our affairs at heart.' But Balliol knew that times had changed, that, at fifty-three(ish), he too was not getting any younger. And so he asked Philip 'to prosecute, or cause to be prosecuted, our said affairs, especially those we have against the king of England, in the way which shall seem good to you … bringing to an end in the first place your own matters, if so it should seem good to you, either by a peace, or by truce, or abstinence, in such manner that if you bring your own affairs to a conclusion, you would be pleased forthwith to prosecute ours, and to bring it to an end in the way you best may. May God give you a good and long life.'[339]

Despite his use of his royal title, Balliol had given up on becoming king in any meaningful sense; for the next twelve years, until his death in 1314, he lived a quiet, frugal life in Picardy, selling off bits and pieces of his French possessions to make ends meet and receiving the occasional financial gift from Philip, who still found it useful until at least 1308 to describe him as king of Scotland.[340] Since John was well aware in 1302 that Philip was about to make a deal with Edward, his own 'affairs' probably amounted to little more than a vain hope that his French lord might persuade the English king to give him back his vast family estates in Northumberland, which would have pulled him out of the penury that his whole sorry Scottish adventure had brought Balliol to.

In the light of the changed political landscape, on 2 December 1302, the French and English kings had concluded a truce that made no reference to the Scots, a turn of events that Edward was keen for his sheriffs of 'that land [*of Scotland, or at least the southern part of it controlled by his own officials*]' to broadcast.[341] In Robert (7)'s submission document, it had suited Edward – for the obvious reason that he was at that particularly difficult time prepared to encourage Robert in his quest for a throne – to describe

Scotland as a kingdom, but now it had been decisively and deliberately stripped of any royal pretensions.[342]

There was to be no direct extension of the truce with the Scots, which had expired on 1 November 1302, and a week later the first orders were sent out summoning an English army to Berwick by the end of May 1303. Arrangements – and finance – for this campaign had been thrashed out at a parliament held in London at the end of October, which Robert attended. Despite his promise to the tenants of Melrose Abbey living in his earldom, he was not allowed to shirk his responsibilities, receiving a personal letter from the king in April 1303 demanding that he 'come with all the men-at-arms that he can,' along with 1000 footsoldiers chosen from Kyle, Cunningham – both of which belonged to James the Steward – Cumnock and Carrick (modern Ayrshire), and another 1000 from Carrick and 'Galloway' – which perhaps included Annandale – at his own discretion and which he should lead out himself.[343]

The Scots – led by John Comyn, the Guardian, and Simon Fraser, a Scottish knight who defected from Edward's service in 1301 – knew they should make use of the window of opportunity between the end of the truce in November 1302 and the inevitable arrival of Edward's army in the late spring or summer of 1303. Since the English garrisons of the south-west were repaired and packed with men, the Guardian decided to target the south-east; he was even prepared to ride out in the depths of winter, attacking Roxburgh castle in early January 1303 so that its occupants lived 'daily in peril of our lives.' Though unable to make much headway against Roxburgh's mighty walls, on 20 January the Scottish army took Edward's brand new fortress at Selkirk. Encouraged, Comyn then rode with his men nearly sixty miles further west to another new pele, this time protecting the royal manor house at Linlithgow, but could not repeat his success.

The Scots headed south to Biggar, which lies on an important east-west route, perhaps to wait and see what the English might do from either direction. Finally, on 23 February, Comyn received news that an English force, recently reinforced from the north of England, had headed out of Berwick and now lay, in three brigades set at a distance of six miles from each other, around Roslin just south of Edinburgh. Choosing a number of 'picked men who preferred to die rather than be shamefully subjected to the English nation,' the Guardian led them twenty-five miles through the night before ambushing the main English brigade and skirmishing with the other two in hard-pressed contests. A number of English were killed and many others taken prisoner, including the English commander, Sir John Segrave. The battle of Roslin was a huge morale-boost for the Scots.

Edward's men, on the other hand, found it hard to muster enthusiasm for a job that was both dangerous and seriously under-funded.[344]

Roslin also cemented John Comyn's reputation as a valiant and effective military leader. He was singled out for praise because 'In these victories the bravery and gallant exhortation of their leader stood them in good stead,' while he and his captains were described as 'war-like men, stalwart and endowed with every virtue.' Later Scottish commentators marvelled at their sheer determination, their ability to overcome the winter, their resilience in the face of the long overnight ride and the superior numbers of English: '… it should also be remarked that on thoroughly weighing every gallant feat of arms and dashing exploit in battle in former chronicles, we do not find that it ever happened that so many were defeated in detail by so few three times in one day without any interval of refreshment.' Another reported that: 'After exposure to the winds by removing their helmets and being cooled by the fresh air, and after replacing their wounded horses with other fresh ones, the Scots [overcame] the attacks of their enemies with the help of divine strength rather than human power.'[345] Though the future King Robert would certainly never admit it, he learned much from his great rival's approach to warfare. The element of surprise, the use of Scotland's difficult terrain, and disdain for the traditional campaigning season – all of these tactics were ones the future king would mould into a lethal and effective military ethos. But it was John Comyn who showed him the way.

****

Edward crossed the border on 16 May 1303, four days before a final and perpetual Anglo-French peace was ratified by King Philip in Paris.[346] On 25 May, the Scottish embassy in France wrote a desperate letter back to Scotland, in the full knowledge of this treaty, urging Comyn and the rest to continue their resistance, believing Philip when he said that he would strive to make a peace for them too that would be 'useful for the kingdom.' The recent battle at Roslin, so Soules and the others said, had only served to increase the honour of the Scots 'in various places in the world.'[347]

Comyn tried his best, but Edward had a new and devastating military objective, for this year he finally intended to cross the river Forth himself for the first time since 1296. For the Scots, it seemed that he meant 'to occupy it fully and permanently with his forces, and to make it submit to him entirely and finally, or to destroy its inhabitants utterly and to reduce the land itself to a completely irredeemable desert.'[348] The 1303 campaign certainly dealt a hammer blow to Scottish resistance, though even that was not necessarily the end of the struggle.

Transporting his very own pontoon bridge with him from England – the bridge at Stirling having still not been repaired after the battle there in 1297 – the king crossed the Forth to reach Clackmannan on the river's northern bank on 10 June. Four days later the Scots 'had entered Annandale and Liddesdale and elsewhere within the marches in the county of Cumberland with a great multitude of armed men.'[349] The Scottish intention was, as it had been in 1301, to attack garrisons left vulnerable by the withdrawal of men to the main English army in the hope that this would distract Edward from his original purpose. It may also have pleased some of the Scottish leaders that at least one of these garrisons [Lochmaben] happened to be in Bruce territory.

Robert (7) had been told to bring his 2000-plus contingent to the king at Roxburgh in May. There he would surely have found it impossible to avoid his father, who had dragged himself north with the king and was due to stay with the army until the middle of October. But at least Robert would also be able to catch up with one of his younger brothers, Edward, who had joined the Prince of Wales's household.[350] In many ways, it must have felt an awful lot like 1296.

Just to underline the similarities, part of the Scottish army led by Sir Simon Fraser crossed the border to raid round Carlisle in mid-June 1303, while another contingent marched through Galloway 'persuading' those who had recently submitted to Edward to change their allegiance back again. One of its leaders was Sir William Wallace, recently returned from the continent. Wallace's army then turned back east, 'harassing' the countryside between Caerlaverock and Dumfries, before heading down through Annandale to join up with Fraser's force south of the border. Their main aims seem to have been to cause havoc and mayhem, certainly, but more specifically to stop supplies from reaching English garrisons in south-west Scotland.[351]

Edward, who was about to strike out from Perth into enemy territory, was not to be distracted, but he did realise – thanks to all manner of plaintive letters of distress from his officials – that the situation along the south-western border was serious. And so he sent back from his own army the captain of Cumberland, Westmorland, Lancaster and Annandale, Sir John Botetourt, to deal with the Scottish threat under the overall command of the royal lieutenant in the south, Sir Aymer de Valence, who also happened to be John Comyn the Guardian's brother-in-law.

Robert (7) and his contingent went with Botetourt.[352] By 24 August Valence's army had reached the west coast and the castle of Inverkip – which belonged to Bruce's neighbour, James the Steward, who was still in France – before returning to Glasgow around 10 September.[353] If the intention was to draw the Scots away from their attacks on English garrisons over eighty miles away, then they seem to have succeeded, for the situation at Lochmaben and Dumfries didn't deteriorate any further.

By this time Edward had reached as far as the coast between Aberdeen and Inverness. Then, on 24 September as he made his way back south, he spent at least two nights in John Comyn's island fortress of Lochindorb, making a dramatic point about who controlled Scotland that the Guardian was unlikely to miss. The fact that neither Comyn nor his cousin, the earl of Buchan, were named as leaders of the Scottish armies in the south-west suggests that they were still north of the Forth, perhaps organising the harrying of any English foolish enough to cross their path in sufficiently small numbers.[354]

Nevertheless, Edward's ability to walk all over their lands and sleep in their castles was truly shocking, for this was 'Free Scotland', the part that financed Scottish resistance and kept the Scots in touch with the continent. And the king was not above taking revenge on anyone who defied him – one of the earl of Buchan's manors and some of his lands were certainly set on fire.[355] The Guardian's only hope was that, when the king returned to England at the end of the campaigning season, the garrisons he left behind could be ejected once more. But after six years of war, that prospect cannot have been an attractive one.

In fact, Scottish dismay was serious enough for a dramatic response; only two days after the king's symbolic stay at Lochindorb, Sir Aymer de Valence – now at Linlithgow – wrote to say that he 'is treating with the great lords of Scotland to bring them to the king's will, and hopes to be successful, by God's help, but cannot say for certain.'[356]

And he was right to be wary for, only two days later, he had to confess that negotiations had not gone well, though this was not due to any diplomatic failings on his part. Rather, the Scottish envoys at Linlithgow had seen with their own eyes the profound distress of the Irish soldiers in Valence's army, who had 'nothing to live on except ready money, unless they rob the people who have sworn allegiance to the king; and they see clearly that no man cares for them or their lives, so they have packed their baggage to go home.' Despite having 'come to treat in good form for peace,' the Scots 'broke off their business by reason of the scarcity that they saw among the said people.'[357] In other words, there was hope that the English army would fall apart just as it had done every other year and that Edward's hold on Scotland north of the Forth would prove just as short-lived.

But Scottish optimism did not last long. Though the king failed to do much more than take a long, furious look at Stirling Castle – now the only major fortification still held against him – from the nearby monastery of Cambuskenneth in late October 1303, he and his beleaguered officials somehow managed to pull enough financial rabbits out of the hat to allow him to move on to winter quarters at Dunfermline Abbey in early November. He was joined there by his queen, who was moved to present a gold brooch worth 100 shillings [over £4000 today] at the famous shrine there of her namesake, St Margaret, wife of Malcolm III and mother of David I.[358]

Edward Bruce, Robert's younger brother, along with the rest of the Prince of Wales's household, rode north to Perth on 25 November as part of a separate court, probably in the hope that this might nudge Comyn and 'his company' – who, despite Edward's efforts over the summer, were 'in their lands beyond the mountains where none ... who came on horseback could approach them' – into peace negotiations.[359] The king was still very keen for his son to oversee the end of the war, even if this was not going to be brought about by a spectacular military victory and even if he himself intended to be consulted every step of the way.

Sure enough, by the end of December messengers were galloping between Dunfermline and Perth and beyond as the Guardian tentatively sought to know King Edward's mind. On 11 January 1304 English negotiators were appointed to go to Kinclaven, a royal castle on the banks of the River Tay twelve miles north of Perth, where Comyn had agreed to meet them. The process was more or less complete a month later and on 16 February the prince led a victory parade south to Dunfermline, where the Scots swore homage and fealty to Edward I yet again. On 21 February, back in Perth, Prince Edward dined on herrings and 'stockfish' washed down with wine in the company of 'Sir John Comyn with his knights and part of his retinue.'[360]

The submission agreement finally signed off by both sides contained an implicit recognition that the Scots had put up a good fight and were certainly not beaten, in contrast to 1296. Like Bruce two years earlier, no-one – with one glaring exception – was to lose life or limb or suffer imprisonment or disinheritance. But Edward reserved the right to impose penalties for past misdeeds and to settle the 'land' of Scotland as he saw fit. The Scots still in France were to be urged to come home and submit by 12 April 1303, which they mostly did, though some dragged their feet. Only Sir John Soules couldn't stomach the thought of giving up, never setting foot in his native land again.[361]

Wallace was the only named exception to these terms; the king wanted Sir William to grovel at his feet, to throw himself on his royal mercy with no guarantee that he would receive it. The former Guardian did try to submit, but he would not come to Edward without any promises and went on the run.[362] Perhaps Edward wanted a scape-goat; perhaps he had been genuinely shocked by the brutal murder of his sheriff of Lanark and could not forgive Wallace for being the first to resurrect an independent Scottish government. We will never know. At the same time, there were a number of Scots who, like Sir William, felt that submission was not the only option. Edward and his men still had work to do.

Robert (7) and Sir John Botetourt left Sir Aymer de Valence in the late summer of 1303, spending eight days in the first half of September riding round the sheriffdoms of Linlithgow, Lanark and Peebles 'and elsewhere south of the Forth to ordain and appoint sheriffs and other officials on the part of the king.' It was agreed that Robert himself would become sheriff of Lanark, as well as Ayr.[363] Six months later and he was still well to the fore in mopping-up efforts during the dying months of Scottish resistance. He had been summoned to attend a parliament at St Andrews in March 1304 – one called largely to pave the way for the outlawing of the garrison at Stirling and Sir William Wallace and Sir Simon Fraser – but asked the king's forgiveness for not being able to attend. Thankfully, he had a very good excuse, because he had joined an English force to 'follow the enemy.'

Their target was Wallace and Fraser, who were still in southern Scotland, perhaps already lurking in Selkirk Forest near Fraser's lands, which lay around Peebles. Edward was very pleased with Robert and the rest for their work on a task that the king viewed as vitally important and it earned Bruce a complimentary 4 gallons of wine. But there was a hint of menace in the royal pleasure:

Know that for the great diligence and care that you have used and do use in our affairs from day to day, and because you are thus agreed to follow the enemy, we thank you as earnestly as we can, and pray and require especially, as we confide in you, who are our good people, and have well begun the said business, that you will complete it, and that you leave not either for negotiation or for any other thing until you follow diligently your intention to pursue the enemy, and to put an end to affairs before your departure from those parts. For if you complete that there which you have begun, we shall hold the war ended by your deed, and all the land of Scotland gained. So we pray you again, as much as we can, that whereas the robe is well made, you will be pleased to make the hood; and by your letters, and by the bearer of these, send us back your answer hereupon without delay, together with the news of your parts.[364]

Edward was keen to employ every method at his disposal, supplementing the direct route – the heavily armed and mobile posse to which Robert belonged – with a more devious one – 'a certain Scottish boy' who was sent on a number of occasions 'to the castle of Stirling and elsewhere to infiltrate Sir Simon Fraser and Sir William Wallace and others of the king's enemies.'[365] Both probably played their part in the close encounter of 5/6 March, which Edward must have been pleased, but frustrated, to hear about as he made his way up the Fife coast to St Andrews; the English had managed to catch up with Fraser and Wallace at Happrew near Peebles, 'discomfiting' them. But still the Scotsmen eluded capture.

It's not clear if Robert was at Happrew, but he was certainly very busy throughout March and April south of the Forth, receiving urgent letters from the king, who had now turned his attention on the forthcoming siege of Stirling castle whose garrison refused to submit without permission from King John. One of Robert's most difficult tasks, which Edward viewed as vitally important- 'on no account do you desist from using all the pains and deliberation you can' – was arranging for the king's enormous and unwieldy siege engines to be moved safely into position.[366] By 22 April 1304 Edward had arrived outside the castle walls and everything was set.

But even as the king enjoyed the final act of this interminable war, so the seeds of a new and far more testing conflict had already been sown. By the end of April, as Robert joined the throng of Scots and English gathered together outside Stirling castle's walls in a deliberate show of unity, he already knew that his father had died just south of the border on his way to Annandale.[367] And that changed everything.

Chapter Ten

The man who would be king

In which, on the news of his father's death, Robert starts working his way towards the empty throne, but finds himself thwarted by John Comyn of Badenoch, who also manages to exclude Bruce from King Edward's government of Scotland. To make matters much, much worse, Comyn is now putting forward his own credentials to take the crown when the time was right as nephew of King John and a tried and tested Scottish leader.

The Stone of Scone set within the coronation chair, Westminster Abbey. Edward presented the stone, plundered from Scone Abbey in 1296, to his namesake and predecessor, Edward the Confessor. Used last at the coronation of Queen Elizabeth II in 1953, it lay at Westminster until 1996, when it was taken with much pomp and ceremony to Edinburgh castle where you can see it today.

In the early summer of 1304 Robert Bruce, seventh lord of Annandale and earl of Carrick, was approaching his thirtieth birthday. In the prime of life, with extensive estates in Scotland, England and Ireland, a young wife with excellent connections on which to sire a son, and the esteem of his royal master, he could have spent the rest of his life in comfort and privilege.

But he did not hesitate for a moment. As the siege engines whipped their lethal missiles at Stirling castle, Robert found a quiet place on Thursday 11 June at the abbey of Cambuskenneth to meet discretely with Bishop Lamberton of St Andrews. There they finalised an agreement that made a mockery of the bishop's homage and fealty, offered to Edward only a month earlier, not to mention Robert's own, entirely voluntary submission two and a half years before and the oath of loyalty he would make three days later for his father's lands. Under the extraordinary penalty of £10,000 [nearly £8 million today] for breaking it, the agreement bound the two men to support each other against all others, without mentioning the obvious, necessary exception – their lord, the king of England. In this it was conspicuously unlike the Turnberry band sealed by Robert's father and grandfather fifteen years earlier.[368] No specific enterprise was mentioned, but there can have been only one thing on their minds. This was a silent revolution – a tacit acknowledgement by Scotland's most senior churchman that Scotland's future as an independent kingdom now lay with Bruce.

Not that Robert meant to make a move immediately – that would have been suicidal. The Scots had only just submitted to Edward and those oaths had been given freely, not forced out of them in the wake of a military defeat. But the king was now in his mid-sixties and everyone could see that he was not nearly as vigorous as he once was. The unanswerable question is whether Bruce canvassed only Lamberton or whether he had a word with other Scottish notables. It was certainly possible.

In the meantime, Robert could look forward to enjoying the combined incomes of an impressive array of properties including Carrick and Annandale in Scotland, Hatfield and Writtle in Essex, Tottenham in Middlesex, and Caldecote in the honour of Huntingdon, the first of the Bruces to possess such an extensive and varied inheritance. There was a brand new pigeon-house at Hatfield to be stocked, a garden and a third of the profits of a watermill at Tottenham and two parks at Writtle, which his grandfather had once enjoyed, as well as the more usual agricultural and commercial accoutrements of lordship. The downside was that he now owed the king £518 5s 8d [over £400,000 today] for the debts of his father 'or his ancestors,' Robert (6) having managed to increase these more than five-fold from the £99 he had been liable to pay when Robert (5) died.[369]

On 20 July 1304 the Stirling garrison finally offered to surrender, but they were not allowed to come out until the king's fearsome new engine, the 'War Wolf', had proved what it could do. The final agreement was made with those that survived on 24 July and six days later the king was looking forward to going hunting with his goshawks and sparrow-hawks once he finally reached the south of England.[370] He had spent more than a year in Scotland but now, at last, could look forward to a less physically strenuous life, except in the pursuit of pleasure.

Nevertheless there was still much work to be done to sort out Scotland off the campaign trail. In this Edward seems to have learned many of the lessons of 1296, when his decision to place the government of his new conquest overwhelmingly in the hands of Englishmen, combined with his own distraction over his continental campaign, made his regime unpalatable from the word go. His task in 1304-5 would have daunted a lesser man, for he intended to listen to complaints and queries from all quarters, including those who had served him loyally and well over the previous eight years of war and now faced expulsion from the lands they had only just won, because the agreement made with Sir John Comyn meant that all property was to be handed back to their original Scottish owners.[371]

But while the king was prepared to allow the Scots to keep many of their distinctive laws and customs, he had no qualms about reforming anything that seemed either too primitive or gave too much power to anyone other than himself. One of the first things he'd done as king of England had been to organise inquiries into English noble rights and privileges in the firm, and not entirely unwarranted, belief that many of these had been 'acquired' from the crown over the centuries.[372] Not surprisingly, he was keen to ensure that the kind of quasi-royal power in noble hands he had been at pains to end south of the border should not continue north of it. And in this Edward soon found himself at odds with Robert Bruce.

When King David brought the first Robert to Scotland over 180 years before, he had given him extensive powers to carve out his lordship of Annandale and agreed that no royal official would set foot within its borders. Instead Scottish kings had to make do with choosing one of

Bruce's Annandale tenants to process royal demands, answering to his sheriff at Dumfries. As a parting shot as he began the long journey home in August 1304, Edward ordered a jury to look into these rights and, at the end of the month, eight knights and seventeen others, all local, confirmed that the Bruces held them "'by the title of antiquity', viz, from the time of William, King of Scotland and all his successors uninterruptedly to this day."[373]

But just because the lords of Annandale had always had these rights didn't necessarily mean that Edward would allow them to continue in *his* Scotland. The king was unusually indecisive on this issue, however, and three months later, in November 1304, Robert had to petition him for an answer for the second time.[374] Perhaps even Edward had enough sense to realise that tinkering with an ancient status quo was likely to be seen as a grave injustice by Bruce; at the same time, the king couldn't quite bring himself to confirm them, leaving Annandale in something of a legal limbo. To add injury to insult, its revenues – now a respectable £194 2 shillings 6 ¾ pence [about £170,000 today] compared with the £23 13 shillings 4 pence they'd brought in in 1299 – were still being collected for the crown even as Robert was experiencing the same kinds of problems as everyone else in getting payment for his royal duties, asking – politely – in the spring of 1305, if he might recover what he was owed for looking after the sheriffdoms of Ayr and Lanark.[375]

And yet it was not Edward's failure to reward Robert properly for his loyalty that ultimately pushed Bruce into seizing the throne, for we have the agreement with the bishop of St Andrews to suggest that his royal aspirations, from the very moment of his father's death, were, as ever, far more important to him than remaining a trusted friend to the king. In truth, as we will see, it was not what *Edward* did or didn't do that governed Robert's actions in the coming months. Within the bounds of his highly-developed sense of his own royal importance, the king was the very model of medieval statesmanship, negotiating a tortuous path towards a final settlement of what he was careful now to call the *land* [rather than kingdom] of Scotland, after which, he presumably hoped, he would never have to give too much thought to his northern province again.

In the meantime, Edward was even prepared to appoint two Scots – John, earl of Atholl and William, earl of Ross – as keepers of Scotland beyond the Rivers Forth and Spey respectively, though the Englishman, Sir John Segrave, was to hold Scotland south of the Forth.[376] It must have been with considerable relief and satisfaction that he announced on 8

November 1304 that 'the war in Scotland [had] come to an end,' not least because 'the king, sir Edward had felt his labours.' Instead of going hawking in the south, he was now languishing at the royal manor of Burstwick near Hull. As all of England knew, he 'takes there his sojourn a while for his health.'[377]

And Bruce knew it too, for he was with him every step of the way, following the king south in November 1304 to attend to his own affairs in England as head of the family, including the customary confirmation of various charters granted by his ancestors.[378] Then, in February 1305, he attended a parliament at Westminster as Edward's adviser on Scotland's government, along with Bishop Wishart of Glasgow and Sir John Moubray, to ensure that, where possible, a forthcoming Scottish parliament might be held according to Scottish law and custom. Though Moubray was cousin and close ally of John Comyn, Bruce and Wishart obviously outnumbered him and Robert was no doubt pleased that the balance of power, even if wielded under the king's strict control, lay in his favour. He was also now enjoying the revenues of the earldom of Mar on behalf of his young nephew, Donald, and had been granted the keepership of three royal forests in the north-east of Scotland.[379] Life under an ailing Edward I wasn't all bad.

This trio of Scots laid their advice about when and where a Scottish parliament should take place, as well as explaining who usually attended, before the king at Westminster on 26 March 1305. Edward listened attentively, but in the end, despite being asked 'to have a care for the well-being of the people of Scotland,' decided to hold it in London. He was not being deliberately difficult, but knew he was in no fit state to make the long journey north yet again. Indeed the king's increasing frailty was probably behind this 'Scottish' parliament's postponement from 15 July to 15 August and then again until 8 September.[380]

The Scottish delegates to London were chosen at an assembly held at either Scone or Perth in May 1305, which Bruce and Wishart were sent north to oversee.[381] This was presumably the first Scottish gathering that Robert had attended since he submitted to Edward more than three years before. But if he thought he could just pick up where he left off, he was sadly mistaken, for now he was confronted with the repercussions of leaving the Comyns to dominate Scottish politics since he gave up the guardianship in 1300. It didn't help that key Bruce allies were absent – the earl of Atholl remained at his post as royal lieutenant north of the Forth, while James the Steward was only just back from France and desperately negotiating with Edward so that he could submit and get his lands back.[382] But, in the end, it was surely Robert's own fault that the ten selected were almost all members of the Comyn faction, or at least – with the exception of Bishop Lamberton – no friends to Bruce. He couldn't even get picked himself, and neither could his friend, Bishop Wishart, though John Moubray made it on to the list. Robert had just lost his ability to influence Scottish affairs under Edward I.

This was certainly bad enough, but he may have hoped for much more from this assembly. He had already concluded a potentially treacherous agreement with Bishop Lamberton under Edward's very nose during the siege of Stirling. A year later and it would surely have been tempting for Bruce to canvas his fellow nobles while they were gathered together, to ask for their support if he should make a bid for the throne, not least in the light of the king's deteriorating health. He would have done it secretly, of course, well out of earshot of Edward's English officials. But there would have been nothing subtle about the response from John Comyn.[383]

If much of Robert Bruce's influence in Scotland had ebbed away since the last time they met, then Comyn's had only increased. Like Robert, he was now head of his family, but presided over a far more powerful and influential network. He had been Guardian probably for the entire period between 1298 and 1304 and had won a battle at Roslin that bolstered his credentials as an effective military leader. He was also King John's nephew as well as having royal blood of his own through a line of descent from King David I's uncle, Donald III, all of which surely brought John Comyn to the conclusion that *he* was Balliol's natural successor by blood, assent and fitness to rule, when the time was right.[384] He could also make it perfectly clear that, unlike King John, he would be a very different kind of ruler, dynamic, innovative and effective.

Figure 5: John Comyn's descent from King Donald III

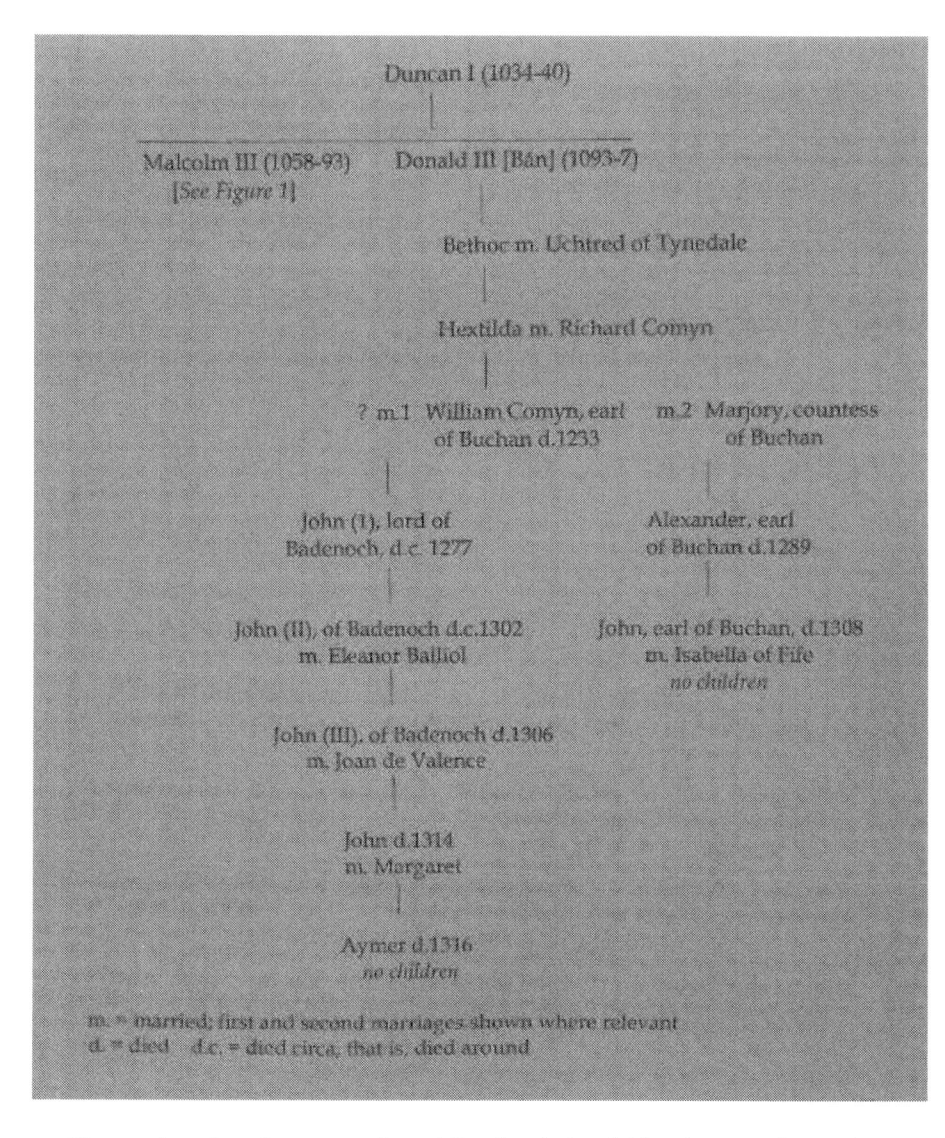

```
                    Duncan I (1034-40)
                           |
        ┌──────────────────┴──────────────────┐
Malcolm III (1058-93)         Donald III [Bán] (1093-7)
[See Figure 1]                         |
                              Bethoc m. Uchtred of Tynedale
                                       |
                              Hextilda m. Richard Comyn
                                       |
                    ┌──────────────────┴──────────────────┐
            ? m.1  William Comyn, earl      m.2  Marjory, countess
                   of Buchan d.1233              of Buchan
                      |                              |
            John (I), lord of                 Alexander, earl
            Badenoch, d.c. 1277               of Buchan d.1289
                      |                              |
         John (II), of Badenoch d.c.1302    John, earl of Buchan, d.1308
             m. Eleanor Balliol                m. Isabella of Fife
                      |                           no children
         John (III), of Badenoch d.1306
              m. Joan de Valence
                      |
                 John d.1314
                 m. Margaret
                      |
                 Aymer d.1316
                  no children

m. = married; first and second marriages shown where relevant
d. = died   d.c. = died circa, that is, died around
```

The notion that the next ruler of Scotland should be the grandson of a man who had lost the battle for the crown more than a decade before was frankly laughable. If anyone had the right to ask the Scottish political community to support a new bid for the throne in due course then it was not a Bruce. And so Robert came face to face with the fact that John Comyn was an immovable obstacle to his ambitions even now that Balliol was no longer in the picture. Indeed, despite stories that Bruce and Comyn made an agreement for one to become king and the other to be richly rewarded with lands, Robert in fact had very little to bargain with.[385] This was not 1297, when he commanded an important political faction of his own, one which could not be ignored. Since he gave up the guardianship in 1300, the Comyns had become the only real political power in Scotland, a fact that even King Edward was now ready to acknowledge. This was a game-changer. The question now was: what, if anything, could Robert do about it?

****

Meanwhile, the inexorable settlement of Scotland went on. Before parliament finally met in September 1305, there was one important piece of business to finish off. Sir William Wallace had been left a lonely fugitive when Sir Simon Fraser submitted in the early summer of 1304. A few months later, in September, he was chased by members of the garrison near the port of Dundee, where he had presumably been trying to find a ship out of Scotland.386 He then disappeared for almost a year but was finally captured near Glasgow on 5 August 1305. Now the king could indulge in the blood-letting that the politics of subduing Scotland over the last eighteen months had made unwise. Wallace was rushed south and put on trial in Westminster Hall on charges of treason, charges that the former Guardian did not deny, instead vehemently asserting that there was no crime since the English king was not Scotland's lord. But Edward's lawyers had no time for such an argument. Sir William was immediately dragged to Smithfield and brutally executed on 23 August 1305 as part of the entertainment put on for Londoners during the St Bartholomew Fair.[387]

Only a few weeks later, the Scottish representatives chosen in May met in parliament at Westminster to set the seal on their final absorption into Edward's empire. One of their most important tasks was to decide on who should become sheriffs – those delegated by the king to keep the peace throughout the country – since Edward was pleased to allow most of them to be Scots. Not surprisingly, given those who had been chosen to attend, a large proportion were men with connections to the Comyns while Robert lost both of the sheriffdoms he currently controlled. The only 'Bruce man' given an important role was Sir Roger Kirkpatrick, an Annandale knight who became justiciar of Galloway, sharing the role with another Scot but a consistently pro-English one, Sir Walter Burghdon.

In a move that was at least as likely to have been Edward's idea as the Scottish commissioners', Robert did become one of twenty-one Scots chosen to advise the new lieutenant in Scotland – the king's nephew, John of Brittany – among an otherwise overwhelmingly Comyn set of appointees. But this scarcely left Bruce with very much to show for his recent years of conspicuous service to the English crown. Even his control of the earldom of Mar – uncomfortably sandwiched between John Comyn's lordship of Badenoch and the latter's cousin and namesake's earldom of Buchan – may have come under pressure from his Scottish rivals, judging by the fact that Robert was abruptly told in September 1305 to put one of its main strongholds, Kildrummy castle, 'in the keeping of one for whom he shall answer.'[388]

It was all now a far cry from the important role Bruce had played as a trusted royal official, riding out in a small, handpicked company of knights on secret missions, overseeing the king's siege engines, appointing sheriffs and advising Edward on Scottish affairs. Few fourteenth century noblemen, let alone one with such a deeply ingrained belief in his own destiny, would have found it easy to be pushed aside, especially by those who not only still had to prove their loyalty, but were his bitter political rivals.

And yet this wasn't a deliberate snub on Edward's part – the king was, to a large extent, allowing the Scots to sort themselves out as much as possible. His overriding concern was, quite naturally, to protect his reconquest, even if that meant listening to many of those who had fought long and hard against him. And while John Comyn himself was given no official role apart from membership of the new lieutenant's council, there was a place in local government for many of his councillors and close friends – the very people who had, until January 1304, run Scotland under his guardianship. So if that meant offending men like Bruce, or those Englishmen deprived of the Scottish lands they'd been promised, then so be it.

There is certainly no suggestion whatsoever that the king suspected Robert of disloyalty; given the length of time Edward had already spent on Scotland and the precarious state of his health, he was unlikely to stand for any hint of treachery. The blunt truth of the matter is that the king no longer had much need for Robert Bruce, whereas he had long experience of just how important the Comyns were to Scotland's government. We might, with the considerable benefit of hindsight, see that as foolish and short-sighted, but the fact of the matter is that Robert was just not that important to either the majority of Scots or their English master.

And yet the king was surely naïve if he imagined that the long, hard years of warfare could be erased overnight even among his own people. He had harnessed English feelings of superiority over the Scots to persuade men to commit to his armies and pay for the war effort and found that some of his subjects were failing to put these xenophobic feelings behind them now that peace was the order of the day. On 14 October 1305 he had to send an order to all his sheriffs in England 'that no one shall say to any men of that land [*Scotland*] passing through the sheriff's jurisdiction in their inns, on the road, or elsewhere any insults or contumelious words, or otherwise inflict wrong, annoyance or damage upon them, or sell to them victuals or other necessaries dearer than to others of the realm.'[389] Some of those from north of the border who had come south to parliament in September had obviously been badly treated on their way to and from London for the simple reason that they were Scots. Such antipathy was entirely understandable, but it would not help to bind the two nations together as peaceful subjects of King Edward.

And though Scotland's ruling classes had accepted Edward's peace, for some this was surely a matter of expediency, a temporary respite. Beneath them were still more Scots, the men and women for whom the nobility supposedly spoke, who also felt that too much water had flowed under the bridge for them to accept English rule willingly. Pockets of resistance lingered even after John Comyn agreed the terms of general submission. In late March 1304, the men of the Lennox were still considered rebellious despite the fact that their earl had already accepted Edward as his lord. The king's clerks, busy on royal business throughout 1304, needed an armed escort because 'the men of the parts beyond the Mountains, and in Galloway and Carrick' – whose earl was Robert Bruce himself – 'had not yet fully come to the king's peace.' And Sir Alexander Comyn, who, despite being brother to the earl of Buchan, had always served King Edward, was worried that 'in the discharge of his office during the war he may have displeased some of the people of his country, to the king's benefit, and now in peace time they may impeach him…' Even as Scotland was being 'settled' permanently at Westminster in the autumn of 1305, the keeper of Scotland between the Forth and the Grampian mountains, Sir Alexander Abernethy, claimed that he had been forced to keep an armed retinue 'lest he might be surprised by a sudden outbreak.'[390]

Most worrying, on 23 January 1306 Sir John Botetourt and his men were appointed justices 'to hear certain trespasses against the peace.' On 10 February the sheriff of Edinburgh, Sir John Kingston, one of the justices north of the Forth, Sir Robert Keith, and the sheriff of Northumberland were ordered to do the same.[391] Resentments, feelings of injustice and terrible prejudices brought to fever pitch in the furnace of a long and brutal war had not magically disappeared on either side of the border with the drying of a seal on a piece of parchment or the saying of an oath of loyalty.

But for the king, it really was that simple, mostly because he was determined that it would be and hints of trouble were, in his view, mere details that would be mopped up by Scotland's government. He did not particularly care if the Scots were happy – the Welsh had not been happy when he conquered them in the 1280s, rebelling as recently as 1294, but they were knuckling under now. And he was being much, much more tolerant of Scottish national pride than he ever had been towards the Welsh, allowing the Scots their idiosyncratic laws (or some of them) and ways of government. Heck, he would even let them call his chief financial officer in Scotland chamberlain rather than treasurer, as it was in England, even if the man who held the post was English and, like the Scottish chancellor, needed someone to keep him right on the Scottish procedure he was supposed to preside over.

It was just a question of time for things to settle down and everyone to get used to the new regime, even if, once again, Edward's choice as lieutenant – John of Brittany – proved reluctant, just like the earl of Surrey, to set foot in Scotland. But even that was not the end of the world; on 16 February 1306 two Scots – Bishop Lamberton and Sir Robert Keith – were appointed to take the lieutenant's place until he arrived, along with the Englishman, Sir John Kingston.[392]

But there was to be no time for things to settle down. Though the news had not yet reached London, six days earlier Sir John Comyn had been murdered. And Robert Bruce, earl of Carrick and lord of Annandale was the man who had wielded the knife.

CHAPTER ELEVEN

Resolution

In which Robert kills John Comyn and takes the throne of Scotland. Despite a confident start, he is soon facing enemies on all sides and is defeated at the battle of Methven on 19 June 1306, less than three months after becoming king. Retreating into the hills, he soon has to leave his wife and daughter, who are captured trying to escape to Norway. One brother and numerous friends are brutally killed by an irate Edward I. By the end of the year, Robert has somehow evaded capture, disappearing into the far north-west of Scotland. Few expected him to return.

February, as depicted in the *Très Riches Heures du Duc de Berry* (1412-1416)

The winter of 1305-6 had been another testing one with freezing conditions causing hardship and misery. Ice and frozen snow lay from mid-December till the end of January even in southern England, killing fish in the lakes, birds in the woods and cattle in the fields.[393] Men and women across the British Isles may have wondered what they had done to deserve such punishment, but the Scots had their own particular reasons for thinking they must have displeased God, for the weather was just one more burden they had to bear. Or at least that's what Scottish writers were keen to stress, claiming that continuing English oppression was the reason why the Scottish people needed a leader of their own to lead them into freedom:

After the king's [Edward I's] departure, the English nation was dominant in every part of Scotland, and cruelly afflicted the Scots in a great many different ways under a dire yoke of bondage with insults, wounds and killings. God in his mercy took pity on the miseries and continuous complaints and griefs of the Scots, and in the usual manner of his fatherly kindness raised up for them a saviour and champion, that is one of their fellow-countrymen called Robert de Bruce, who saw them lying in a pool of misery and utterly lacking any hope of help or salvation.[394]

There may be an element of truth in this cry for help, though at least some of the responsibility for the 'dire yoke of bondage' lay with the Scots themselves. The years of war, along with the lack of clear, firm and impartial leadership over the whole country for nearly twenty years, had inevitably taken its toll. Nobles had gotten into the habit of maintaining armed retinues for their own protection, which might also be used to defend their interests more generally. Such retinues had mostly been disbanded when their leaders came to Edward's peace, but those native lords who became royal officials – often continuing in the offices they'd previously held under the Guardians – did not necessarily give up theirs.[395] And a few of them were certainly accused of violent and disruptive behaviour.

Sir Reginald Cheyne, justiciar north of the Grampian Mountains, and Sir Duncan Frendraught had connections to the Comyns but it is difficult to know whether their activities represent a deep-rooted and long-standing abuse of power or whether the John Comyn of Badenoch in particular now found himself without sufficient authority to rein in men loosely associated with him. Their actions could also be viewed as excessive zeal in bringing in revenue for King Edward, though 'wasting and consuming crops,' according to one allegation, was unlikely to help those that owed money to pay up. Frendraught was also accused of protecting a group of 'thieves and robbers' near Arbroath who 'lately plundered Thomas le Graunt of his goods and chattels and cut off one of his hands …'[396]

Two bad eggs do not make a rotten omelette, of course, and we don't know the outcome of the cases brought against them, though the fact that it was Edward's lieutenant – the absent John of Brittany – who was supposed to look into them did not augur well. Even John Comyn's cousin, John Moubray, admitted that that there was a problem, begging the king to 'send into Scotland some man of authority to protect his lieges there against the injustice of their rulers.'[397] And while he wrote this once war had broken out all over again, he was clearly referring to more general issues of law and order for which Edward was ultimately responsible.

Moubray had put his finger on the nub of the matter – now that Scotland belonged once more to the English king, forming just one part of an empire that spread across the totality of the British Isles and Ireland and on into south-western France, Scottish interests – and problems – had to compete with all the other issues demanding the king's attention if his officials proved less than willing or able to govern fairly. There can be little doubt that the apathy and indolence of men like Surrey and Brittany at the very top gave those officials below them little incentive to behave honourably, even if some did. For those Scots with grievances it was easy to package them up as English oppression, even if those who were actually doing the oppressing might be rather more home-grown. If anyone from the king down thought that Scotland was truly settled at the beginning of 1306, they needed to think again.

****

We will never know exactly why Robert Bruce and John Comyn met in the Greyfriars Church at Dumfries on 10 February 1306, nor the precise sequence of events that led to the murder of Scotland's most important and influential nobleman. Both sides almost immediately launched a war of words every bit as ferocious as the actual conflict that broke out in the wake of Comyn's death, which makes it impossible to be sure of much beyond the outcome of that extraordinary day. Even one of Bruce's earliest biographers, writing some seventy years after the event, gives his version but immediately qualifies it by saying: 'Nonetheless some men still say that that quarrel happened otherwise; but whatever caused the quarrel, he [*John Comyn*] died because of it, I know for certain.'[398]

And yet, the simplest telling of the story may come closest to the truth and certainly fits best with what we know of Robert Bruce long before he stuck a dagger into his rival, as well as with the few facts emerging from the murk of deliberate lies and determined obfuscation. Comyn was at his castle of Dalswinton seven miles north of Dumfries – possibly preparing to attend a session of the justiciars of Galloway – when Bruce, then at Lochmaben, asked to see him. They agreed to meet in the church of the Greyfriars in Dumfries, perhaps because John was wary of any gathering involving Robert, but surely also because it was a suitably neutral venue. Certainly Comyn cannot have believed he had much to fear from Bruce; he arrived not wearing armour, perhaps unarmed and with only two companions, his uncle Robert and his valet, Richard Galbraith (Colubrath).

But Bruce was both armed and armoured. They met in the cloister, probably just the two of them, while their men – in Robert's case, his old friend, Sir Alexander Lindsay and the three Seton brothers, Christopher, John and Humphrey – lingered nearby. If the two former Guardians uttered more than a greeting to each other, then it was the briefest of conversations – the various versions of the story that this meeting was really about Comyn betraying to Edward an agreement backing Bruce's bid to become king in return for lands, or vice-versa, are pure propaganda designed to portray John as a traitor and justify his death. They cannot be true, not least because the English king clearly didn't know that Robert intended to seize the throne even once he'd been told about the murder.

Bruce kicked out at John almost immediately, unbalancing him before running him through with a sword or knife. Presumably Comyn cried out and his uncle ran to defend him but was then killed by Robert's brother-in-law, Christopher Seton. There is no need to believe that John was finished off on the high altar, which was added to make Robert's actions appear even more blasphemous [anti-Bruce accounts], or the story that Sir Roger Kirkpatrick came back to 'mak siccar' (make sure) that Comyn was dead [pro-Bruce accounts], which was intended to shift the blame for the murder away from the man who would soon become king. Even John Barbour, author of *The Bruce*, says that 'he [*Robert*] ... with a knife took his life on that very spot.'[399]

It is not hindsight to suggest that Bruce arranged the meeting with Comyn explicitly in order to kill him but the lack of any other credible explanation. Unless we believe – and we cannot – the stories of Comyn's treachery, then we are left with the rather pathetic scenario that Robert wanted to meet John to upbraid him because Comyn had pushed him out of Edward's favour, but ended up killing him in hot blood because John proved his usual annoying and provocative self. Throughout Robert's ten-year career in public life, he had been entirely and consistently focused on the Bruce right to rule Scotland. He always, so far as we can tell, acted with cool calculation in the interests of that belief. So why would he jeopardise his entire career to date by killing his rival *in a church* because he was annoyed that he hadn't received a sufficient share of the crumbs thrown to the Scottish nobility by Edward I? He had never lost his temper with Comyn before – it was John who grabbed him by the throat in 1299, not the other way around – so why would he do so now, within touching distance of the opportunity to go for the throne once the English king was dead?

Robert did not even risk the combined and ferocious ire of Edward I, the Comyns and almost the entire ecclesiastical establishment of Western Europe because he knew that John didn't want him to become king. Rather, it was Comyn's own credentials to be king – implicit in the 'one of us gets the throne/the other gets the land' stories and rather more explicit in snippets from Scottish chronicles written around this time[400] – that sealed John's fate. Striking before Edward was dead was obviously highly dangerous, but waiting might prove even more terminal to Bruce's ambitions now that Comyn was putting his own plans in place. Robert must have known that there were preparations afoot to justify John's claim to the Scottish throne and would then quite naturally conclude that plans were also afoot among the Comyns and their allies to pursue it at the right time. His only option was to get in first.[401]

As for the sacrilegious element of the murder, it was obviously not ideal that they were to meet in a church, but there was little he could do about it if he was to persuade John Comyn to meet him. It is possible that Robert had a more pragmatic attitude towards killing – and killing on holy ground – than many of his contemporaries thanks to the years spent with his Gaelic foster family. Politics in the Irish Sea World was a lot riskier for society's leaders than in England and much of Scotland, where Norman practices of honourable surrender and ransoms prevailed, and even the Anglo-Irish had embraced this very different martial culture in their dealings with the native Irish. In 1274, the year of Robert's birth, the new king of Connaught 'was slain, in the church of the Friars at Roscommon, by his kinsman …' Three years later the native lord of Thomond was pulled apart by horses at the instigation of the son of the Anglo-Irish earl of Clare, despite having 'taken vows by bells and relics to retain mutual friendship.'[402] No doubt both deaths were shocking across Irish society, involving as they did the breaking of trust in the sanctity of religious buildings and promises. But they did not result in the immediate casting out of those who perpetrated them, even if the chances of their coming to an equally violent end must certainly have increased.

Death as a weapon against political rivals was still used thirty years later even in the Gaelic West Highlands. Around 1299 Alasdair Óg Macdonald – whose charter Bruce had witnessed when he was eight – 'the best man of his tribe in Ireland and Scotland for hospitality and prowess, was slain … with a countless number of his people' by his rival, Alasdair Macdougall.[403] This is not meant to excuse what Robert did in Dumfries on 10 February 1306, which was undoubtedly viewed as a terrible, shocking thing even by those who might have been sympathetic to his cause. But it may help us to understand why he seems to have viewed it as a necessary means to the only end he had ever cared about.

And what happened next looks far too well-planned for a meeting between two rivals that supposedly went violently, but entirely unexpectedly, wrong. Once Robert and his men had finished with Comyn, they rode a mile along the River Nith to Dumfries castle and quickly seized it from the sheriff and constable, Sir Richard Siward. They were joined by Sir Roger Kirkpatrick, who, along with Sir Walter Burghdon, had been holding a court nearby as justiciars of Galloway, probably in order to hear 'trespasses against the peace' just like Sir John Botetourt and their fellow justices in the east. Burghdon and the other English officials were made prisoner, as was Sir Richard Siward. Siward's own castle of Tibbers, seventeen miles to the north-west of Dumfries, was taken shortly afterwards, along with John Comyn's castle of Dalswinton.

Next on the list was the royal castle at Ayr and James the Steward's castle at Inverkip, while further afield Robert's supporters took Rothesay castle on the island of Bute (also the Steward's). The royal castle of Dunaverty on Kintyre and Bruce's own castle of Loch Doon in Carrick had been provisioned 'for a long time' in March 1306, suggesting that they too were made ready shortly after Comyn's murder or perhaps even before. Altogether, these strategically important fortresses would help Bruce to control the sea-routes in and out of the west of Scotland.[404] Targeting them was not the work of a man who had made a mistake, whose hand was forced, but were rather the prelude to the main act, which Robert was surely already planning.

Edward was, as yet, unclear as to exactly the threat posed to his painstakingly created Scottish settlement, but he soon knew John Comyn was dead, granting Sir John Moubray control of his lands in England on 23 February, because the dead man's son, another John – the English king's first cousin, once removed, through the boy's mother, Joanna de Valence – was too young to inherit. Edward also realised, no doubt with a heavy heart, that the situation was serious enough to warrant his own less-than-vigorous presence in the north, ordering in supplies for the royal store at Skinburness near Carlisle 'to the king's use in the fresh rebellion of the Scots' on 20 February, only ten days after the murder. This was followed by a demand for further provisions to be sent to Berwick and Skinburness 'against the arrival of the king and his magnates and others of his subjects who are going there to repress the malice of certain Scots who have lately risen against him in Scotland' at the beginning of March. The campaign was to be organised in a hurry, with everything to be in place by Ascension Day (27 May). In the meantime, the garrison at Carlisle was strengthened and properly provisioned, just in case.[405]

To begin with, however, Edward found it hard to believe that Comyn's murderer and the ringleader of those who 'are doing their utmost to trouble the peace and quiet of our land of Scotland' was Robert Bruce.[406] He wanted to know the facts, despatching two friars on 5 March to Dumfries 'to inquire into the murder of John Comyn.'[407] What the king absolutely did not want to believe – though he should have known better, with his long experience of the Bruces – was that Robert had his eye on the empty throne of Scotland.

But his officials in the north knew otherwise, for Robert soon told them so himself, grimly assuring the government in Berwick 'that he would take castles, towns and people as fast as he could, and strengthen himself as fast as he could, until the king [*Edward*] had notified his will concerning his [*Robert's*] demand, and if he would not grant it to him, he would defend himself with the longest stick that he had.' This prompted an urgent message from Berwick to their colleagues in southern England urging them to ignore misinformation from Scotland and stating in no uncertain terms that 'no matter what any man has given you to understand of the said earl of Carrick [*Robert*], he is [nevertheless] attempting to seize the kingdom of Scotland and to be king.'[408]

The mention of Bruce's demand to Edward reveals as much about Robert's thinking as anything else emerging from this fraught and febrile period of Scottish history, suggesting as it does that his intention now was to ask the English king to reconsider making him ruler of Scotland under English overlordship ten years after Edward had got rid of the last Scottish king. Robert surely cannot have been asking for permission to become a totally independent monarch in the mould of Alexander III. With the English king's support, it would have been possible to persuade the pope to go easy on any penance for the sacrilegious murder *and* to force the rest of the Comyn affinity to back off. This was what the Bruces would once happily have settled for, what they thought they had been promised in 1296 and what Robert himself had tentatively agreed with Edward I when he submitted in 1301/2.

Even so, it was surely not what he had been planning when he made the agreement with Bishop Lamberton two years before, but once Robert realised he would have to kill Comyn or risk seeing him take the throne, seeking Edward's protection surely became an attractive option. Perhaps too, he calculated that the English king, not to mention the English people, would, at a pinch, prefer a Bruce kingship under Edward's ultimate authority rather than launch yet another full-scale war so soon after the end of the last one. That would also mean that he could keep the rich English estates he had only just inherited, which would be useful given that much of Scotland itself had been devastated by years of war and less able to pay royal taxes.

But Robert soon changed his mind, largely because of the deafening silence from the Lord Paramount of Scotland, who still refused to view what was happening in the north as anything other than a continuation of the kind of kingless uprisings that he had dealt with between 1297 and 1304 and was clearly absolutely against the revival of Scottish kingship on any terms. But Bruce also received encouragement to think well beyond a crown bestowed on him by the king of England. On Saturday 5 March,[409] he met with Bishop Wishart, who now dared to absolve him for his sacrilegious murder of John Comyn, even if the pope was unlikely to prove so forgiving. The bishop gave Robert a firm talking-to, urging him to be guided by the Scottish clergy and 'to go to secure his heritage by all the means that he could.' Wishart had no time for making deals with Edward, whose overlordship had proved so disastrous for Scottish independence during the reign of King John. If Robert wanted the support of the Scottish church, then he needed to go for broke. The pair then ate together and Bruce took the first steps on his way to Scone to be made king.[410]

Wishart did not go with his protégé – he was an old man, a veteran of the fight for Scottish independence who had been the first to stand up and openly challenge Edward's right to be overlord of Scotland, but perhaps he also felt he could be of more use directing military operations of his own, besieging Kirkintilloch castle and seizing the royal castle at Cupar.[411] He had clearly been waiting for years for the moment when a Scottish king would once more be enthroned, not only providing Robert with appropriate attire for his inauguration but sending to Scone 'a banner with the royal coat of arms that used to belong to the king of Scots [*Alexander III*], which banner the bishop had long kept hidden in his treasury …'[412]

But, despite such stalwart support and Robert's own efforts to secure a base of loyal subjects from his own lands, as well as in and around Glasgow and parts of the far west, Bruce's inauguration was scarcely a resounding endorsement of his right to rule. The scale of the challenge ahead of him was acknowledged by those writing about it at the time, partly in order to make his eventual triumphs seem even more extraordinary. But there is much truth to the assertion that:

he also devoted himself to a struggle against one and all in the kingdom of Scotland, with the exception of a very few well-disposed to him, who in comparison with the multitude of the other side were like a drop of water reckoned against the waves of the sea, or a single grain of any seed against a great number of grains of sand.[413]

On the day in which Robert Bruce was made king – the Feast of the Annunciation (25 March), which was then also the first day of the New Year – no bishop seems to have presided over any part of that first ceremony, though the abbots of Scone and possibly of nearby Inchaffray were in attendance. Also missing were the two earls – Fife and Strathearn – who traditionally led the man who would be transformed into a monarch to his throne. However, Isabella, aunt of the young earl of Fife, was determined to play her part, placing a gold coronet on Robert's head the following day. She would soon pay dearly for her resolute belief in her family's ancient responsibilities, but must have already known that she would never see her husband – the murdered Guardian's cousin, John Comyn, earl of Buchan – again.[414] The earls of Atholl, Mar, Lennox and Menteith may also have attended, but it was scarcely an unqualified and triumphant return of an independent Scottish king.

Nevertheless, the bishop of St Andrews – still one of King Edward's lieutenants pending the arrival of John of Britanny and among those gathered at Berwick to co-ordinate the government's response to the murder of Comyn – slipped away overnight, reaching Scone in time to perform a mass on 27 March, Palm Sunday. He brought with him James the Steward's eldest son, despite King Edward explicitly requesting that the boy be handed over to his Chamberlain of Scotland.[415] As Scotland's senior bishop, Lamberton gave a legitimacy and authority to proceedings that would otherwise have been lacking. And now that Robert was king, he too had a sanctity and authority that was denied to lesser men. If he could live long enough to wield it.

King Robert certainly had much work to do, given that many – if not most – of his more senior and powerful subjects would not break their recent oaths to King Edward, wished him dead for what he had done to John Comyn or, at the very least, were profoundly shocked by the sacrilegious path he had taken to becoming king. They may also – and at least as importantly – have remained far from convinced that he had any of the attributes likely to make a success of this extremely dangerous enterprise. And that was before considering the response of Edward's men in Scotland and the inevitability of a full-scale English invasion in the coming months.

And yet there were Scots for whom personal oaths of loyalty made by their social superiors and the fall-out of the murder of Scotland's most powerful man counted for less than the possibility of ridding the kingdom of the shackles of over-bearing, intrusive and expensive English rule which the inauguration of a Scottish king promised. These were landowners of modest means, the men (and women) hit hardest by the unprecedented demands for their money and contributions to military service that Edward would once more expect from his Scottish subjects and whom Bruce, along with Bishop Wishart and James the Steward, had already fought for in 1297. From across the country and not just in areas where the Bruces and their allies held sway, they came, if not exactly in droves, then certainly in sufficient numbers to provide some comfort to the new king. Interestingly, too, he also had the support of at least one of his tenants from Essex, Gilbert Mauduyt, whose loyalty to his lord extended to rebellion against the king of England.[416]

Robert knew he had a window of weeks or hopefully even months before any English campaign could get off the ground and he determined to hit his Scottish enemies as quickly as possible. Although the earldoms of Atholl and Mar in the north-east might be viewed as Bruce-friendly, much of northern Scotland was not and, immediately after his inauguration, the Scottish king rode out 'getting friends and friendship in order to support what he had begun' through Perth, Dundee, Forfar, over the Grampian mountains to Aboyne and east to Aberdeen.[417] This was tough campaigning against his own people at a time of year – April into May – when snow might still linger in the higher mountain passes.

At Perth he left the citizens in no doubt that there had been a revolution by imprisoning local officials and demanding £54 of royal rents (about £40,000 today). These townsfolk were thus first to find themselves in that unenviable position between a rock and a hard place when Edward's Scottish chamberlain later forced them to hand over £142 (over £100,000) for their 'disloyalty'.[418] Robert took Aberdeen too, but these rapid successes – in the south-west immediately after Comyn's murder and in the north-east after his inauguration – were soon exposed as beginner's luck based as much on a degree of paralysis among his many enemies.

And that was about to change. News of Bruce's crowning reached Edward, currently bed-bound in Winchester in the far south of England, on 5 April 1306, less than two weeks later. The old man reacted with fury, entirely unable to fathom why Scots who had come to his peace up to four times already should break their solemn oaths yet again and why a man to whom he had been entirely magnanimous should betray him so profoundly.[419] What Robert Bruce had done in reviving Scotland's kingship might be undone, but it could never be forgiven and on 10 April his family's ancient lordship of Annandale with its main seat at Lochmaben was granted to Edward's son-in-law, the earl of Hereford. Grants of more Bruce lands and some of those of his supporters followed in the coming weeks and months.[420] And so too John Comyn – whose murder was now revealed as the prelude to this final treacherous act – began to be reshaped into a martyr for his loyalty to the English king in a torrent of royal commands to deal with his murderer.

Edward realised at last that Scotland could not wait for a full-blown campaign. On 5 April 1306 he appointed Sir Aymer de Valence as royal lieutenant between York and the river Forth, fundamentally changing the rules of this new war with the order for Valence to 'raise the dragon,' a terrifying banner that meant anyone, however noble, who fought against it could expect no mercy. So far as the king was concerned, the Scots had sought his peace and were now throwing their sacred oaths – freely given – back in his face. Sir Henry Percy was once more to provide back-up on the western border using Carlisle as a base. Heading the list of those the English king hoped would soon endure a similar fate to Sir William Wallace were Bruce himself and those who had been with him at Comyn's murder – Sir Alexander Lindsay and the three Seton brothers, whose excommunication the English king also requested from the pope.[421] It was a list that would soon grow much longer.

Edward was keen to attack Robert on his home ground while the Scottish king was in the north-east, but was now aware that his options were limited by Bruce's pre-emptive strikes on strategic positions in the south-west throughout February and March. Supplies that the English king had ordered to be split between Ayr and Skinburness were now all to go to Skinburness south of the border, while English seamen were told to stick to the high seas well away from the coasts of Galloway and Carrick.[422] Orders were also sent to the barons of the northern counties of England and southern counties of Scotland to call out their men to ride with Valence within eight days, should he request it. In the meantime – given that Sir Aymer was still making his way to Berwick – the former Scottish Guardian, Sir Ingram d'Umfraville and Sir John Moubray – both Comyn stalwarts who had once been implacable in their opposition to Edward I – ventured into King Robert's earldom of Carrick. All tournaments, jousts and tiltings were to be cancelled as England's men-at-arms prepared to go to Scotland.[423] The war was back on.

But Edward was far from completely blinded by self-righteous anger, though he had plenty of that to spare. Only those great lords who had betrayed him personally by breaking their oaths and, particularly, killing one of their own who had wished to stay loyal (as the official line on John Comyn now had it) would suffer the full force of the law. Already the king was willing to forgive 'the middling [*mesne*] men of the land of Scotland, who have risen in insurrection, but are willing to come in.'[424] Prising them away from their lords was a strategy that he had already used with some success in the first war,[425] knowing full well that it would be an uphill struggle for Bruce to cobble together an army without them.

But what he probably didn't know as yet was that these were precisely the kind of men who were slipping away to support King Robert, unencumbered as they were by any personal relationship with King Edward. Such men – and the women who stood in the historical shadows beside them – now had fifteen years' experience of English rule, off and on, since Edward first intervened in Scottish affairs in 1291. They had been given little reason to like it.

With an apparently energetic and dynamic Scottish king now leading out an army and determined to make his kingdom fully independent once more, it was perhaps time to think again. But this was no obvious and straight-forward decision. Though Robert had played a part in the struggle against English rule in the first war, it was over six years since he'd been Guardian and for many the new king was largely an unknown quantity; it might have seemed best to wait until he proved he was worth following. Nevertheless Bruce would prove adept at harnessing the anti-English sentiment that had grown hard and enduring in the breast of many a Scot over the last ten years, along with the kind of instinctive patriotism that seems to have moved Sir William Wallace and had perhaps inspired Robert himself to try to persuade the knights of Annandale to join him in 1297 in defending 'his own flesh and blood.'

But despite Edward's obsession with their conduct, most of the Scottish nobility remained, at best, aloof from the new king. This was an issue that Robert was prepared to tackle head-on, however, sending his men to track down John Comyn of Buchan's brother-in-law, the earl of Strathearn, before being persuaded to break the earl's safe-conduct and threatening him with death unless he swore homage and fealty. Despite robustly asserting that he was not in the habit of chopping and changing his allegiances once he had made an oath, Strathearn had no choice but to take King Robert as his lord.[426] And while he was the most high profile Scot on the receiving end of these forceful tactics, he was surely not the only one as the Scottish king's chief commanders rode round east-central Scotland at the head of small companies demanding homage and fealty, just as Edward I had once done. But time would tell whether loyalty forcibly extracted in this way actually meant anything.

Valence crossed the border on Whitsunday (22nd May). A week or so earlier he had written to the English king asking for more money, sweetening his request with the promise that he 'was on the point of making an expedition against the enemy.' Edward received the letter around 24 May and promised more funds, though preferably from Scotland itself. His own health was deteriorating and, despite promising on 17 May that he and the Prince of Wales both intended 'to be in these parts to put down the rebellion of the Scots,' he now realised that he had to delegate command to his son 'to seek King Robin' – one of the many contemptuous names for Bruce – in the hope that he himself could 'follow as soon as possible.' Young Edward had just been knighted, aged twenty-two, along with three hundred other young men with much pomp and splendour.[427]

Valence's small army numbered over 500 horsemen, nearly 2000 footsoldiers and 140 crossbowmen,[428] a decent, but comparatively mobile, fighting force. Leaving Berwick, he headed first to Selkirk Forest, burning Sir Simon Fraser's lands there around the beginning of June. King Edward, who had become very fond of Simon when Fraser entered his service in 1297 as the price of his freedom after the battle of Dunbar, felt personally betrayed by his return to the Scottish side in 1301. Like Bruce, there was to be no way back for him after this second betrayal.

Indeed, Edward was keen to highlight the new rules of engagement, the heavy price to be paid by those who had spurned his generosity in 1304-5, ordering Valence on 12 June to burn out 'all enemies on his march [*the eastern border*], including those who turned against him in this war of the Earl of Carrick, and have since come to his peace as enemies and not been guaranteed [*found others to provide financial reassurance of their good behaviour*], and to burn, destroy, and waste their houses, lands and goods in such wise that Sir Simon and others may have no refuge with them as heretofore.' At the same time, Valence was to tread a fine line so as not to discourage the loyal, but to 'spare them and their houses and goods.'[429]

By the time he got this letter, however, Sir Aymer had already moved further north towards Perth, presumably because his informants had told him that King Robert was in the vicinity. On the way (9 June), he captured Bishop Lamberton at his house at Scotlandwell, a result that pleased King Edward mightily, along with the news that Bishop Wishart had also been taken.[430]

Bruce had his own spies and was aware that he might soon be tested, pulling together an army full of 'fierce young fellows easily roused against the English.'[431] The Scottish king now had at his disposal a rudimentary chancery (secretariat) staffed by royal clerks capable of sending out letters ordering a muster on his behalf. The earl of Strathearn received one of them, which placed him in a terrible quandary for, like the citizens of Perth, he now sat between the rock of King Robert's determination that he should join him and the hard place of King Edward's equal determination that he must not. Alas, choosing either might prove fatal.

The earl made his decision, ignoring King Robert's letter summoning him to fight and later claiming he had been on the point of setting off to join Sir Aymer de Valence at Perth. However, the Scottish king's men came for him once more deep in the western recesses of his earldom, which strongly suggests that he had actually been intent on keeping his head down, hoping both sides would go away. Strathearn had learned his lesson this time, refusing a safe conduct and only agreeing to go to Robert if hostages were left to ensure he came back in one piece. He repeated his refusal personally to the Scottish king, who had no choice but to let him go home.

With Valence safely tucked up behind Perth's walls, the Scottish army appeared outside the town 'in great numbers in white' on 19 June. The news of the dragon banner seems to have spooked Robert and his men, for the Scottish king ordered everyone to cover themselves with white linen, presumably so that they could not be easily identified by their coats of arms and targeted later on. This, together with the treatment of Strathearn, hints at Robert's insecurity, even if he was supported by 'many who were valiant in action, and barons who were bold as boar.'[432] Despite being a crowned king, he still needed to coerce and cover up, though Strathearn ultimately taught him the limits of coercion unless Bruce really was prepared to make a habit of killing senior noblemen.

Valence – advised by friends of John Comyn – decided to lay a trap, heartened by the fact that so few were ranged against him and knowing as he did that Robert had very little experience of leading men in battle. He told Bruce's messenger that he would not fight that day, because it was a feast day but agreed to come out the next morning. The Scottish king believed him and withdrew a few miles west towards Methven to forage for food.

To entirely discount the possibility of attack was extreme folly and Robert and his men were completely taken by surprise when Valence came at them during the long June night. Though some managed to scramble onto their horses, it was a rout and even the king was lucky to escape when either Sir John Haliburton or Sir Philip Moubray – Scotsmen, but in Valence's army – seized his reins. Thankfully for Bruce, Haliburton dropped them when he realised who it was or Moubray was fended off by Sir Christopher Seton. Robert's nephew, Thomas Randolph, was captured, but another Scot – Sir Adam Gordon – urged his release so long as he made his homage and fealty to King Edward and was kept closely guarded in Inverkip castle, now recaptured.[433]

Others were not so lucky. On 4 August – a month and a half after the battle – sixteen of them were hanged on Edward's orders – 'from spite,' says John Barbour, seventy years later, but it was more that the English king had lost all patience with those who had taken him as their lord only to betray him yet again. Two were knights, who would never have dreamed that the death of a common criminal might be their fate, along with the 'false king's' standard bearer, Alexander Scrymgeour, who had been confirmed in this office by both Wallace and Bruce when they had served as Guardians, Robert's marshal [in charge of the army], his chaplain, and Adam Turry, Simon Fraser's messenger. Fraser himself managed to escape, along with King Robert, his brothers, Neil, Thomas, Alexander and Edward, and the earls of Atholl, Lennox and Menteith.[434]

This was a bitter blow, not least because Robert was entirely to blame for not posting sentries. Those who heard John Barbour's popular poem on his life and reign, *The Brus*, written in the 1370s, were now treated to a romantic rendition of the Scottish king's time in the wilderness, when he and his men – and his queen and daughter too – 'spent many days as outlaws, suffering hardship …, eating flesh and drinking water.'

But in truth, there was nothing romantic about his situation, for if it was believed that Robert could scarcely save himself, he was unlikely to persuade his subjects that he could look after them. 'His own men began to be weighed down by their wearisome lot, and the victorious side to be greatly strengthened by the victory given to them.' Even Barbour admits that: 'He dared not go to the open [country] since all the commons rejected him; to [save] their lives they felt compelled to pass to the English peace again. It's often like that – no-one can trust the commons except the person who can be their protector. That's how they treated him then, for he could not protect them from the enemies; they turned to the other side. But serfdom, which they had to suffer, made them yearn that things would go well with him.' And who can blame them, for after all, protecting his people was precisely what a king was for.[435]

The victors at Methven fell over themselves to inform the English king of their victory. The winner was a 'boy' sent by Geoffrey Moubray – whose family owned the lands and castle at Methven – who reached Edward 'in great haste' at Woburn Abbey in Bedfordshire on 25 June, having travelled more than 400 miles in less than a week. Three more messengers arrived before the end of the month, while Sir Aymer de Valence clearly had better things to do – his envoy, 'bringing the king news of the battle between the English and Scots at Perth', did not reach Edward until early July.[436] Though the English king remained in the south, the Prince of Wales was now on his way north with the main army.

So far as Edward was concerned, the battle was a vindication of his own rights in Scotland and it was only a matter of time before the traitor, Robert Bruce, was captured. He already had the pope's sentence of excommunication against those who had taken part in the murder of the martyr, John Comyn, to which he added the earl of Atholl and Simon Fraser, whom he felt he had personally betrayed him. On 28 June, in light of the news of the battle, the king spelled out in more detail what should happen to such traitors – they were not to be executed straight away but kept in prison 'till he declares his pleasure on their fate.'[437] This cannot have meant that Edward was prepared to be lenient, but more likely that he wanted them to stew for a while wondering just how cruel he intended to be. It remained to be seen, however, whether such harsh penalties acted as a deterrent or provoked sympathy and hardened resolve among those who now had no choice but to keep fighting just to stay alive.

After Methven, Robert seems to have gone north – though no-one was really very sure – having been joined by his family, including his wife, Elizabeth de Burgh, his daughter, Marjory, who was about ten years old, his sisters and Isabella of Fife who crowned him and now had nowhere to go. The women supposedly gave the king 'great comfort and all kinds of solace,' which were deemed to be one of femalekind's main attributes, at least according to a middle-aged monk. They 'spent many days as outlaws, suffering hardship in the Mounth [*an outcrop of hills at the far eastern extremity of the Grampian mountains*], eating flesh and drinking water.' Robert himself took the night watch, sleeping during the day, but there were spies everywhere and the men looking for them were clearly getting closer.

Alas, the further they rode into the hills, the more they suffered 'a terrible shortage of food,' relying on those who knew how to hunt venison and trap fish – pike, salmon, trout, eels, even minnows – with their hands, a rudimentary kind of fishing called *gumphling* or *guddling* in the Scots language.[438] But by late July 1306, after a good few weeks of skulking, Bruce may have heard the bad news from south-west Scotland, for on 11 July Prince Edward had personally supervised the submission of the garrison inside Robert's own castle of Lochmaben. Sir Richard Siward's castle of Tibbers, captured by Sir John Seton immediately after Comyn's murder, was presumably recaptured around this time; Seton was sent to Newcastle where he was executed in August. The prince continued on his way north with many of the young men recently knighted with him, all of whom had sworn to avenge the murder of John Comyn in a fit of chivalric fervour. They set off towards Perth, presumably in pursuit of the fugitive Scottish king, burning and devastating towns and villages without mercy as they went.[439]

Robert now perhaps came to the obvious conclusion that he was bringing danger to his own family, while the women – unused to living outdoors – were no doubt slowing him down. It was time to say goodbye to his wife and daughter, those on whom the future of his dynasty depended. Probably in her late teens, Queen Elizabeth was not much older than her step-daughter Marjory and, judging by the lack of children in their first four years of marriage, must have been still too young for proper marital relations when she and Robert first wed in 1302.

But though she was now old enough to endure childbirth, this was scarcely the time to be bringing children into the world. Elizabeth supposedly rebuked her husband after his inauguration, responding to his proud assertion that 'Yesterday we were earl and countess, today we are king and queen' with the cutting reply that 'I think you are the king of summer, but perhaps not of winter. I fear we are like the flowers in the fields today but tomorrow will be put in the oven, still blooming, and because you broke your oath so as to be called king, you will lose both earldom and kingdom.'[440] There was some sympathy in England for the young woman's predicament, given that she was the daughter of Edward's friend, the earl of Ulster, though this flowery dressing-down smacks of imaginative wishful thinking on the part of the chronicler. What little remains to us about Elizabeth de Burgh suggests an absence rather than the forceful presence these words conjure up.

Putting the women into the safe-keeping of his brother Neil, the plan was clearly to get the women away from the frontline and they headed towards the formidable castle of Kildrummy in Mar some forty miles north-west of the mountains they had been hiding in. Robert himself fled south and west, perhaps in order to re-establish himself in his own lands, but most likely, given how few now followed him, in order to raise more men if that were at all possible.

But he had many enemies in the west too, and on 11 August 1306 he crossed paths with one of them – John Macdougall of Lorne – at Dalrigh [dail righ – king's field] just south of Tyndrum and the route out to the west coast. John was son and heir of Alexander Macdougall who, in 1299, had killed Bruce's ally, Alasdair Óg Macdonald of Islay. Though travelling on horseback, Macdougall's men dismounted when they caught up with Bruce and his men, slicing at their horses with their great axes. Once again, King Robert only just escaped, legend having it that he lost the brooch from his cloak as he pulled desperately away from his would-be captors. He would not have been allowed to flee a second time if he'd been recognised, for John of Lorne was John Comyn's cousin. Some of Bruce's men were to be reminded of this second humiliation for the rest of their lives thanks to the scars carved onto their skin by Macdougall axes.[441]

Not surprisingly, this fresh defeat only confirmed the suspicions of many that the so-called king of Scotland was unlucky at best, or, at worst, had incurred God's severe displeasure for fairly obvious reasons.

Knowing King Edward as they did, Bruce's most prominent supporters were well aware that there was probably no going back, but staying with the Scottish king was scarcely a sensible option and some chose to leave his side and take their chances on their own – it was said that 'fear overtook all of them, and they were all separated from one another and scattered throughout various places.'[442]

Many of them did not last long. In mid-August Sir Simon Fraser was finally caught and taken by twenty-four Welshman serving Prince Edward to his father, who had made it as far north as Newbrough in Northumberland. There the ailing king pronounced the sentence himself, sending his former favourite down to London to entertain the people there with his brutal execution. Though he had taken no part in the murder of Comyn, Sir Simon was hung, drawn and quartered like his friend Wallace around 7 September, his head joining Sir William's skull on London Bridge. But, however entertaining the spectacle, it still made some Englishmen uncomfortable, that a nobleman should suffer such a fate – 'In him, through his falseness,' said one chronicler, clearly perplexed that things had come to such a terrible pass, 'perished much worth.'[443] This was as much about the ransom he should have brought the man who actually captured him as Sir Simon's personal qualities.

Figure 6: King Robert's family

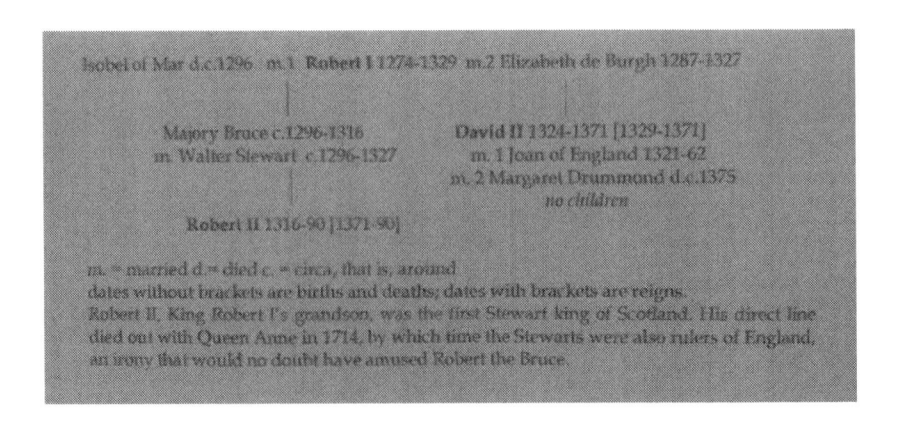

Isobel of Mar d.c.1296   m.1   Robert I 1274-1329   m.2 Elizabeth de Burgh 1287-1327

Marjory Bruce c.1296-1316
m. Walter Stewart c.1296-1327

David II 1324-1371 [1329-1371]
m. 1 Joan of England 1321-62
m. 2 Margaret Drummond d.c.1375
no children

Robert II 1316-90 [1371-90]

m. = married d. = died c. = circa, that is, around
dates without brackets are births and deaths; dates with brackets are reigns.
Robert II, King Robert I's grandson, was the first Stewart king of Scotland. His direct line died out with Queen Anne in 1714, by which time the Stewarts were also rulers of England, an irony that would no doubt have amused Robert the Bruce.

But there was worse to come for Robert's family and supporters. Even before the skirmish at Dalrigh, Bruce realised that his womenfolk were still in danger, for the Prince of Wales was making his way towards Kildrummy in hot pursuit. The Scottish king sent John, earl of Atholl – one of his earliest and most trusted supporters – to tell Robert's brother Neil that the women must all leave the castle and indeed get away from Scotland altogether, most probably into the safe-keeping of their sister, Isobel Bruce, the dowager-queen of Norway. Atholl managed to get them to the coast and on board a ship, but they were driven back ashore by the wind. With their enemies closing in, they sought sanctuary in the shrine to St Duthac at Tain.[444]

The English king's fury towards Robert now found some outlet in the punishment of his women. The queen was treated comparatively leniently, as befitted a daughter of the earl of Ulster even if she was the wife of a traitor. But Elizabeth was still to remain a prisoner at Burstwick near one of the early Bruce properties of Holderness in Yorkshire in the keeping of two local women, whom Edward decreed should be 'elderly and not at all merry,' along with two valets, one of whom was sent by her father, and a page, who was to be 'restrained and not given to causing mischief', punishment enough for a teenage girl.

Edward first of all decreed that Marjory Bruce, whom he'd failed to get his hands on as a baby nine years earlier, should be very securely locked up in a cage in the Tower of London and not allowed to speak to anyone or be let out except by the constable of the Tower. Thankfully he relented slightly and the girl was sent to the convent at Watton, twenty-five miles north of her step-mother. Robert's sister, Christian, despite being married to Sir Christopher Seton who had been with Bruce at the murder of John Comyn, was also sent to a nunnery at Sixhills in Lincolnshire.

But Isabella of Fife had crowned the traitor and for that Edward could never forgive her. He sent orders to Berwick that a strong cage should be built in one of the towers in the castle there and that an Englishwoman or two from the town who were above suspicion should serve Isabella her food and drink. They alone were allowed to talk to her, and she certainly wasn't allowed to communicate with anyone 'of the nation of Scotland.' Given that she was a countess, it was to be comfortable, but God help those charged with her keeping if she were to escape. Bruce's sister Maria was to be similarly housed in a cage in Roxburgh castle, though we have no idea what she said or did to offend King Edward so deeply.[445]

Even so, they were spared the worst of it. Neil Bruce stayed to defend Kildrummy with other Bruce stalwarts when Atholl came to take the women away but by late August found themselves besieged by Aymer de Valence and the Prince of Wales. Nevertheless, the castle's walls were stout and the English outside them received some disturbing news 'concerning certain secret and arduous business touching the king while he was sick.' On 17 August Edward – now being carried slowly and painfully in a litter – managed only the five excruciating miles between Hexham and Newbrough. Even that seems to have been too much for him, for he stayed at Newbrough for the best part of three weeks.[446]

If the English king had died in August/September 1306, then Kildrummy might have been saved. As it was, by 10 September the siege was over and the castle taken, suggesting that stories of a traitor within who seized some embers 'glowing hot' and pitched them high into a pile of grain in the great hall so that the whole place caught fire were true.[447] Though the garrison negotiated their surrender, Neil was taken to Berwick and executed. Sir Alexander Lindsay – who had been at the murder of Comyn – and Sir Robert Boyd were reported to have been taken too, but they must have escaped, for Lindsay would certainly otherwise have been hung, drawn and quartered.[448]

Given the impressive networks of spies employed by both sides, King Robert may well have been told of the terrible fate meted out to so many of his closest friends and family, often as punishment for his actions rather than their own. He certainly knew that he and those that stayed with him were in mortal danger on all sides. Now 'the king saw how his folk were placed, and what afflictions they suffered; [he] saw winter was nearly upon them and that in no way could he risk lying in the cold, or waking for the long nights, in the hills.'[449] In fact, it was still only August, but he certainly needed to get away, and quickly, before the nights really did turn cold in another six weeks or so.

But where to go? Annandale was already lost to him and Sir Henry Percy had been making inroads into Carrick – which King Edward had given to him – since the end of July. In early August a flotilla of boats was launched against Robert's castle in the middle of Loch Doon, which was held for the Scottish king by his brother-in-law, Sir Christopher Seton. The castle fell a week or so later, once more thanks to treachery, and in it were found many of Bruce's papers and even his own private seal. Seton and his brothers John and Humphrey were, with terrible inevitability, hung, drawn and quartered at Dumfries, where they'd helped to murder John Comyn only six months before.[450]

King Robert seems to have hoped to see through the winter in Kintyre which juts out into the North Channel between Scotland and Ireland, putting his fate in getting there in the hands of a distant relative, Sir Neil Campbell, whose lands lay around Loch Awe about eighteen miles from the altercation with John Macdougall at Dalrigh. There were few Robert could trust now, for even those he viewed as his own subjects might inform his enemies of his whereabouts. He had no boats, which would have helped him to travel quickly and easily along the many rivers and lochs of the west Highlands and were certainly needed to get to Kintyre, which, though a peninsula, had to be approached by sea to avoid a long and difficult overland journey.

The Scottish king had also got rid of his horses, perhaps because he could no longer feed them and also to attract less attention. He did not even deserve the insult 'King Hobbe' – a favourite epithet bandied about by his enemies because of the stocky little ponies or 'hobby' horses ideal for riding through Scotland's hill country that he had come to rely on. These intrepid mounts had carried him and his men far in these days of wandering, but for the many ranged against him, both Scots and English, it was easy to portray them as scarcely a mode of transport worthy of a knight and a king. Those who might have spied Bruce and his friends traipsing through the hills on foot would surely have imagined they were vagabonds and certainly not honest men.

While Campbell went off to find water transport, Robert and his men took to the hills east of Loch Lomond, where they chanced to meet the earl of Lennox, whose lands these were. Lennox had not seen the king since Methven and it is clear from his delight at seeing Bruce alive and well that rumours of Robert's death were circulating widely. Whether it was manly or not, they were all moved to tears, which was quite understandable given what they had been through and the hardships and dangers they still faced, even if the king himself was largely to blame for their trials and tribulations.[451]

Word came that Campbell had found a galley to carry them to Kintyre and they set sail, with Lennox accompanying them in his own boat. They probably sailed down Loch Long, past the mouth of the River Clyde and James the Steward's island of Bute. None were exempt from rowing duty, 'For all were at it, knight and boy, [and] none could have any relief from steering and rowing [that] helped them in their passage.[452] But they were spotted nonetheless and boats, probably from the garrison at Inverkip, held for King Edward by the Berwickshire knight, Sir Adam Gordon,[453] set off in pursuit. The earl of Lennox lagged behind to draw them off, supposedly throwing everything bar arms and armour overboard so as to make his galley lighter and speedier. He soon caught up with Robert, who had landed safely at Dunaverty castle right at the bottom of Kintyre, but the Scottish king must already have known that he should not linger there for long now that his enemies might guess where he was going.

This priceless information was quickly relayed to Sir Henry Percy, who was only some sixty miles south of Inverkip in the process of subduing 'his' earldom of Carrick. Percy immediately asked for siege engines to be sent by sea to Dunaverty from Skinburness and had reached Kintyre himself, in an impressive company that included King Edward's nephew, Thomas, earl of Lancaster, probably in mid/late August. They stayed there, besieging the castle, for the best part of six weeks, finally gaining entry at the end of September. But, much to their horror and disbelief, their prey was long gone.[454]

Robert had probably headed north, hopping straight to the next island – Islay – which was Macdonald territory. Since the death of Alasdair Óg in 1299, the Bruces could no longer rely on the new chief – Alasdair's brother, Donald – and the Scottish king now had to force him to provide hospitality. And so it was not safe to tarry here either, for 'he feared treason all the time, and therefore, as I heard men say, he trusted in nobody completely until he knew them through and through. But whatever fear he had [of people] he presented a smiling face to them.'[455]

Robert's intention was almost certainly to keep going north, but fate – in the form of 'contrary winds' which could scupper the best-laid plans – intervened and he was blown south, to the island of Rathlin of the coast of Antrim, now in Northern Ireland. This was an even more dangerous place to end up, because it was then part of the earldom of Ulster, which belonged to Robert's father-in-law, Richard de Burgh. And Richard would have had few qualms about handing his daughter's husband over to King Edward. Of course, if we believe the legend, then it was just as well, for otherwise Robert might never have met the spider whose infinitely patient web-spinning persuaded him to take courage and try again to regain his kingdom.

But that would imply that Bruce had given up – indeed Sir Walter Scott, in his *Tales of a Grandfather*, where the spider story most famously appears, has the Scottish king declare his intention to 'transport himself and his brothers to the Holy Land, and spend the rest of his life in fighting against the Saracens,' a suitably pious and penitent desire. Seeing the spider, he resolves to let her decide his fate – if she succeeds, he will fight on, but if she fails, he 'will go to the wars in Palestine, and never return to my native country more.'[456]

But, even now, it is hard to imagine Robert feeling ambivalent about his kingship, not when every political move he ever made was designed to enhance his chances of gaining the throne; not when his brother, his brother-in-law and a number of close friends had already paid the ultimate price for that ambition and his wife, daughter and sisters languished in captivity. Whether he had fully understood the implications of Bishop Wishart's advice to have himself made king on his own terms, not Edward's, is impossible to know. But that he should have considered giving up was surely unthinkable. He was not entirely penniless either, sending men to collect the rents of his earldom of Carrick due at Martinmas [29 September 1306] even once he had been forced to flee from Kintyre. Such effrontery may have prompted Percy – who had been besieging Dunaverty – to hurry back to what were supposed to be his lands.[457]

And so, for the rest of 1306 and several months of 1307, King Robert disappears, not least into legend, and few must have expected to ever hear of him again, either because he was dead or because he had chosen exile somewhere he might never be found. Bruce's brief foray into kingship squared with the rest of his career so far – full of bravado and decisive action but marred by mediocre, if not downright poor, military leadership. It was a wonder and a marvel that he had survived this long and it must have been a source of great annoyance to King Edward that the traitor had slipped through his fingers yet again, for surely God ought to have delivered him up quickly and easily. For those who knew how it would all work out, these terrible months of hardship were Robert's divine punishment for John Comyn's murder. For them, his redemption and deliverance were never in doubt. But for those at the time, including Bruce himself, the road ahead must have seemed very rough indeed.

INDEX

Aardenburg, Flanders
  English army at, 102
Aberdeen
  attacked by Robert Bruce (7), 152
Scottish parliament at, 122Aberdeen, bishop of
  in minority of Alexander III, 26
Abernethy, Alexander
  keeper of Scotland north of the Forth, 140
Acre, Levant, 28
Agincourt, battle of, 121
Alan, lord of Galloway, 20, 21
Alexander II, king of Scots, 20, 23
  death of, 23
  death of wife, 21
  invades England, 20
Alexander III, king of Scots, 23, 24, 149
  banner of, 150
  death of, 38
  death of eldest son, Alexander, 32
  death of younger son, David, 32
  inauguration of, 24

knighted by Henry III, 25
  makes arrangements for succession, 37
  marriage to Yolande de Dreux, 38
  minority of, 23, 24, 26
  objects to marriage of Robert Bruce (6) and Marjory of Carrick, 29
  performs homage to Henry III, 25
  swears homage and fealty to Edward I, 31
Alexander, eldest son of Alexander III
  death of, 32
Amersham, Walter
  chancellor of Scotland, 85
Ancrum, palace of bishops of Glasgow, 91
Angus, earl of
  role before battle of Falkirk, 97
  swears homage to Edward I, 73, 80
Annan, Bruce castle and settlement, 10, 16, 18, 27, 29, 39, 67

Annan, William of, clerk of Robert Bruce (5), 22
Annandale, Bruce lordship of, 10, 13, 15, 16, 17, 20, 22, 62, 68, 71, 72, 73, 78, 88, 94, 99, 105, 119, 124, 126, 130, 132, 133, 134, 152, 162
  attacked by Scots, 126
  revenues of, 134
  taxation in, 112
Annandale, knights of, 17, 42, 118, 154
  reject appeal to join Robert Bruce (7), 88
Arbroath
  robbers near, 144
Argyll, bishop of
  attests grant of Alasdair Óg Macdonald, 37
Ashridge, monastery of
  English parliament at, 50
Asnières, Treaty of, *See* Edward I, Philip IV
Atholl, John de Strathbogie, earl of
  ?present at inauguration of Robert Bruce (7), 150
  absent from Scottish assembly, 1305, 135
  ally of the Bruces), 48
  appointed keeper north of the Forth, 134
  escapes after battle of Methven, 157
  in English prison, 85
  leader of Scottish army, 72, 75
  role during conquest of 1296, 76
  sent to Kildrummy, 160
  sentence of excommunication against, 157
  supports Bishop Lamberton as Guardian, 111
  with Scottish army in Selkirk Forest, 106
Ayr
  Prince Edward's army at, 113
Ayr, castle of
  granted to Henry Percy, 81
  strengthened during civil war of 1286, 43
  taken by Robert Bruce (7), 147
Ayr, William of, clerk of Robert Bruce (5), 28
Baddow, Edmund
  esquire of Robert Bruce (6), 73
Baddow, William
  esquire of Robert Bruce (6), 73
Bailleul, Picardy
  final residence of King John, 115
Balliol, Dervorguilla, lady of Galloway, 21
  death of, 46
  her castle of Buittle taken by Robert Bruce (5), 43
Balliol, Edward, son of King John
  in English custody, 80
Balliol, Eleanor, wife of John Comyn, 2nd lord of Badenoch, 40
Balliol, John, father of John I, king of Scots, 21
  and English civil war, 27
Balliol, John, lord of Barnard castle, lord of Galloway, king of Scots, 46, 149
  agrees treaty with Norway, 69

167

and Macduff case, 64
arguments in Great Cause, 54
attends English parliament on Scottish affairs, 66
basis of claim to the throne, 40
concludes treaty with France, 71
conditions of imprisonment in England, 104
debts of, 66
final years of, 123
first parliament, 61
hands over his rights to Philip of France, 123
imprisoned in England, 80
inaugurated at Scone, 57
judged rightful king of Scots, 57
lodged at Malmaison, 104
meets with Wallace, 110
moved around in France, 110
name absent from Scrymgeour charter, 103
parliament of, 69
relationship with Anthony Bek, bishop of Durham, 49
relationship with Edward I, 60, 63
released from English prison into papal custody, 104
renounces homage and fealty to Edward I, 75
retreats before Edward I, 78
seeks absolution from pope for oaths to Edward I, 66
seizes Bruce earldom of Carrick, 62
sends embassy to France, 69
stripped of kingship, 79
submits to Edward I, 79
swears homage and fealty to Edward I, 57
transferred from pope to Philip of France, 115
tries to smuggle Scottish crown and great seal out of England, 104
wins arguments against Robert Bruce (5), 55
Balliol, William
envoy to France, 122
Bannockburn, battle of, 98
Barbour, John
author of *The Brus*, 156
Bardolf, Robert
knight of Robert Bruce (6), 73
Barnard Castle, Northumberland, seat of the Balliol family, 21, 49
Bek, Anthony, bishop of Durham, 60, 97
active in Scotland, 1291, 52
attends King John's inauguration, 57
in English army, 72
orchestrates submission of King John, 79
relationship with John Balliol, 49
role in negotiations between Edward I and Scots, 47
sent to negotiate with King John, 70
Berwick, castle and town of, 18, 53, 54, 75, 76, 77, 80, 82, 86, 88, 91, 92, 93, 109, 112, 113, 124, 148, 150, 153, 154, 161, 162
provisions sent to, 148
put into custody of men of Fife, 72

168

siege of, 74
venue for Great Cause, 53
Berwickshire
  still in English control, 90
Biggar
  Scots at, 124
Birgham, agreement at, 1289, 45
Boniface VIII, pope, 119
  ally of Scotland, 95
  needs Edward I's friendship, 122
  reprimands Bishop Wishart of Glasgow, 122
  sends letter to Edward I on Scottish question, 112
  writes to Edward I demanding King John's release, 104
  writes to King John for William Lamberton as bishop of St Andrews, 103
Bordeaux, Gascony, 41
Boreham, Essex
  manor belonging to Maud Burnell, 68
Botetourt, John
  appointed justice in Scotland, 140
  appoints sheriffs with Robert Bruce (7), 129
  takes English force to deal with Scots in south-west, 126
Bothwell, castle of, 116
  falls to English, 114
Boyd, Robert
  reportedly captured, 162
Brechin, castle of
  site of King John's submission, 79
Breton, Archibald le

knight of Robert Bruce (6), 73
Britanny, John of, nephew of Edward I
  appointed royal lieutenant of Scotland, 139
  bad choice as royal lieutenant, 141
  continuing absence of, 144
  royal lieutenant of Scotland, 150
Bruce, Adam, eldest son of Robert Bruce (1), 13
Bruce, Alexander
  escapes after battle of Methven, 157
Bruce, Bernard, brother of Robert Bruce (5), 27
Bruce, Christian, wife of Christopher Seton
  capture and imprisonment, 161
Bruce, Edward
  escapes after battle of Methven, 157
  fostered in Ireland, 36
  goes to Perth with Edward, prince of Wales, 128
  member of household of Edward, prince of Wales, 126
Bruce, Isobel, wife of Eric II of Norway, 161
  marriage of, 56
Bruce, Maria
  capture and imprisonment, 161
Bruce, Marjory, daughter of Robert Bruce (7)
  birth of, 82

169

capture and imprisonment of, 161
goes on the run after battle of Methven, 158
to be a hostage for her father, 90

Bruce, Neil
besieged in Kildrummy castle, 161
captured and executed, 162
defends Kildrummy castle, 161
escapes after battle of Methven, 157
takes royal women to Kildrummy castle, 159

Bruce, Robert, 1st lord of Annandale, 9, 11, 15
aftermath of battle of the Standard, 13
at battle of the Standard, 12
career of, 13
gift of Annandale by David I, 10
gift of lands from Henry I, 9

Bruce, Robert, 2nd lord of Annandale, 13, 17
builds Lochmaben castle, 16
cursed by St Malachy, 16
eldest son marries illegitimate daughter of William I, king of Scots, 18
reaction to Scottish invasion of England, 17

Bruce, Robert, 3rd lord of Annandale, 20

Bruce, Robert, 4th lord of Annandale
death of, 20
loyal to Scottish king, 20
marriage to Isabella of Huntingdon, 19

Bruce, Robert, 5th lord of Annandale, 22, 23, 24
accepts overlordship of Edward I, 52
also known as the Competitor, 42
and Eighth Crusade, 28
and English civil war, 27
argues that Scotland should be split among heirs of David, earl of Huntingdon, 56
arguments in Great Cause, 54
asserts rights of 'Seven earls of Scotland' to choose king, 50
at Birgham, 46
basis of claim to the throne, 40
birth of, 20
claims he was named heir to Alexander II, 21, 50
cross-border landholding, 65
death of, 67
debts of, 30, 68, 133
description of, 39
envoy to Edward I, 44
gathers Scottish and Irish nobles at Turnberry, 41
in minority of Alexander III, 26
joins household of Henry III of England, 26
known as 'the Noble', 20
launches civil war on south-west Scotland, 1286, 42
loses arguments to Balliol, 55
made keeper of Carlisle castle, 27
marriage to Christina of Ireby, 29

not at King John's inauguration, 60
places himself under Edward I's protection, 50
Plan B in Great Cause, 55
plotting to acquire Garioch, 46
prepared to go to war over claim to throne, 40
serves Edward I in Wales, 30
status in Scotland, 23
success and failure in civil war of 1286, 43
summoned to fight for Edward I, 67
swears homage to King John, 62
threatens civil war after death of Maid, 48

Bruce, Robert, 6th lord of Annandale, earl of Carrick
?claim to throne overlooked, 119
?writes to bishop of Vicenza on King John's release from English prison, 105
and Eighth Crusade, 28
arranges his father's ransom, 27
asks Edward I to make him king, 77
at Birgham, 46
becomes knight of Edward I, 30
birth of, 22
campaigns in Wales, 30, 67
complains that he has been kept out of Annandale, 119
daughter Isobel marries Eric II of Norway, 56
death of, 130
debts of, 30, 63, 65, 67, 73, 82, 96, 133
does homage to Edward I, 68, 73, 80
envoy of Alexander III, 30
fails to swear homage to King John, 61
gets lands back after revolt of Robert Bruce (7), 92
given Bruce claim to the throne, 62
given powers to bring men of Annandale to Edward I's peace, 78
in Norway, 62
intended to go with Edward I to continent, 92
joins English army, 72
joins his father in civil war, 1286, 43
living mostly in the south of England, 88
loses all Scottish lands, 68
loses earldom of Carrick, 63
made keeper of Carlisle, 30
marriage to Marjory, countess of Carrick, 28
marriage to Maud Burnell, 68
not at King John's inauguration, 60
part of Turnberry band, 1286, 41
planning to go to Scotland, 89
restored to Scottish estates, 78, 81
rides with Anthony Bek, bishop of Durham, 72
role in conquest of Scotland, 76, 80
stands in for Alexander III, 31

summoned to fight for Edward I, 67, 96
unhappy at father's second marriage, 30
Bruce, Robert, 7th lord of Annandale, earl of Carrick, king of Scots, 9, 92
?canvases for support to take throne, 136
?challenge from Comyns to his control of Mar, 139
?not at Turnberry, 1286, 42
?present at Great Cause, 54
?submission to Edward I includes acknowledgement of claim to throne, 118
actions after murder of Comyn, 147
agrees truce with England as Guardian, 109
ambitions for the throne, 132
and patriotism, 154
appeals to knights of Annandale to join him, 88
appointed advisor to John of Brittany, 139
appointed sheriff of Ayr and Lanark, 129
appoints sheriffs with John Botetourt, 129
appraisal of life on death of his father, 132
arranges to meet John Comyn at Dumfries, 145
assessment of career, 1305, 139
at Lochmaben, 99, 145
attacked by John Comyn, 107
attacks enemies, 151
attacks father's lordship of Annandale, 105
attends English parliament, 124
attends King John's parliament as earl of Carrick, 62
attends parliament at Westminster to advise Edward I, 135
attends Scottish assembly at Scone or Perth, 135
becomes Guardian of Scotland, 102
birth of, 34
bishop of Glasgow and Alexander Lindsay to guarantee his loyalty, 91
burns Ayr, 99
burns William Douglas's lands and seizes his family, 88
career noted in Guisborough Priory chronicle, 16
career up to 1298, 102
comes out on Scottish side, 99
confirms Wallace's grant of Dundee to Alexander Scrymgeour, 103
birth of daughter Marjory, 82
debts of, 74
defeated by Aymer de Valence at Methven, 156
disappears, 165
earldom of Carrick occupied by the English, 117
earldom of Carrick restored to him, 120
early life, 37
early successes illusory, 152
Edward hoping to target his lands, 112

Edward I challenges his rights in Annandale, 133
Edward I pleased with, 129
escapes to Kintyre, 162
expected in Berwick, 91
finally becomes earl of Carrick, 81
flees from Dunaverty castle, 164
foster family, 35
given earldom of Carrick, 62
given powers to bring men of Carrick to Edward I's peace, 78
goes to Glasgow to join Scottish lords, 105
granted custody of earldom of Mar, 135
granted keepership of royal forests, 135
hiding near Loch Lomond, 163
hunting William Wallace and Simon Fraser, 129
in English army, 73
inauguration of, 150
influence of Courtrai on, 122
joins revolt with Robert Wishart, bishop of Glasgow and James the Steward, 88
joins Scots besieging Stirling castle, 109
keen to exploit power vacuum in Scottish politics, 87
kills John Comyn, 141, 145
lack of horses, 163
lack of support as king, 150
leaves womenfolk and heads west, 158
likelihood of going on crusade in 1306, 164
little military success, 109
loses all Scottish lands, 68
loses earldom of Carrick, 63
loses position as sheriffs of Ayr and Lanark, 138
loyalty in late 1297, 94
makes agreement with Bishop Lamberton of St Andrews, 132
marries Isabella of Mar, 63
movements after battle of Methven, 158
nicknamed 'King Hobbe', 163
not chosen as envoy to Westminster parliament, 136
part of English regime in Scotland, 119
prepares to take the throne, 148
reaction to scrapping of Scottish kingship, 78
realises John Comyn is obstacle to his becoming king, 137
receive letter from Philip of France as Guardian, 103
receives revenues of earldom of Carrick, 165
rejected by ordinary Scots, 157
restored to Scottish estates, 78, 81
returns to south-west Scotland, 108
reunited with family, 126
revives Scottish government, 155
seeking payment as sheriff of Ayr and Lanark, 134

173

seeks lands of Ingram d'Umfraville, 118
sentence of excommunication against, 157
situation in 1296, 85
skirmish with John Macdougall of Lorne, 159
spider story, 164
steps down as Guardian, 110
stupidity at battle of Methven, 157
submits to Edward I, 118
submits to Percy and Clifford, 89
support of 'middling folk' for, 153
suspected of disloyalty by bishop of Carlisle, 87
swears homage to Edward I, 73, 80
to bring footsoldiers to serve in English army, 124
to hand over his daughter as a hostage, 90
to lose hostages to Henry Percy, 81
to put Edward I's siege engines into position at Stirling, 130
unwilling to call out army of Carrick, 120
upbringing, 34
why he killed John Comyn, 146
with John Botetourt's force, 127
with John Soules besieging Turnberry castle, 115
with Scottish army in Selkirk Forest, 106

Bruce, Robert, eldest son of Robert Bruce (2)
marriage to illegitimate daughter of William, king of Scots, 17
Bruce, Thomas
escapes after battle of Methven, 157
Bruce, William
knight of Robert Bruce (6), 73
Bruces
relationship with the Comyns, 76
Bruges, Flanders, 120
Buittle, Balliol castle of, 43
granted to Henry Percy, 81
taken by Robert Bruce (5), 1286, 43
Burgh, Elizabeth de, daughter of earl of Ulster, wife of Robert Bruce (7)
capture and imprisonment, 161
goes on the run after battle of Methven, 158
marriage to Robert Bruce (7), 120
supposedly rebukes her husband, 159
Burgh, Richard de, earl of Ulster, 164
at Turnberry, 1286, 41
Burghdon, Walter
appointed justiciar of Galloway, 138
justiciar of Galloway, 147
Burnell, Maud, wife of Robert Bruce (6), 68
Burstwick, manor of, Yorkshire, 161

Edward I at, 135
Bute, James the Steward's island of, 163
Caddonlee, Selkirkshire
  musterpoint of Scottish army, 72
Caerlaverock, castle of, 126
  owned by Maxwells, 109
  Scottish garrison causes problems for English garrison at Lochmaben, 109
  taken by English, 111
Caithness, Alan, bishop of
  envoy to Edward I, 46
Caldecote, Cambridgeshire,
  Bruce lands of, 132
Cambuskenneth, abbey of, 128, 132
Campbell, Neil
  finds galley for Robert Bruce (7), 163
  helps Robert Bruce (7) to escape, 162
Cardross, King Robert's manor house of, 36
Carham, priory of, Northumberland
  devastated by Scottish army, 76
Carlisle, 27, 109, 152
  attacked by Scottish army, 72
  keepership given to Robert Bruce (6), 30, 69
  Scots raid to, 126
Carlisle, bishop of
  defending south-western border, 94
  suspicious of Robert Bruce (7), 87
Carlisle, William
  knight of Robert Bruce (6), 73
  in charge of Carlisle, 72
Carrick, earl of, 28
  in minority of Alexander III, 26
Carrick, earldom of
  description of, 29
  Irish lands belonging to, 29
  revenues from, 165
Carrick, Gilbert of
  ally of the Bruces, 62, 63
Châtillon-sur-Marne
  temporary residence of King John, 110
Chester, castle of
  Andrew Murray escapes from, 89
Cheyne, Reginald
  justiciar north of the Grampian mountains, 143
civil war
  possibility after 1286, 40
Clare, Thomas de, of Thomond, nephew of Robert Bruce (5)
  at Turnberry, 1286, 41
Cleveland, Yorkshire
  Bruce lands in, 9
Clifford, Robert
  background of, 89
  campaigns in Annandale, 94
  defending south-western border, 94
  given Caerlaverock castle, 119
  gives up keepership of Galloway, 109
  in charge of Galloway, including Lochmaben, 105
  to put down revolt with Henry Percy, 89
Clyde, river, 163

175

Coldstream, priory of, Berwickshire
   English army at, 74
Comyn family
Comyn, Alexander, brother of earl of Buchan
   on English side, 140
Comyn, Alexander, earl of Buchan, 24
   chosen as guardian, 1286, 39
   sheriff of Wigtown, 43
Comyn, John, 2nd lord of Badenoch, 24, 43
   accused of abuse of power by Bruces, 50
   and English civil war, 27
   chosen as guardian, 1286, 39
   death of, 123
   envoy to Edward I, 44, 46
   joins household of Henry III of England, 26
   married to Eleanor Balliol, 40
   released to return to Scotland, 88
   submits to Edward I, 79
Comyn, John, 3rd lord of Badenoch, 133, 157, 162
   ?active in northern Scotland, 127
   ?less authority after 1303, 143
   agrees to meet Robert Bruce (7) in Dumfries, 145
   agrees truce with England as Guardian, 109
   at Dalswinton, 145
   at Glasgow with other Scottish lords, 105
   attacks Robert Bruce (7), 107
   becomes a martyr for loyalty to Edward I, 153
   can't work with Bishop Lamberton as Guardian, 111
   credentials to be king, 136
   becomes Guardian of Scotland, 102
   deserts English army, 102
   Edward, prince of Wales swears to avenge his murder, 158
   escapes English army and returns to Scotland, 96
   God punishes Robert Bruce (7) for his murder, 165
   in Scottish army, 72
   leader of Scottish army, 75, 124
   makes peace with Edward I, 128
   marries Joanna de Valence, 53
   murdered by Robert Bruce (7), 141, 145
   obstacle to Robert Bruce (7) becoming king, 137
   receives letter from Philip of France as Guardian, 103
   sends scouting party to south-east Scotland, 106
   sole Guardian of Scotland, 123
   urged by Scots in France to continue the fight, 125
   victor at battle of Roslin, 125
   with Scottish army in Selkirk Forest, 106
Comyn, John, earl of Buchan
   ?active in northern Scotland, 127
   at Glasgow with other Scottish lords, 106
   envoy to France, 122
   given Bruce lordship of Annandale, 71

leader of Scottish army, 72
leads part of Scottish army to south-west Scotland, 72
leads Scottish army, 113
negotiates with men of Galloway, 111
property set on fire, 127
released to return to Scotland, 88
submits to Edward I, 78
with Scottish army in Selkirk Forest, 106
Comyn, Robert, uncle of John Comyn, 3rd lord of Badenoch killed by Christopher Seton, 145
Comyn, Walter, earl of Menteith, 22
controls Alexander III, 24
Comyn, William, chancellor to David I, 23
Comyn, William, earl of Buchan, 23
Comyns
acquire Badenoch, 23
arrival in Britain from Normandy, 23
attitude to William Wallace, 107
choose most envoys to Westminster parliament, 136
dominance of Scottish politics, 42, 66, 135
exiled from Scotland, 85
fail to deter revolt of Andrew Murray, 89
in minority of Alexander III, 26

loyalty suspected by English government, 91
military tactics of, 111
re-establishing dominant position in Scotland, 100
relationship with the Bruces, 76
relationship with William Wallace, 96
supporters appointed as advisors to John of Brittany, 139
Coucy, Marie de, mother of Alexander III, 25
Courtrai, battle of, 120
importance of, 121
Crambeth, Matthew, bishop of Dunkeld
envoy to France, 69, 122
permanently stationed in France, 122
Cressingham, Hugh, treasurer of Scotland, 85
killed at battle of Stirling Bridge, 93
receives loan from England, 86
unhappy with state of Scotland, 90
Cruggleton
lands of John Comyn, earl of Buchan, 111
Crusade, Eighth, 27
Cryps, Walter
cook of Robert Bruce (6), 73
Cumberland, 13, 20, 25, 89, 94
attacked by Scots, 126
Cunningham, Robert
constable of Caerlaverock castle, 109
Cupar, castle of

177

taken for Robert Bruce (7) by Bishop Wishart of Glasgow, 150
Dalrigh, Argyll
  Robert Bruce (7) defeated by John Macdougall of Lorne, 159, 162
Dalswinton, Comyn castle of, 145
  falls briefly to English, 113
  Scottish army at, 114
  taken by Robert Bruce (7), 147
David I, king of Scots, 10, 17, 23, 24, 133
  invades England, 12
  loses battle of the Standard, 12
  rules Cumberland and Northumberland, 13
David II, king of Scots, 15
David, younger son of Alexander III
  death of, 32
Douglas, James
  seized by Robert Bruce (7) as a boy, 88
Douglas, William
  imprisoned in Berwick castle, 91
  joins revolt of Robert Bruce (7), Robert Wishart, bishop of Glasgow and James the Steward, 88
  joins William Wallace, 87
  keeper of Berwick castle, 74
  lands burned and family seized by Robert Bruce (7), 88
  role in conquest of 1296, 77
  submits to Edward I, 75

Dover castle. *See* Bruce, Robert, 5th lord of Annandale
dragon banner, 152
Dreux, Yolande de
  gives birth to stillborn child, 42
  marries Alexander III, 38
  pregnancy of, 40
Dryfesdale, Annandale, 24
Dumfries, 16, 43, 89, 111, 112, 126, 127, 134, 147, 162
  taken by Robert Bruce (5), 1286, 43
Dunaverty, castle of, Kintyre, 165
  besieged by Henry Percy, 164
  provisioned by Robert Bruce (7) after murder of John Comyn, 147
  Robert Bruce (7) seeks shelter there, 163
Dunbar, battle of, 76
  celebrated by English, 84
  prisoners from battle released to serve with Edward I on the continent, 92
Dunbar, earl of
  at Turnberry, 1286, 41
  in minority of Alexander III, 26
  role before battle of Falkirk, 97
  swears homage to Edward I, 73, 80
  to lose hostages to Henry Percy, 81
Dundee, castle and port, 20, 103, 138, 151
  attacked by Robert Bruce (7), 151

178

besieged by William Wallace, 92
Dunfermline, abbey of
Edward I at, 128
new tomb built for St Margaret, 24
royal mausoleum at, 32
treaty with France ratified there, 71
Dunipace, Falkirk
English army at, 114
Dunkeld, bishop of. *See* Crambeth, Matthew
in minority of Alexander III, 26
Durham, bishop of. *See* Bek, Anthony
Durham, cathedral of, 13, 49, 75
Durham, Ralph
clerk of Robert Bruce (6), 73
Durward, Alan, 24
in minority of Alexander III, 26
Earls of Scotland, seven. *See* Robert Bruce, 5th lord of Annandale
Edinburgh, castle of, 26, 53, 97
council meeting, 1286, 38
strengthened during civil war of 1286, 43
Edward I, king of England, 26, 36
?acknowledges Robert Bruce (7)'s claim to the throne, 118
abolishes Scottish kingship, 77
agrees truce with Scots, 112, 116
and civil war, 27
and Eighth Crusade, 27, 28
and marriage of the Maid with his son, 45

angry that Robert Bruce (7) hasn't been captured, 165
asked to quell disorder in Scotland, 144
asserts overlordship over Scotland, 51, 57
attends marriage, knighting and homage of Alexander III of Scotland, 25
attitude to Comyns, 138
attitude to Robert Bruce (7), 139
attitude to Scotland, 83
becomes king, 28
brings an army to Scotland, 96, 125
concludes Treaty of Asnières with Philip of France, 116
conditions attached to marriage of Maid of Norway to his son, 47
consults Parisian scholars, 54
death of son John, 28
decrees what should happen to traitors after Methven, 157
description of, 84
determines to winter in Scotland, 114
discovers Franco-Scottish treaty, 79
encourages 'middling folk' to submit, 153
fails to winter in Scotland, 116
failure of continental campaign, 95
gains in 1300, 112
goes after King John, 78

179

hardline policy towards those who supported Robert Bruce (7), 155
health of, 135, 154, 162
informed of murder of John Comyn, 148
looks after interests of Maid of Norway, 43
looks forward to end of Scottish campaigns, 133
moves north of Perth, 126
negotiates Treaty of Salisbury, 44
negotiating peace treaty with France, 104
orders army to muster, 69, 111
orders inquiry into Bruce rights in Annandale, 134
plans Scottish campaign, 95, 148
postpones Scottish campaign, 105
reaction to news of inauguration of Robert Bruce (7), 152
ready to depart for the continent, 92
receives Alexander III's homage and fealty, 31
receives letter from pope demanding King John's release, 104
receives letter from pope on Scottish question, 112
relationship with Philip IV of France, 65
relationship with Scotland after death of Alexander III, 40
reopens Great Cause, 54
responds to pope about his rights over Scotland, 114
Robert Bruce (7) appeals to him to make him king, 148
seizes lands and wool of Scots in England, 69
settles Scotland, 133
summons King John and Scots to fight against France, 66
takes Bothwell castle, 114
takes earldom of Fife under direct control, 72
takes Lochmaben castle, 99
unable to campaign north of the Forth, 115
viewed as able to keep the peace in Scotland, 49
wins battle of Evesham, 27
wins battle of Falkirk, 98
Edward, prince of Wales
besieges Kildrummy castle, 161
besieges Turnberry castle, 113
given military responsibility, 112
heads towards Kildrummy, 160
knighted, 154
on campaign in Scotland, 1306, 158
on way north against Robert (7), 157
to negotiate with Scots, 128
Eleanor, of Castile, wife of Edward I
death of, 50
Elgin
English army at, 80
England, 12
anti-Scottishness in, 140

north badly affected by Scottish raids, 106
English
attitudes to Scotland, 84
expelled from Scotland, 72
Eric II, king of Norway, 32
competitor for the throne of Scotland, 52
makes agreement with Robert Bruce (5), 55
marries Isobel Bruce, 56
reluctance to send Maid to Scotland, 43
Evesham, battle of, 27
Falaise, treaty of, 18
used to justify English overlordship, 52
Fife, Duncan, earl of
chosen as guardian, 1286, 39
Fife, earl of, 24
absent from inauguration of Robert Bruce (7), 150
in minority of Alexander III, 26
Fife, earldom of
taken under Edward I's direct control, 72
Fife, Isabella of, wife of John Comyn, earl of Buchan
capture and imprisonment, 161
goes on the run after battle of Methven, 158
present at inauguration of Robert Bruce (7), 150
Flanders
clothmakers of, 15
Flanders, duchy of, 92
Fleet, water of, Galloway

skirmish between English and Scots, 112
Flemish
defeat French at Courtrai, 121
Forfar
attacked by Robert Bruce (7), 151
Forth, river, 12, 90, 93, 109, 115, 125, 126, 127, 128, 129, 130, 134, 135, 140, 152
France
defeated by Flemings at Courtrai, 121
Fraser, Simon
captured and executed, 160
chased by English force at Happrew, 130
escapes from battle of Methven, 156
lands burned by Aymer de Valence, 154
leader of Scottish army, 124
leads raid round Carlisle, 126
on the run, 129
sentence of excommunidation against, 157
Fraser, William, bishop of St Andrews, 43
accused of abuse of power by Bruces, 50
chosen as Guardian, 1286, 39
concerns over civil war, 48
envoy to Edward I, 44
leads deputation to Edward I, 40
supporter of John Balliol, 49
Frendraught, Duncan
accused of violent behaviour, 143

Gaels, culture, attitudes and attributes, 11, 12, 29, 36, 146
Galbraith (Colubrath), Robert, valet of John Comyn
  at murder of Comyn, 145
Galloway, lordship of, 11, 13, 20, 43, 49, 80, 86, 105, 111, 112, 114, 115, 118, 124, 126, 138, 153
  granted to Henry Percy, 81
Garioch, Aberdeenshire, 20, 46, 56
Gascony
  duchy of kings of England, 31, 41, 42, 44, 64, 65, 66, 84, 105
Gevrey-Chambertin
  temporary residence of King John, 110
Ghent, Flanders, 120
Glasgow
  English army at, 113
Glasgow, bishop of. *See* Wishart
Gloucester, earl of, 26, 27
Gloucester, Isabella of, wife of Robert Bruce (5), 21, 27
  death of, 28
goedendags
  Flemish clubs, 121
Gordon, Adam
  constable of Inverkip castle, 163
Graham, David
  demands seizure of William Wallace's lands and goods, 106
Graunt, Thomas le
  robbed and assaulted, 144
Great Cause, 53, 54, 55
Greyfriars, church of, Dumfries
  site of meeting between Robert Bruce (7) and John Comyn, 144
Guardians. *See* Bruce, Robert, 7th lord of Annandale, earl of Carrick, king of Scots; Comyn, John, 2nd lord of Badenoch; Comyn, John, 3rd lord of Badenoch; Comyn, Alexander, earl of Buchan; Fife, earl of; Fraser, William; Lamberton, William, Soules, John; Steward, James the; Umfraville, Ingram de; Wallace, William; Wishart, Robert,
Guisborough Priory, 9, 13, 16, 67, 68
Haliburton, John
  nearly captures Robert Bruce (7) at Methven, 156
Happrew, Peebles
  William Wallace and Simon Fraser chased at, 130
Harby, Leicestershire, 50
Hartness (Hartlepool), county Durham
  Bruce lands of, 9
Hastings, Henry, 20
Hastings, John, competitor in Great Cause
  argues that Scotland should be split among heirs of David, earl of Huntingdon, 56
Hatfield, Essex, Bruce lands of, 20, 67, 68, 132
Henry I, king of England, 9
Henry II, king of England, 18
Henry III, king of England, 21, 23, 25, 27

and civil war, 26, 27
claims overlordship over Scotland, 24, 25
death of, 28
does homage and fealty to French king for Gascony, 31
Henry V, king of England
victor at Agincourt, 121
Henry, earl of Northumberland, 13
Hereford, castle of, 27
Hereford, earl of, son-in-law of Edward I
given Bruce lordship of Annandale, 152
Herries, Robert, steward of Robert Bruce (5), 22, 28
Hexham, Northumberland
devastated by Scottish army, 76
Edward I at, 162
Holland, Florence, count of
competitor for the throne of Scotland, 52
delays Great Cause, 53
failure of his claim in Great Cause, 56
makes agreement with Robert Bruce (5), 55
hunting, 36
Huntingdon, David, earl of, 18, 19
given lands by King William, 20
Huntingdon, Isabella of, wife of Robert Bruce (4), 19, 20
Huntingdon, John, earl of, 20, 21
Huntingdon, Margaret of, wife of Alan, lord of Galloway, 21
Hutton, Berwickshire

English army at, 74
Inchaffray, abbot of
?at inauguration of Robert Bruce (7), 150
Inverkip, James the Steward's castle of
garrison pursues Robert Bruce (7), 163
in English hands, 156
taken by English, 127
taken by Robert Bruce (7), 147
Ireby, Christina of
marriage to Robert Bruce (5), 29
Islay, Macdonald island of
Robert Bruce (7) seeks refuge there, 164
Jedburgh, abbey of, 38, 98
Jerusalem, kingdom of, 27
John I, king of England, 20
John, son of Edward I. *See* Edward I
Keith, Robert
appointed justice in Scotland, 140
appointed temporary royal lieutenant, 141
Scottish warden of Selkirk Forest, 112
Kilconquhar, Adam of
first husband of Marjory, countess of Carrick, 28
Kildrummy, castle of, Mar
fall of, 162
Neil Bruce takes royal women to, 159
Kilkerran, church of, Argyll, 37
Kincardine, castle of
site of King John's submission, 79

King Hobbe. *See* Bruce, Robert, 7th lord of Annandale
Kinghorn, Fife, 38
kingship
  attributes of, 13
Kingston, John, sheriff of Edinburgh
  appointed justice in Scotland, 140
  appointed temporary royal lieutenant, 141
Kintyre, 162, 163
  Robert Bruce (7) making for, 163
Kirkcudbright, Adam of, physician of Robert Bruce (5), 22, 28
Kirkintilloch, castle of
  taken for Robert Bruce (7) by Bishop Wishart of Glasgow, 150
Kirkliston, West Lothian
  English army at, 97
Kirkpatrick, Roger
  appointed justiciar of Galloway, 138
  involvement in muder of John Comyn, 145
  justiciar of Galloway, 147
Lamberton, William, bishop of St Andrews, 134, 149
  agreed truce with England as Guardian, 109
  appointed temporary royal lieutenant, 141
  attends inauguration of Robert Bruce (7), 150
  attitude to King John, 103
  brings message from Philip of France back to Scotland, 103
  brings news of King John's release back to Scotland, 105
  captured by Aymer de Valence, 155
  envoy to France, 122
  made third Guardian with Comyn and Bruce, 108
  makes agreement with Robert Bruce (7), 132
  problems with John Comyn, 111
  Scottish envoy to continent, 95
  Scottish envoy to Westminster parliament, 136
  with Scottish army in Selkirk Forest, 106
Lancaster, Thomas, earl of
  besieges Dunaverty castle, 164
Lanercost, priory of, 39
Lennox, Malcolm, earl of, 163
  ?present at inauguration of Robert Bruce (7), 150
  ally of the Bruces, 62, 63
  escapes after battle of Methven, 157
  leader of Scottish army, 72
  offers to negotiate with Scots before battle of Stirling Bridge, 93
  reunited with Robert Bruce (7), 163
  travels with Robert Bruce (7) to Kintyre, 163
Lewes, battle of, 27
Liddesdale
  attacked by Scots, 126
Lindsay, Alexander
  at murder of John Comyn, 145
  reportedly captured, 162

to guarantee loyalty of Robert Bruce (7), 91
Lindsay, Simon
  knight of Robert Bruce (6), 73
Linlithgow, royal manor of, West Lothian
  attacked by Scots, 124
  Aymer de Valence at, 127
  English army at, 97, 116
Llewellyn, Madog ap
  leader of Welsh revolt, 1294, 67
Loch Awe
  Campbell lands at, 162
Loch Doon, Robert Bruce (7)'s castle of
  captured, 162
  provisioned after murder of John Comyn, 147
Lochindorb, Comyn of Badenoch castle
  Edward I slept here, 127
Lochmaben, Bruce castle and settlement at, 16, 18, 24, 43, 46, 89, 99, 105, 108, 109, 112, 118, 119, 126, 127, 145, 152
  besieged by Scots, 114
  captured by Edward, prince of Wales, 158
Lomond, Loch, 163
Long, Loch, 163
Louis IX, king of France, 27, 28
Macdonald, Alasdair Óg, of Islay, 37, 64
  at Turnberry, 1286, 41
  hostage to Alexander III, 37
  loyalty of Macdonalds after his death, 164
  murder by Alasdair Macdougall, 147

Macdonald, Angus, of Islay
  at Turnberry, 1286, 41
  fails to swear homage to King John, 61
Macdonald, Donald, of Islay
  head of the family, 164
Macdougall, Alasdair, of Argyll, 159
  murders Alasdair Óg Macdonald, 147
Macdougall, John, of Lorne, 162
  defeats Robert Bruce (7), 159
Macduff of Fife
  takes court case to Edward I, 64
Magna Carta
  reissued in 1297, 95
Malachy, saint and bishop of Down
  curses Robert Bruce (2), 16, 28
Malcolm III, king of Scots, 10, 11
Malmaison, castle of bishop of Cambrai
  King John's temporary home, 104
Mar, Donald, earl of
  ally of the Bruces, 48, 62, 63
  daughter marries Robert (7), 63
  leader of Scottish army, 72
  places himself under Edward I's protection, 50
  role in conquest of 1296, 76
Mar, Donald, earl of, Gartnait's son
  ?present at inauguration of Robert Bruce (7), 150
  custody of earldom given to Robert Bruce (7) during his minority, 135

185

Mar, earldom of, 139
Mar, Gartnait, earl of
  brother-in-law of Robert Bruce (7), 63
Mar, Isabella of, wife of Robert Bruce (7), 63
  death of, 82
Margaret, daughter of Henry III of England, wife of Alexander III of Scotland, 23
Margaret, Maid of Norway, granddaughter of Alexander III
  birth of, 32
  death of, 47
  departure from Norway, 47
  marriage of, 44
  potential marriage to Edward I's son, 45
Margaret, St, wife of Malcolm III, 24, 128
Margaret, wife of Alexander III
  death of, 24, 26, 32
Margaret, wife of Eric II of Norway
  death of, 32
Marguerite, sister of Philip of France, wife of Edward I
  at Dunfermline, 128
Marjory, countess of Carrick, 28
Mauduyt, Gilbert, of Essex
  joins Robert Bruce (7), 151
Maybole, Carrick, 120
Melrose, abbey
  lands in earldom of Carrick, 120
Menteith, earl of
  ?present at inauguration of Robert Bruce (7), 150
  at Glasgow with other Scottish lords, 106
  at Turnberry, 1286, 41
  escapes after battle of, 157
  in English prison, 85
  leader of Scottish army, 72, 75
  with Scottish army in Selkirk Forest, 106
Methven, battle of, 156
Montfort, Simon de, 26
Montrose
  site of King John's submission, 79
Moubray, Geoffrey, of Methven
  informs Edward I of victory at Methven, 157
Moubray, John
  asks Edward I to deal with disorder, 144
  attends parliament at Westminster to advise Edward I, 135
  chosen as envoy to Westminster parliament, 136
  given custody of John Comyn's son, 148
  nearly captures Robert Bruce (7) at Methven, 156
  riding with Aymer de Valence, 153
Murray, Andrew
  death of, 93
  joins up with William Wallace, 92
  relationship to Comyns, 93
  starts revolt in north of Scotland, 88
  wins battle of Stirling Bridge, 93

Newbrough, Northumberland
  Edward I at, 162
Newcastle, Northumberland, 57, 69, 158
Norham, castle of, Northumberland, 51, 57
Norman culture, attitudes and attributes, 10, 11, 12, 13, 17, 23, 29, 36, 146
Normandy, 9, 12, 18, 23, 208
Northumberland, 12, 13, 25, 29, 50, 52, 73, 75, 76, 80, 81, 90, 92, 160
Northumberland, sheriff of
  appointed justice in Scotland, 140
O'Brian, Turlough, king of Thomond, 41
Paisley, abbey of, 37
Peebles
  Scottish army at, 106
Penrith, honour of, Cumberland, 25
Percy, Henry, keeper of Galloway, 165
  background of, 82
  based at Carlisle, 152
  granted earldom of Carrick, 162
  not receiving payments as keeper of Galloway, 86
  pursues Robert Bruce (7) to Kintyre, 164
  to arrest disturbers of the peace, 87
  to put down revolt, 89
  to put down revolt with Robert Clifford, 89
Perth, 128, 157, 158

attacked by Robert Bruce (7), 151
Aymer de Valence at, 155
English army at, 78
Scottish assembly at, 135
Philip IV, king of France, 119
  ally of the Scots, 65, 95
  concludes Treaty of Asnières with Edward of England, 116
  concludes treaty with Scotland, 71
  needs Edward I's friendship, 122
  relationship with Edward I, 64
  writes supportively to Bruce and Comyn as Guardians of Scotland, 103
  writes to Edward I, urging King John's release, 103
primogeniture in Scotland, 23
Prudhoe, castle of earls of Angus, Northumberland, 73
Quitclaim of Canterbury, 18
Randolph, Thomas, nephew of Robert Bruce (7)
  captured at Methven, 156
Rathlin, island of
  Robert Bruce (7) probably blown there, 164
Richard I, king of England, 18
Richard of Cornwall, brother of Henry III of England, 21
Richmond, Yorkshire, 18
Ripe, Sussex, Bruce lands of, 22
Roslin, battle of, 124
Ross, William, earl of
  appointed keeper north of the Spey, 134
  in English prison, 85

leader of Scottish army, 72, 75
Rothesay, James the Steward's castle of, island of Bute
  taken by Robert Bruce (7), 147
Rothing, William
  knight of Robert Bruce (6), 73
Roxburgh, castle of, 161
  attacked by Scots, 124
  English track Scottish army in south-east Scotland, 106
Roxburghshire
  still in English control, 90
Rutherglen
  parliament at, 111
Salisbury, treaty of, 44
Scone, 149
  meeting after death of Alexander III, 39
  parliament at, 61
  Scottish assembly at, 135
  site of royal inaugurations, 49, 57
Scone, abbot of
  at inauguration of Robert Bruce (7), 150
Scotland
  English regime collapsing, 90
  no longer referred to as a kingdom, 124
  pays taxes to Edward I, 85
  unhappy with Edward I's government, 86
Scotlandwell
  house of bishops of St Andrews, 155
Scots
  agree truce with Edward I, 112, 116
  conditions of peace with Edward I, 1304, 128
  continued resistance among, 140
  dumped as allies by Philip of France, 122
  feelings about English occupation, 143
  impact of war on, 143
  military tactics of, 99
  respond to pope over English claims of overlordship, 114
Scott, Walter
  author of Tales of a Grandfather, 164
Scrymgeour, Alexander, royal standard bearer
  executed, 156
  given lands and office of constable of Dundee, 103
Segrave, John
  appointed keeper south of the Forth, 134
  leader of English force, 124
Selkirk Forest
  archers of, 98
  burned by Aymer de Valence, 154
  provides refuge for Scots, 90
  Scottish army in, 106
  Wallace and Fraser in, 129
Selkirk, castle of
  taken by Scots, 124
Seton, Christopher
  at murder of John Comyn, 145
  captured and executed, 162
  kills Robert Comyn, 145
  married to Christian Bruce, 161
  saves Robert Bruce (7) at Methven, 156
Seton, Humphrey

Seton (cont.)
at murder of John Comyn, 145
captured and executed, 162
Seton, John
at murder of John Comyn, 145
captured and executed, 158, 162
sheep
importance to Scottish economy, 16
sheep scab, 69
Siward, Richard
sheriff of Dumfries, 147
Sixhills, convent of, Lincolnshire, 161
Skinburness, 164
provisions sent to, 148
Sluys, port in Flanders, 92
Smithfield, London
site of William Wallace's execution, 138
Soules, John, 125
ally of the Bruces, 62, 63
becomes Guardian, 113
besieges Turnberry castle, 115
envoy to France, 69
gives up guardianship, 122
leads Scottish army, 113
St Andrews
parliament at, 129
St Andrews, bishop of. *See* Fraser, Lamberton
St Duthac's, Tain
capture of earl of Atholl and family of Robert Bruce (7), 161
St John, John de
accepted Robert Bruce (7)'s submission to Edward I, 118
attends King John's inauguration, 57

keeper of Galloway, 119
Standard, battle of, 12, 13, 14
Steward, James the, 43
ally of the Bruces, 62, 63, 64
at Glasgow with other Scottish lords, 106
at Turnberry, 1286, 41
chosen as guardian, 1286, 39
envoy to France, 122
expected in Berwick, 91
joins revolt with Robert Bruce (7) and Robert Wishart, bishop of Glasgow, 88
not allowed to submit to Edward I, 135
offers to negotiate with Scots before battle of Stirling Bridge, 93
sides against the Bruces in civil war of 1286, 43
submits to Percy and Clifford, 89
supports Bishop Lamberton as Guardian, 111
to guarantee loyalty of Robert Bruce (7), 91
to lose hostages to Henry Percy, 81
with Scottish army in Selkirk Forest, 106
Stewart, Andrew, eldest son of James the Steward
taken by Bishop Lamberton to Robert Bruce (7), 151
Stewart, John, of Jedburgh,
commands Scottish archers at Falkirk, 98
Stirling Bridge, battle of
aftermath of, 93
Stirling, bridge at

still destroyed, 126
Stirling, castle of, 18, 32, 128
   English garrison under Scottish attack, 109
   English siege of, 132
   falls to Scots, 110
   parliament at, 62, 69
   Scottish garrison surrenders, 133
   supply line under attack from William Wallace, 106
Stone of Destiny
   removed from Scone, 80
Stracathro, church of
   site of King John's submission, 79
Strathearn, earl of, 24
   absent from inauguration of Robert Bruce (7), 150
   forced to join Robert Bruce (7), 154, 155
   in minority of Alexander III, 26
   leader of Scottish army, 72
Surrey, earl of, lieutenant of Scotland, 83, 141
   absent from Scotland, 90
   arrives in Scotland, 91
   leaves Berwick with army, 92
   loses battle of Stirling Bridge, 93
   sent to negotiate with King John, 70
Thomond, western Irish kingdom, 41
Tibbers, Richard Siward's castle of
   captured by Edward, prince of Wales, 158
   taken by Robert Bruce (7), 147

Topcliffe, Yorkshire
   seat of the Percy family, 82
Torthorwald, Adam, knight of Annandale, 28
Tottenham
   Bruce lands of, 132
Tunis, North Africa. See Louis IX
Turnberry band, 41, 43, 132
Turnberry, castle and settlement in Carrick, 29, 34, 37, 41, 42, 80, 113, 114, 115, 116, 117, 118, 120
   meeting at, 1286, 41
Turry, Adam, Simon Fraser's messenger
   executed, 156
Tyndale, liberty of, Northumberland, 25, 81
Ulster, earl of, Richard de Burgh, 36
Umfraville, Ingram de
   envoy to France, 69, 122
   lands in Carrick sought by Robert Bruce (7), 118
   leads Scottish army, 114
   made Guardian with Bishop Lamberton and John Comyn, 111
   made Scottish sheriff of Roxburgh, 108
   riding with Aymer de Valence, 153
Upsetlington, Berwickshire, 51
Valence, Aymer de, 157
   appointed royal lieutenant between York and Forth, 152
   at Perth, 155
   besieges Kildrummy castle, 161

campaign against Robert Bruce (7), 1306, 154
captures Bishop Lamberton of St Andrews and Bishop Wishart of Glasgow, 155
defeats Robert Bruce (7) at Methven, 156
given Bothwell castle, 114
receives Scottish envoys to treat for peace, 127
royal lieutenant in southern Scotland, 127
takes English force to western Scotland, 127
to ride against Robert Bruce (7), 153

Valence, Joanna de, wife of John Comyn, 3rd lord of Badenoch, 53, 148

Vicenza, bishop of
King John given into his care, 104

Wales
uprising in, 67

Wallace, Malcolm, brother of William Wallace
defends his brother, 106
in retinue of Robert Bruce (7), 105

Wallace, William
attacking Stirling castle supply line, 106
attacks and kills sheriff of Lanark, 86
battleplan, 1298, 96
capture and execution of, 138
chased by English force at Happrew, 130
chosen as guardian of Scotland, 94
collusion with great lords of Scotland, 88
comparatively unknown, 88
excepted from peace agreement, 1304, 129
gathering army in Selkirk Forest, 90
goes with army to Dundee, 92
government of, 95
invades north of England, 94
joins up with Andrew Murray, 92
leader of Scottish army, 126
leaves Scotland for France, 109
loses guardianship, 98
made a knight, 94
on the run, 129
patriotism of, 154
preparations for battle of Falkirk, 98
protects property of Robert Wishart, bishop of Glasgow, 91
relationship with Comyns, 96
visits King John in France, 110
wins battle of Stirling Bridge, 93

War Wolf
Edward I's siege engine, 133

Wark, castle of, Northumberland
English army at, 73

Watton, convent of, Yorkshire, 161

Westminster Abbey
given stone of Destiny, 80

Westminster, London, 22
parliament at, 135

Wigtown, 43
Wigtown, castle of

granted to Henry Percy, 81
taken by Robert Bruce, 6th lord of Annandale, earl of Carrick, in civil war of 1286, 43

William I, king of England, 9

William I, king of Scots, 17, 134
 agrees Treaty of Falaise, 18
 invades England, 17, 20

William II, king of England, 9

Winchelsea, Sussex, 92

Winchester
 Edward I at, 152

Wishart, Robert, bishop of Glasgow, 43
 attends parliament at Westminster to advise Edward I, 135
 attends Scottish assembly at Scone or Perth, 135
 captured by Aymer de Valence, 155
 chosen as Guardian, 1286, 39
 encourages Robert Bruce (7) to take throne on own terms, 149
 envoy to Edward I, 44, 46
 envoy to France, 69
 expected in Berwick, 91
 imprisoned for disloyalty of Robert Bruce (7), 91
 joins revolt with Robert Bruce (7) and James the Steward, 88
 not chosen as envoy to Westminster parliament, 136
 objects to English claims of overlordship, 51
 property protected by William Wallace, 91
 reprimanded by pope, 122
 still in prison, 104
 submits to Percy and Clifford, 89
 to guarantee loyalty of Robert Bruce (7), 91
 tries to help Scots take Roxburgh castle from inside, 106

Woburn Abbey, Bedfordshire
 Edward I at, 157

Writtle, Essex, Bruce lands of, 20, 28, 34, 68, 132

York, 24

Yorkshire, 9, 10, 12, 14, 16, 17, 18, 82, 85, 91, 161

Ypres, Flanders, 120

BIBLIOGRAPHY AND SHORT GLOSSARY

The ACCOUNTS of the Great Chamberlains of Scotland, volume I, Edinburgh, 1836

ACTS of the Parliaments of Scotland, Cosmo Innes, editor, volume I, Edinburgh, 1844

ANDERSON, Alan O, editor, *Scottish annals from English chroniclers, AD 500 to 1286*, London, 1908

-----, *Early Sources of Scottish History AD 500 to 1286*, volume II, Edinburgh & London, 1922

ANNALES of Nicholas Trivet, Thomas Hog, editor, London, 1845

ANNALS of the Four Masters see website section below

ANNALS of Ulster see website section below

BARBOUR, John, *The Brus*, AAM Duncan, editor, Edinburgh, 1997

BARROW, G W S, *Robert Bruce and the Community of the Realm of Scotland*, Edinburgh, 2005

BEAM, Amanda, *The Balliol Dynasty 1210-1364*, Edinburgh, 2008

BLAKLEY, Ruth M, *The Brus Family in England and Scotland, 1100-1295*, Woodbridge, 2005

The BOOK of Pluscardine, F J H Skene, editor, volume II, Edinburgh, 1880

BOWER, Walter, *Scotichronicon*, DER Watt, editor, volume V, Aberdeen, 1990; volume VI, 1991

BROUN, Dauvit, *Scottish independence and the idea of Britain*, Edinburgh, 2007

BUCHANAN, George, *History of Scotland*, James Aikman, editor, Glasgow, 1827

CALENDAR of Charter Rolls, 1300-1326, volume III, London, 1908

CALENDAR of the Close Rolls, 1279-88, London, 1902

CALENDAR of Close Rolls, 1288-96, London, 1904

CALENDAR of Close Rolls, 1296-1302, London, 1906

CALENDAR of Close Rolls, 1302-1307, London, 1908

CALENDAR of Documents relating to Scotland, Joseph Bain, editor, volume I, Edinburgh, 1881; volume II, 1884; volume III, 1887; volume IV, Edinburgh, 1888

CALENDAR of Documents relating to Scotland, Grant G Simpson and James D Galbraith, editors, volume V, Edinburgh, 1986

CALENDAR of Inquisitions Miscellaneous, volume I, London, 1916

CALENDAR of Patent Rolls, 1258-66, London, 1910

CALENDAR of Patent Rolls, 1266-72, London, 1913

CALENDAR of Patent Rolls, 1272-81, London, 1901

CALENDAR of Patent Rolls, 1292-1301, London, 1895

CALENDAR of Patent Rolls, 1301-1307, London, 1898

CHARTULARY of the priory of Guisborough, London and Edinburgh, 1894

CHRONICA et Annales by Johannis de Trokelawe, Henry Thomas Riley, editor, London, 1866

CHRONICLES of the Age of Chivalry, Elizabeth Hallam, editor, New York, 2000

The CHRONICLE of Lanercost, Herbert Maxwell, editor, Glasgow, 1913

CHRONICLES of the Picts and Scots, W F Skene, editor, Edinburgh, 1867

The CHRONICLE of Pierre de Langtoft, Thomas Wright, editor, volume II, London, 1868

CHRONICLE of the Scottish Nation by John of Fordun, William F Skene, editor, volume I, Edinburgh, 1872; volume II, 1872

CHRONICON Domini Walteri de Hemingburgh, Hans Claude Hamilton, editor, vol. 2, London, 1849

CHRONICON, Galfridi le Baker de Swynebroke, Edward Maunde Thompson, editor, Oxford, 1889

CLANCY, Thomas Owen, editor, The Triumph Tree. Scotland's earliest poetry AD 550-1350, Edinburgh, 1998

CONTAMINE, Philippe, War in the Middle Ages, Michael Jones, translator, Oxford, 1984

DOCUMENTS and Records Illustrating the History of Scotland, Francis Palgrave, editor, volume I, London, 1837

DOCUMENTS Illustrative of the History of Scotland, 1286-1306, Joseph Stevenson, editor, volume I, Edinburgh, 1870; volume II, 1870

DUFFY, Sean 'The Bruce brothers and the Irish Sea World, 1306-1329', Cambridge Medieval Celtic Studies, 21, 1999

DUNCAN, AAM, 'The Bruces of Annandale, 1100-1304,' Transactions of the Dumfries and Galloway Natural History and Antiquarian Society, 3rd series, 1964

----, *The Kingship of the Scots, 842-1292*, Edinburgh, 2002
----, 'The Community of the Realm and Robert Bruce: A Review', *Scottish Historical Review*, 45, Edinburgh, 1966
----, *The Making of the Kingdom*, Edinburgh, 1975
EARLY *Yorkshire Charters*, William Farrer, editor, Edinburgh, 1915
EARLY *Scottish Charters prior to AD 1153*, Archibald Campbell Lawrie, editor, Glasgow, 1905
FACSIMILES *of National Manuscripts of Scotland*, Joseph Robertson, editor, volume II, Edinburgh, 1870
FAVIER, J, *Philippe le Bel*, Paris, 1978
FLORES *Historiarum*, Henry R Luard, editor, volume III, London, 1890
FOEDERA, Thomas Rymer and Robert Sanderson, editors, volume I, parts I and II, 1745
GASCON *Calendar of 1322*, Camden 3rd series, volume LXX, GP Cuttino, editor, London, 1949
GEOGRAPHICAL *collections relating to Scotland collected by Walter Macfarlane*, Arthur Mitchell, editor, vol. 1, Edinburgh, 1906, Scottish History Society, vol. LI
GOLDSTEIN, R James, 'The Scottish Mission to Boniface VIII in 1301: a reconsideration of the context of the Instructiones and Processus,' *Scottish Historical Review*, volume 70, no.189, Edinburgh, April 1991
GRANT, Alexander, 'The death of John Comyn: what was it about?', *Scottish Historical Review*, volume 86, No. 222, Part 2, Edinburgh, Oct 2007
HASKELL, Michael A, *The Scottish Campaign of Edward I, 1303-4*, Masters Thesis, Durham University, 1991 [http://etheses.dur.ac.uk/6101/]
HISTORIA *Rerum Anglicarum* by William of Newburgh, Book 2, in *Chronicles of the Reigns of Stephen, Henry II and Richard I*, Richard Howlett, ed., volume I, London, 1884
HOLLISTER, Charles Warren, *Henry I*, New Haven, 2003
INSTRUMENTA *Publica sive processus super fidelitatibus et homagiis scotorum domino regi angliae factis AD MCCXCI – MCCXCVI*, Edinburgh, 1834
ITINERARY *of Edward I, 1272-85*, Henry Gough, Editor, volume I, Paisley, 1900
JONES, Robert, *Knight. The warrior and world of chivalry*, Oxford, 2011
Les JOURNAUX *de Tresor de Philippe IV*, J Viard, editor, Paris, 1940
KEEN, Maurice, editor, *Medieval Warfare: A History*, Oxford, 1999
The KNIGHTS *of Edward I*, C Moor, editor, volume I, London, 1929; volume II, 1929; volume III, 1930; volume IV, 1931; volume V, 1932

LAING, H, editor, *Supplemental Description Catalogue of Ancient Scottish Seals, Royal, Baronial, Ecclesiastical and Municipal, Embracing the Period from A.D. 1150 to the Eighteenth Century*, Edinburgh, 1866

LIBER Quotidianus Gardrobae Contrarotulatoris Garderobae, John Topham, editor, London, 1787

LIBER Sancte Marie de Melrose, Cosmo Innes, editor, volume I, Edinburgh, 1837

LIBER Sancte Thomas de Aberbrothoc, Cosmo Innes and Patrick Chalmers, editors, volume I, Edinburgh, 1848

LINEHAN, PA, 'A Fourteenth-Century History of Anglo-Scottish Relations in a Spanish Manuscript', Bulletin of the Institute of Historical Research, XLVIII, 1975

NEILSON, G, 'Burghs of Annandale: Annan and Lochmaben – their burghal origins,' Transactions of the Dumfries and Galloway Natural History and Antiquarian Society, Series 3, 1915

MATTHEW Paris's English History, JA Giles, editor, volume II, London, 1853; volume III, London, 1854

MISCELLANY of the Spalding Club, volume II, Aberdeen, 1842

MORRIS, John E, *Bannockburn,* Cambridge, 1914

NICHOLSON, Ranald, 'The Franco-Scottish and Franco-Norwegian treaties of 1295', *Scottish Historical Review*, volume XXXVIII, no.126, Edinburgh, October 1959

ORD, J Walker, *The History and Antiquities of Cleveland*, London & Edinburgh, 1846

ORPEN, Goddard Henry, *Ireland under the Normans, 1216-1333*, volume IV, Oxford, 1920

OWEN, DDR, *William the Lion, Kingship and Culture, 1143-1214*, East Linton, 1997

The PARLIAMENTARY Writs and Writs of Military Summons, Francis Palgrave, editor, volume I, London, 1827

The ORIGINAL Chronicle of Andrew of Wyntoun, David Laing, editor, Edinburgh, 1872

PENMAN, Michael, *Robert the Bruce*, New Haven, 2014

PRESTWICH, Michael, *Edward I*, New Haven, 1988

----, 'The Battle of Stirling Bridge. An English perspective,' in EJ Cowan, editor, *The Wallace Book*, Edinburgh, 2012

The RED Book of Menteith, William Fraser, editor, volume II, Edinburgh, 1880

REGISTER of the Great Seal of Scotland, J M Thomson, editor, volume I, Edinburgh, 1882

REGISTRUM de Dunfermelyn, Edinburgh, 1842

REGISTRUM de monasterii de Passelet, Cosmo Innes, editor, Edinburgh, 1832

RISHANGER, William, *Chronica et Annales*, Henry Thomas Riley, editor, London, 1865

ROTULI Parliamentorum, volume I, London, 1767

ROTULI Scotiae in turri Londinensi, volume I, London, 1814

SAYLES, GO, 'The Guardians of Scotland and a parliament at Rutherglen,' *Scottish Historical Review*, volume 24, Edinburgh, 1927

The SCALACRONICA of Sir Thomas Gray, Glasgow, 1907

SCOTT, Walter, *Tales of a Grandfather*, abridged by Elsie Gray, London, c.1928

The SIEGE of Caerlaverock, Nicholas Harris Nicolas, editor, London, 1828

SMALLWOOD, TM, 'An unpublished early account of Bruce's murder of Comyn,' *Scottish Historical Review*, volume 54, no.157, part 1, Edinburgh, April 1975

SMITH, Alexander, *A Summer in Skye*, London, 1865

STONES, ELG, 'The submission of Robert Bruce to Edward I, c.1301-2,' *Scottish Historical Review*, volume 34, no.118, part 2, Edinburgh, 1955

----, 'An Undelivered Letter from Paris to Scotland [1303]?], *English Historical Review*, 80, no.134, Oxford, 1965

----, *Anglo-Scottish Relations, 1174-1328*, Oxford, 1970

STONES, ELG and Simpson, Grant G, *Edward I and the Throne of Scotland, 1290-1296: an Edition of the Record Sources for the Great Cause*, volume II, Oxford, 1978

VITA Edwardi Secundi, N Denholm-Young, editor, Edinburgh, 1957

BOWER, Walter, *A History Book for Scots*, DER Watt, editor, Edinburgh, 1998

WATSON, Fiona, *Under the Hammer*, East Linton, 1998

----, 'Settling the stalemate: Edward I's Peace in Scotland, 1303-1305' in M Prestwich, R Britnell and R Frame, eds., *Thirteenth Century England*, VI, Woodbridge, 1997

----, *Edward I in Scotland, 1296-1305*, Ph.D. thesis, Glasgow, 1991 [http://theses.gla.ac.uk/2222/1/1991watsonphd.pdf]

YOUNG, Alan, *Robert the Bruce's rivals: the Comyns, 1212-1314*, East Linton, 1997

YOUNG, Alan and CUMMING, George, *The real patriots of early Scottish independence*, Edinburgh, 2014

Websites

http://www.breakingofbritain.ac.uk/blogs/feature-of-the-month/september-2011-the-guardians-in-1286-and-wallaces-uprising-in-1297/

canmore.org.uk – Historic Environment Scotland's database of historic sites

https://celt.ucc.ie//published/T100001A/ Annals of Ulster

https://celt.ucc.ie//published/T100005A/index.html Annals of the Four Masters

debrustrail.org.uk/ - dedicated to research on the Bruce family in northern England before 1350

measuringworth.com/ukcompare/ I use this to give some rough notion of medieval prices in today's money

db.poms.ac.uk/search/ This is a database of all known people of Scotland between 1093 and 1314 mentioned in over 8600 contemporary documents. The People of Medieval Scotland website is an outcome of three projects, The Paradox of Medieval Scotland (2007-2010) and The Breaking of Britain (2010-2013), funded by the Arts and Humanities Research Council (AHRC), and the Transformation of Gaelic Scotland in the Twelfth and Thirteenth Centuries (2013-2016), funded by the Leverhulme Trust. [Amanda Beam, John Bradley, Dauvit Broun, John Reuben Davies, Matthew Hammond, Michele Pasin (with others), The People of Medieval Scotland, 1093 – 1314 (Glasgow and London, 2012)]

http://www.rps.ac.uk/ Records of the parliaments of Scotland

SHORT GLOSSARY

Anglo-Irish – those who lived in Ireland after the Norman invasions of the 1160s but were of Norman/English extraction.

Bailiwick – the area over which a royal official has jurisdiction.

Banneret - knight with his own banner and troops.

Canon – like a monk, a canon lived by a religious rule but was more active in work and involved in wider society.

Dowry – money or property brought by a bride to her husband on their marriage.

Excommunication - exclusion from participation in the services and sacraments of the church.

Galley – a low, flat ship with one or more sails and up to three banks of oars commonly used on the western seaboard of Scotland.

Grange - farm with barn used to gather grain owed to a feudal lord.

Lésémajestie - offence against, or disrespect to, the crown.

Manor – an agricultural estate worked by the lord's tenants and including a village and manor-house, as well as other elements – woods, orchards, mills – to make the manor self-sufficient.

Pele – in this period, a palisade or wooden stockade usually attached to a fortification to give the garrison more room to operate in safety.

Relief – the fine paid by an heir to inherit property.

Sasine – possession of feudal property.

Serfdom – this was a form of slavery which would soon die out in medieval Western Europe. But here it is being used as a short-hand for oppression more generally.

Stockfish – unsalted fish, usually cod.

PICTURE CREDITS

Statue of Robert the Bruce (1929) in front of the gates of Edinburgh Castle. Photograph by Ad Meskens - Own work, CC BY-SA 3.0, https://commons.wikimedia.org/w/index.php?curid=15817964.

Pilkington Jackson's monumental statue of Robert the Bruce at Bannockburn. Photograph by Kim Traynor, CC BY-SA 2.0, https://commons.wikimedia.org/w/index.php?curid=14285284.

Guisborough Priory by Thomas Girton, 1801, https://commons.wikimedia.org/w/index.php?curid=5150826.

Seal of David, earl of Huntingdon by Unknown. Not credited in Laing, H, ed., *Supplemental Descriptive Catalogue of Ancient Scottish Seals, Royal, Baronial, Ecclesiastical, and Municipal, Embracing the Period from A.D. 1150 to the Eighteenth Century*. Edinburgh, 1866. The seal appears in plate 4, figure 2. It is noted on page xxv, and described on page 87. Public Domain, https://commons.wikimedia.org/w/index.php?curid=31387534.

Turnberry Castle by John M Leighton in Swan's *Views on the Clyde*, 1830, Public Domain, https://commons.wikimedia.org/w/index.php?curid=33965063.

St Margaret's Hope on Orkney. Photograph by Sylvia Duckworth, CC BY-SA 2.0, https://commons.wikimedia.org/w/index.php?curid=14253672.

Detail showing King John of Scotland by unknown. http://www.bl.uk/catalogues/illuminatedmanuscripts/ILLUMIN.ASP?Size=mid&IllID=42561, Public Domain, https://commons.wikimedia.org/w/index.php?curid=25194992.

Shrine of St Margaret, Dunfermline Abbey, Fife. Photography by Kim Traynor, own work, CC BY-SA 3.0, https://commons.wikimedia.org/w/index.php?curid=16992874.

Anonymous drawing of Edward I. http://www.nndb.com/people/313/000093034/king-edward-i-1-sized.jpg, Public Domain, https://commons.wikimedia.org/w/index.php?curid=6657960

The Tay Bridge at Dundee with St Paul's cathedral in front of it, standing on the site of Dundee castle. Photograph by Paul McIlroy, CC BY-SA 2.0, https://commons.wikimedia.org/w/index.php?curid=13741038.

The battle of Courtrai. This file has been provided by the British Library from its digital collections. It is also made available on a British Library website. Catalogue entry: From the *Chroniques de France ou de St Denis*, BL Royal MS 20 C vii f. 34, Public Domain, https ://commons.wikimedia.org/w/index.php?curid=13350691.

The Stone of Scone in the coronation chair, Westminster Abbey by an anonymous engraver – published in D. Hume, *A History of England* (1859), continued by T. Smollett, E. Farr and E.H. Nolan. Also published in *The Queens of England*, (c. 1889) by Sydney Wilmot Public Domain, https://commons.wikimedia.org/w/index.php?curid=613561.

February, from the *Très Riches Heures de Duc de* Berry by Limbourg brothers - R.M.N. / R.-G. Ojéda, Public Domain, https://commons.wikimedia.org/w/index.php?curid=108562.

Spider's web. Photograph by Fiona Watson.

ACKNOWLEDGEMENTS

Given that I wanted to walk that treacherous tightrope between being academically rigorous (getting my facts as right as possible and my arguments as tight as possible) and appealing to a broad readership with potentially little or no prior knowledge of this period of Scottish and English history, I am extremely grateful to those who agreed to read the book prior to publication. Some are well-versed in the history of Bruce and the Anglo-Scottish wars and can therefore point out errors and less-than convincing arguments; others fit that well-worn category of 'intelligent reader,' strictly enjoined to tell me when the text made no sense or wandered too far from what they thought they had signed up for. My profound and grateful thanks go to Bill Glennie and James Taylor, whose copious notes and comments have saved me from grave error and sloppy arguments. The time and trouble they dedicated to the Bruce cause – or mine – was above and beyond the call of duty and/or friendship and I really can't thank them enough. Despite not warming to the Bruces, Dr Elizabeth Jordan did me a huge service in taking them on, helping me to see where I was presuming too much and persuading me to add a few more family trees to keep all those confusing interrelationships and surfeits of Roberts, Johns, Edwards, etc., under a degree of control. John Jones was kind enough to encourage me in the book's early stages and made the entirely sensible suggestion that I might summarise each chapter at its beginning, something that had never occurred to me. Maitland Kelly surprised me over coffee by outlining one of the key points of the book, which apparently transformed his thinking and reassured me that my arguments were coming across. I would also like to thank Professors Matthew Strickland and Dauvit Broun for listening to me advance some new arguments about Bruce's career, which helped me to articulate them in these pages. I hope they will all forgive me where I have preferred to go my own sweet way - I certainly take full responsibility for every word that ultimately passed through all this rigorous prodding and probing. I would also like to thank my friend, Andy Greig, for generously sharing his knowledge of direct publishing, which I've never tried before. Special and heartfelt thanks go to my reluctant cover model, Finn Hanley, who nonetheless did an excellent job. A further special round of applause (and a big kiss) goes to my husband, Nick Hanley, for encouraging and even funding my impecunious writing career. If I can make even a moderate contribution to our holiday/his retirement fund, then that will make us both very happy.

But I would like to dedicate this book to the man who, above all others, has shaped me as a historian. Professor Archie Duncan took me on as, I believe, his last Ph.D student in 1987, wielding his ferocious red pen and challenging any and every assertion (including those he made himself). As a shy girl brought up to do as she was told, it was the best education I could have asked for, and I find it hard to believe that a man of such intelligence, passion and kindness – a veritable force of nature – is no longer with us. Thank you.

ABOUT THE AUTHOR

Fiona Watson grew up in the shadow of Dunfermline Abbey, the final resting place of King Robert the Bruce. Needless to say, she developed a passion for medieval history, which she studied at St Andrews University, before going on to do her Ph.D. on 'Edward I in Scotland' at Glasgow University. In 1995 she was appointed as a lecturer at Stirling University, becoming a senior lecturer in 2000 before leaving academic life to become a full-time writer in 2006. She has published numerous books and articles throughout her career, but has also communicated her passion for history on television and radio. In 2001 she presented a ten-part television history, *In Search of Scotland*, for the BBC, as well as a number of radio programmes, including *Voices from the Front* (2000), *Are you looking for a fight* (2007), *The real Macbeth* (2007) and *Hooked on History* (2008). She also contributed to a National Geographic documentary on reluctant heroes to coincide with the release of the film, *Lord of the Rings: Return of the King*, which features on the extended version of the DVD, earning maximum cool points with her step-children.

She currently lives in the wilds of Perthshire with her husband and son where she enjoys walking the dog, playing the fiddle and wondering if she could possibly write a novel.

Also by the author:

A History of Scotland's Landscapes (Edinburgh, 2018)

Robert the Bruce, Pocket Giants (Stroud, 2014)

F Watson, Conor Boyle, Jim Campbell and Bright White, *On Dangerous Ground. Bannockburn, 1314* (National Trust for Scotland, 2014)

Macbeth. A True Story (London, 2010)

Scotland: A History (Stroud, 2001, 2002, 2003);

Under the Hammer: Edward I and Scotland, 1296-1305 (East Linton, 1998, 2005).

NOTES

CDS = *Calendar of Documents relating to Scotland*
NRS = National Records of Scotland (in Edinburgh)
RPS = *Register of the Parliaments of Scotland*
TNA = The National Archives (in London)

For the full references to books and articles referred to below, please see the bibliography.

---

[1] Dear reader, if you, like me, feel the urge to guddle about in footnotes to prove to yourself that the author knows what's she's talking about, then please carry on for, apart from anything else, I have placed the arguments behind the conclusions that form the narrative here rather than burden the story I have tried to tell with lots of ifs and buts, not to mention whys and wherefores. But if you are more interested in the story of Robert the Bruce, then I would respectfully suggest that you ignore all this and get back to it. This text is quoted in Clancy, *The Triumph Tree*, p.300. The original comes from Abbot Bower's *Scotichronicon*, pp.320/321.
[2] The Bruces held their estate at Brix from the Dukes of Normandy, though the family's supposed founder – Adam – may well have been responsible for building the stone castle that bears his name and whose remains are hinted at in street names and the odd bit of masonry still to be found there [Blakely, *The Brus Family in England and Scotland*, pp.5-6].
[3] Blakely, *The Brus Family*, pp.8-18.
[4] Charles Warren Hollister, *Henry I*, p.49; G.W.S. Barrow, *Robert Bruce and the Community of the Realm of Scotland*, p.28; William Farrer, ed., *Early Yorkshire Charters*, p.11, p.27-29; J. Walker Ord, *The History and Antiquities of Cleveland*, pp.176-7; http://www.debrustrail.org.uk/.
[5] Blakely, *The Brus Family*, p.21. Robert (1) was a regular witness to King David's charters, occupying a place high up the list of names as an

indication of the favour and status that he enjoyed. See Lawrie, *Early Scottish Charters*, p.307 for a list of the fourteen known charters in which he features.

[6] https://canmore.org.uk/site/66490/annan-mote-of-annan; G Neilson, 'Burghs of Annandale: Annan and Lochmaben – their burghal origins,' p.60. The castle has not been precisely dated, so we can't say for sure that the first Robert Bruce was responsible for it. But he must have built something to live in.

[7] Anderson, *Scottish Annals*, pp.192-3. I have doctored his translation somewhat (these documents would mostly have been in Latin originally) to make it more palatable to the modern ear.

[8] See Anderson, *Scottish Annals*, p.197 onwards for various descriptions of the battle from English sources, which, though informative, paints a distinctly one-sided version of events.

[9] Lawrie, *Early Scottish Charters*, pp.98-99.

[10] See Blakely, *The Brus Family*, pp.28-31 for a fuller discussion of this difficult period.

[11] Broun, *Scottish independence and the idea of Britain*, p.7 onwards.

[12] *Geographical collections relating to Scotland collected by Walter Macfarlane*, ed. Sir Arthur Mitchell, vol. 1, pp.365-6; Lawrie, *Early Scottish Charters*, p.308.

[13] *CDS*, iv, no.1588.

[14] *Chartulary of the priory of Guisborough*, pp.340-1.

[15] *The Chronicle of Lanercost*, pp.112-3.

[16] https://canmore.org.uk/site/66490/annan-mote-of-annan; (Neilson 1915), pp.58, 60, 68.

[17] A glance at Robert (2)'s entry in http://db.poms.ac.uk/record/person/170/# makes it clear that he, at least, was very busy making gifts to the church and receiving in return, consolidating Bruce power and influence within Annandale and the surrounding area. This kind of activity continued even during the brief life of his eldest son, Robert (http://db.poms.ac.uk/record/person/7959/#), but certainly during that of his second son and successor, William (http://db.poms.ac.uk/record/person/754/#), who was a prolific grantor, often in the company of prominent Annandale men.

[18] http://db.poms.ac.uk/record/factoid/60864/# (these men are the witnesses to this charter). See Barrow, *Robert Bruce*, pp.28-29 for a fuller discussion of this point.

[19] For Robert Bruce (2)'s marriage, see http://db.poms.ac.uk/record/person/8224/#. For the marriage of his son Robert, see DDR Owen, *William the Lion*, p.67; Anderson, *Early Sources of Scottish History*, volume ii, p.306; http://db.poms.ac.uk/record/person/7959/#.
[20] *CDS*, I, no.288.
[21] Blakely, *The Brus Family*, pp.36-38. Neilson, 'Burghs of Annandale' argues on p.60 that Robert (2) 'did his duty' to William, but cites no evidence to support his view, presumably because there isn't any.
[22] I use https://www.measuringworth.com/ukcompare/ to calculate current values.
[23] William of Newburgh, *Historia Rerum Anglicarum*, Book 2, in *Chronicles of the Reigns of Stephen, Henry II and Richard I*, ed. Richard Howlett, volume 1, p.185; Owen, *William the Lion*, pp.54-5; http://db.poms.ac.uk/record/factoid/43858/
[24] For Robert Bruce (5)'s earlier moniker see *Walter Bower. A History Book for Scots*, ed. DER Watt, p.164.
[25] Blakely, *The Brus Family*, pp.67-8; 71.
[26] Palgrave, *Documents and Records Illustrating the History of Scotland*, volume 1, p.26.
[27] Dervorguilla Balliol produced no less than four sons, the eldest of which was Hugh, who was probably born before 1238. At her death in 1290, only her youngest – John – was still alive.
[28] http://db.poms.ac.uk/record/person/1938/#; *CDS*, I, no.1683.
[29] *CDS*, I, nos.2671-2.
[30] *CDS*, I, no.1654.
[31] Young, *Robert the Bruce's rivals: the Comyns, 1212-1314*, East Linton, 1997, Chapter Two.
[32] *CDS*, I, no.1763.
[33] *John of Fordun's Chronicle of the Scottish Nation*, ed. William F. Skene, volume 1, pp.290-1.
[34] Giles, ed., *Matthew Paris's English History*, ii, pp.468-9.
[35] Giles, ed., *Matthew Paris's English History*, ii, p.469.
[36] *CDS*, I, no.2013; Anderson, *Early Sources of Scottish History*, pp.583-4.
[37] *Calendar of Patent Rolls, 1258-66*, p.166; *CDS*, I, no.2182.
[38] *Calendar of Patent Rolls, 1258-66*, p.340; *CDS*, I, no.2358. For the potential influence of Robert (5)'s wife Isabella, see *Calendar of Patent Rolls*, p.333. King Henry also made sure to inquire at the same time as Bruce's release into his indebtedness to the Crown, an investigation that

makes clear that Robert (5) was still claiming his £50 as a member of the English king's household [*CDS*, I, no.2369]

[39] Anderson, *Early Sources of Scottish History*, p.644; Giles, *Matthew Paris's English* History, iii, pp.353-5.

[40] *Calendar of Inquisitions Miscellaneous*, volume I, no.613, 808; *Calendar of the Close Rolls, 1279-88*, p.61. See also Blakely, *The Brus Family*, p.81 and A.A.M. Duncan, 'The Bruces of Annandale, 1100-1304', p.98.

[41] *Calendar of Patent Rolls, 1266-72*, p.24, p.218.

[42] See Prestwich, *Edward I*, Chapter 3 for a fascinating analysis of this important period in Edward's life.

[43] http://db.poms.ac.uk/record/person/8198/#. These gentlemen witnessed the gift that Robert (5) made to the abbey of Clairvaux, though Duncan, 'The Bruces of Annandale', p.98 states with some justification that the charter must have been actually granted once he was back in Scotland, in which case we cannot be sure that they all went to the Holy Land. But such an arduous journey would surely have prompted Robert (5) to take his physician with him at the very least.

[44] *Gesta Annalia*, I, Chapter 60 in *Fordun's Chronicle of the Scottish Nation*, ii, pp.299-300.

[45] Buchanan, *History of Scotland*, p.22.

[46] See Barrow, *Robert Bruce*, pp.34-5; Penman, *Robert the Bruce*, p.16.

[47] *Calendar of Close Rolls, 1288-96*, p.488, pp.513-4. See also Barrow, *Robert the Bruce* p.430, fn.24.

[48] See for example, *CDS*, ii, no.51. No. 1690 gives the full extent of Christina's lands.

[49] *CDS*, ii, no.43; no.54.

[50] Prestwich, *Edward I*, London, 1988, p.196.

[51] *Calendar of Patent Rolls, 1272-81*, p.456; *CDS*, ii, no.236, no.268; *CDS*, v, no.48.

[52] See for example, *CDS*, ii, no.84 for Bruce of Annandale's summons to the campaign of 1276, along with a number of other Scots with English lands; *Foedera*, i, 2, 543, in Anderson *Early Sources of Scottish History*, p.675.

[53] A.A.M. Duncan, *The Kingship of the Scots, 842-1292*, p.157.

[54] *Registrum de Dunfermelyn*, no.321, p.217. It has been argued that Carrick was chosen because he was unusually fluent in Norman French among Scottish nobles [Duncan, *Kingship*, p.161], but the Treaty of Salisbury of 1289/90 was written in that language for both the English and the Scots, while it was translated into Latin for the Norwegians.

[55] See Duncan, *Kingship of the Scots*, p.160 onwards for a full discussion of the various accounts of the homage ceremony and their implications.
[56] *Lanercost*, p.9. The monastery at Dunfermline was patronised by King Malcolm III of Scotland and his Saxon wife, Margaret. The abbey was not built until the reign of their son, David I, and they were reinterred there, along with most succeeding kings up until David II, who was at least born in the neighbouring palace.
[57] *Lanercost*, p.40.
[58] *Gesta Annalia*, I, Chapter 63 in *John of Fordun's Chronicle of the Scottish Nation*, volume ii, ed. William F. Skene, Edinburgh, 1872, p.302.
[59] Duncan, *Kingship of the Scots*, p.592.
[60] *Gesta Annalia*, I, Chapter 60, in *Fordun's Chronicle of the Scottish Nation*, ii, p.300.
[61] *Chronicon Galfridi le Baker de Swynebroke*, p.2, p.38, p.178. It is certainly true that this chronicler, who seems to have lived about 1350, knows very little about the Scottish succession and writes utter drivel about it. But, to be fair, he uses another chronicle – the *Continuatio Chronicarum* of Adam Murimuth – for his account of the period up to 1324. Interestingly, Adam does not say anything about King Robert's nationality, so this must be something that Geoffrey le Baker had picked up himself. Geoffrey supposedly came **from Swinbrook** in Oxfordshire [*Chronicon Galfridi le Baker de Swynebroke*, p.v], which lies 111 miles west of Writtle. Given that he was a southern writer, and says not once, but twice, that King Robert was 'of the nation of England', adding on one of those occasions that he was born at Writtle, this does suggest, at the very least, that there was a strong tradition in the south that Bruce was born in Essex, while there is no direct evidence that he was born at Turnberry. The problem about arguing, as Professor Barrow does, that this tradition in fact refers to Robert (6), the king's father, is that Robert (5) didn't get Writtle until 1251 - when his mother died - and Robert (6) was born in 1243 [Barrow, *Robert Bruce*, p.431, footnote 32]. Given that Writtle was Robert (6)'s favourite manor, it is quite believable that his son should be born there and it is interesting too that one of King Robert's Essex tenants, Gilbert Mauduyt, chose to join him after he took the throne and was hanged for his pains. Nevertheless, it was surely the future king's youthful experience of the Gaelic world that was the most formative, rather than the possibility that he might happen to have been born in England.
[62] Jordanus Rufus, who wrote a treatise on the care of horses, quoted in Robert Jones, *Knight. The warrior and world of chivalry*, Oxford, 2011, p.68.

[63] Jones, *Knight*, p.80 onwards.
[64] *The Brus*, pp.252-6.
[65] For a further discussion of this important aspect of Robert Bruce (7)'s upbringing, see Michael Penman, *Robert the Bruce. King of Scots*, p.19 and Sean Duffy, 'The Bruce brothers and the Irish Sea World, 1306-1329', p.70.
[66] *CDS* ii, no. 211.
[67] Penman, *Robert the Bruce*, p.18.
[68] *The Brus*, pp.104-8. The chronicler alleges that it was James Douglas who foraged with Bruce in 1306, which cannot be true, but the point is that the writer is not surprised at a nobleman having such skills.
[69] *Chronicon Domini Walteri de Hemingburgh*, volume 2, p.178.
[70] *Registrum de monasterii de Passelet*, pp.127-9.
71 Fordun, *Chronicle*, ii, p.304.
[72] See A.A.M. Duncan, 'The Community of the Realm and Robert Bruce: A Review', p.185 for a brief discussion of the various dates provided by Scottish chroniclers for this gathering. But it is striking that his preferred one – Abbot Bower's 'ad quindenam post Pascha' (28 April) - is exactly 41 days after the king's body was found, though he also argues that the Bruce claim was put forward at a Scone 'parliament' several weeks earlier (hence the date of 2 April given in other chronicles) and the meeting was then postponed to allow Balliol – the other adult male claimant – to attend.
[73] *Lanercost*, p.43. There seems to have been a seventh Guardian, the bishop of Dunkeld, but he died fairly quickly.
[74] *Lanercost*, p.111-2.
[75] Bower, *Scotichronicon*, vol. 6, p.9; p.5.
[76] *Lanercost*, p.55. This chronicler also states that the Scots asked Edward 'to take charge of their realm,' which was blatantly untrue as they'd just elected Guardians to do that.
[77] See Orpen, *Ireland under the Normans, 1216-1333*, volume 4, Chapter 34. James the Steward held lands in Ayrshire to the north of Carrick.
[78] *The Red Book of Menteith*, vol. 2, pp.219-20.
[79] See Penman, *Robert the Bruce*, p.25.
[80] Various stories have circulated about this momentous pregnancy, including a rather spiteful one from the north of England, which stated that the queen contrived to smuggle in 'the son of a play-actor', and more recent suggestions that it effectively fizzled out into nothing. We can surely conclude that any fit, healthy young woman – as Yolande appears to have been – who thought herself with child and managed to convince

everyone else of that fact must have produced something at the end of it, which sadly can only have been a dead baby.

[81] See Young, *Robert the Bruces Rivals. The Comyns, 1212-1314*, p.114 and elsewhere for the relationship between the Sinclairs and the Comyns.

[82] *The Accounts of the Great Chamberlains of Scotland*, vol. 1, p.56, p.62, p.67, p.74. Barrow, *Robert Bruce*, p.24. In the Chamberlain's accounts, it is John Comyn of Buchan, Alexander's son and heir, who accounts for Wigtown in 1288 after Alexander's death.

[83] The Guardians' administration certainly wasn't perfect – ask the sheriff of Northumberland who was arrested in Scotland in March 1290 and spent a couple of weeks imprisoned in Roxburgh castle. On the other hand, the Guardians ordered his arrest because of complaints from men living on the king of Scotland's lands in Northumberland, who had had their goods seized as payment for alleged debts [Stevenson, *Documents*, volume I, pp.126-8].

[84] That it was the Scots who were the driving force behind the extraction of a binding promise from the Norwegian king to send his daughter within the year even to England is revealed by the fact that as soon as they found out that a papal dispensation might have been issued to allow Margaret to marry Edward's son and heir, the Guardians immediately wrote to Eric pressing him in language that almost veered from the diplomatic to keep his promise or they would 'take the best counsel that God gives us for the state of the realm and the good people of the land' [*Foedera*, I, p.731]. This was surely a heavy hint that they might pass over the Maid's rights to succeed in favour of someone else, a high-risk strategy but one of the few cards the Scots possessed.

[85] *Foedera*, I, p.732. Margaret's dowry was still due to be paid even should she die.

[86] Stevenson, *Documents Illustrative of the History of Scotland*, vol. 1, pp.35-6. See Penman, *Robert the Bruce*, p.28 for a discussion of Bruce (5)'s possible thoughts on the subject of a marriage between his family and the Maid. But it is hard to imagine that the Comyns would have allowed such a possibility and there is no evidence that Edward entertained the idea either.

[87] Stevenson, *Documents*, I, pp.105-111.

[88] Stevenson, *Documents*, I, pp.129-131.

[89] Though the dispensation itself did not arrive in England until after the meeting at Birgham, one of the English ambassadors to Rome, Otto de Grandison, had returned to Edward's court at Quenington in Gloucestershire by 8 March [Duncan, *Kingship*, p.183 fn.37].

[90] *Feodera*, I, p.730. I am well aware that the line I have taken – that the Scots did not know until around 17 March 1290 that Edward had applied for a dispensation to allow his son to marry the lady of Scotland – is a contentious one. The difficulty lies in translating crucial parts of the document sent to Edward on 17 March and even the author of its entry in the Records of the Parliaments of Scotland [RPS 1290/3/2] admits that he/she was unsure. However, that document presents two scenarios to Edward, the first – if the dispensation really had been granted – giving him permission to decide when the marriage should happen (this is the tricky part of the translation, but it doesn't actually alter the argument I am putting forward here). But then they present a second scenario, namely that if it [the dispensation] is to be pursued/striven for [the word is 'purchacer'], then, 'for the great benefits and profit that would arise as a result of this to both kingdoms, we would willingly put our heads together, along with you, to see how it could be brought about [nus, pur les grant biens e profit, que purront de cos avenir al'un e le autre reaume, mettrom volenters conseyl, ensemblement ovesque vous, comment ele seit purchace']. This second scenario was clearly a new – and very welcome - possibility to the Scots, which it would not be if they already knew that Edward had applied for the dispensation.

[91] *Foedera*, I, p.731

[92] *CDS*, ii, no.676, though unfortunately it's not dated.

[93] *CDS*, v, no.78. See Duncan, *Kingship*, pp.184-5 for the gory details of what this actually meant.

[94] Bower, *Scotichronicon* VI, p.4-5. Michael Prestwich mentions one parliament 'early in 1290' but also another due to begin in April, which would fit the bill perfectly [*Edward I*, pp.342-3]. A number of Scots, including the Bruces, would have received regular summonses as English landowners, so they would know that one was imminent.

[95] For detailed argument about the course of these difficult negotiations over the latter half of the summer of 1290 and the, admittedly scant and circumstantial, evidence for the precise date on which news of the Maid's departure from Bergen, see Duncan, *Kingship*, pp.188-194.

[96] *Foedera*, I, p.741. Fraser has been castigated by many for seemingly implying that the man chosen to be king *should* seek Edward's advice, but I think that Professor Duncan is right in stating that someone with the bishop's patriotic credentials was merely acknowledging the English king's European reputation as a diplomat and wise head, credentials that he hoped would stand the Scots in good stead at this critical juncture [Duncan, *Kingship*, p.199].

[97] Fordun, *Chronicle*, ii, p.307.
[98] Beam, *The Balliol Dynasty*, pp.84-5.
[99] Stevenson, *Documents*, I, p.203.
[100] Niccolo Machiavelli himself would not be born for over 150 years, but he would undoubtedly have recognised the kind of duplicitousness employed by both Edward I and Robert Bruce (5). This is not intended to give John Balliol the high moral high ground; he perhaps had less need of such methods, given the straightforward nature of his claim and the political power wielded by his relatives, the Comyns.
[101] There were actually thirteen Scottish earls, but it has been suggested that seven was probably invoked here because it chimed with current practice in choosing the king of the Romans, who traditionally became the Holy Roman Emperor. [Duncan, *Kingship*, p.201]
[102] *CDS*, ii 465
[103] *Lanercost*, p.74.
[104] *Itinerary of Edward I*, volume I, p.76; Ashridge estate is now owned by the National Trust. See Duncan, *Kingship*, pp.202-3 for a blow-by-blow account of some of the events of this period.
[105] Prestwich, *Edward I*, p.356.
[106] Stevenson, *Documents*, I, pp.227-8.
[107] Bower, *Scotichronicon*, vi, p.29; P.A. Linehan, 'A Fourteenth-Century History of Anglo-Scottish Relations in a Spanish Manuscript', pp.120.
[108] *CDS*, ii, no.478.
[109] *CDS*, ii, 480, 483, 485.
[110] Duncan, *Kingship*, p.203. For a complete dissection of what was already a complex series of negotiations made doubly so by the deliberate falsification of the record by the English after 1296, see Chapter Ten, 'The Road to Norham.'
[111] *CDS*, ii, no.482; Duncan, *Kingship*, pp.235-7.
[112] *CDS*, ii, no.484; 516.
[113] On 12 July 1291 Edward held a meeting at Stirling with a group of key Scots, who agreed (allegedly) with 'unanimous good will and consent' that the Guardians and other key Scots, along with an English associate, should undertake to oversee arrangements for a more satisfactory general taking of homage to the English king than the sheriffs had managed [*Instrumenta Publica*, p.14-15, translated in *CDS*, ii, no.508. The order to the sheriffs had gone out almost a month previously, on 15 June (Duncan, *Kingship*, p.254)]. This meeting may, however, have provided the king with more than just the opportunity to express his displeasure. The Scots who came to him there were, with the exception of the

guardian, Bishop Wishart of Glasgow, and the chancellor, Bishop Alan of Caithness (actually an Englishman), a striking coterie of Comyns and their close allies. Two of Comyn of Badenoch's inner circle – his brother-in-law, Sir Geoffrey Moubray, and Sir Patrick Graham – were still with the king when he arrived at Dunfermline on 19 July. And Comyn of Badenoch himself was allowed to bring his nephew, John, son of Alexander Macdougall of Argyll, to perform his homage in the king's chamber in the Dominican friary in Perth six days later, a signal honour given that most of these homages were done in the presence of royal officials rather than Edward himself [*Instrumenta Publica*, p.15-16, p.18]. If the Comyns could be reassured of their place at the heart of Scottish affairs, Edward might have imagined that he could win their support for keeping Scotland under his own direct rule. It was around this time that John, eldest son of Comyn of Badenoch, was married to Joan de Valence, daughter of the earl of Pembroke and Edward's first cousin. This was exactly the kind of preferment that was surely intended to help to persuade Scotland's most important family that they had nothing to fear, and everything to gain, from the lordship of the king of England. Professor Duncan has also noted similar implications in the various grants made by Edward to Scottish notables on 13, 18 and 23 August 1291, the first of which rewarded mostly Bruce supporters with substantial grants of land, but then – having cancelled those grants - in much less valuable gifts of deer to a greater preponderance of Balliol ones. Edward had tried, and failed, to persuade the Bruces to accept his own direct lordship [Duncan, *Kingship*, pp.266-7], the only time his interests clearly ran counter to theirs.

[114] John and Joanna de Valence's son – yet another John Comyn – was a knight and died at Bannockburn in 1314, suggesting his parents married no later than 1292 [see *Figure 5*].

[115] Duncan, *Kingship*, pp.269-73; *CDS*, ii, no.610.

[116] Stones and Simpson, ii, A 72, 72. It might be wondered that the various documents produced on the question of heirs to the throne towards the end of Alexander III's reign as his family dwindled towards extinction were not used as food for thought even among the Scots. However, most of the Scottish royal archive had been taken from Edinburgh castle and deposited at Berwick on Edward's orders and it is to be doubted that anyone was able to rummage through it, though Robert (5) roughly remembered some of what had been set down [*CDS*, ii, no.526].

[117] Duncan, *Kingship*, pp.278-89.

[118] Stones and Simpson, *Documents*, ii, C.88.

[119] The lordship of Galloway, John Balliol's maternal inheritance, had been treated in the English fashion by Alexander II, who divided it among the three daughters of the last lord, with Dervorguilla getting the title. But he did so largely in order to cut the independent-minded region down to size.

[120] Stones and Simpson, *Documents*, ii, C.91-93.

[121] The earls of Mar and Atholl were key supporters of Robert (5) and enthusiastically endorsed the Appeal of the Seven Earls, while Sir John Moray of Stirling was given a five-year lease of the barony of Inverbervie in north-east Scotland on 10 June 1291 for an annual rent of £16 (about £12,000) to be paid at the Bruce port of Dundee [*CDS*, ii, no.495; Duncan, *Kingship*, p.299].

[122] *CDS* ii 635; *CDS* ii 675

[123] Stones and Simpson, *Documents*, ii, C.106.

[124] Stones and Simpson, *Documents*, ii, D.76(B)(iii); D.76(A)(iv).

[125] He had pronounced on this as recently as 17 April 1290 [*Foedera*, I, p.742].

[126] I have put in the most important references to particular pieces of evidence relevant to this tortuous process but if you are really interested in the Great Cause, then I can only direct you to the relevant chapters (10-13) of A.A.M. Duncan's *Kingship of the Scots*. Professor Duncan used to spend at least three hours giving lectures on this subject to undergraduate students, but most of us lesser mortals need something a little more succinct. Nevertheless, the light he has shed on this vital, but deliberately murky, period in Anglo-Scottish relations is quite staggering.

[127] Duncan, *Kingship*, pp.316-7; Stevenson, *Documents*, I, p.372; *CDS*, ii, nos.652-4, 656, 657, 658, 660.

[128] Bower, *Scotichronicon*, volume VI, p.41.

[129] *CDS*, ii, no.645.

[130] *RPS* 1309/2.

[131] Fordun, *Chronicle*, ii, pp.308-9.

[132] The text of this parliament names this individual as Donald, son of Angus, but there was no such person at the time and it was surely a mistake for Angus son of Donald. It was correctly written slightly further on in the original *Acts of the Parliaments of Scotland*, vol. 1, p.92.

[133] Easter ended at Pentecost, when the Holy Spirit descended on the Apostles and other followers of Jesus. It is the seventh Sunday after Easter.

[134] *RPS* 1293/2/20.
[135] *Rotuli Scotiae.*, I, p.18.
[136] James the Steward was sheriff of Ayr from 1289 [*Chamberlains Accounts*, I, p.73], but, not surprisingly, given his friendship with the Bruces, he seems to have lost the office under King John [*Rotuli Scotiae*, I, pp.17-18].
[137] *RPS* 1293/8/8.
[138] He was still being called earl of Carrick until at least late 1296. See, for example, *CDS*, ii, no.850, dated 13 October 1296, where Bruce (6) is described as both lord of Annandale and earl of Carrick, Bruce (5) having died in 1295. This has caused no end of confusion for contemporaries – there is at least one occasion when Bruce (7) is called earl of Carrick during this period [*CDS*, ii, no.823].
[139] Barrow, *Robert Bruce*, p.75; *Rot. Scot.*, I, pp.17-18, p.21; *Foedera*, I, p.761.
[140] Stevenson, *Documents*, I, pp.397-8.
[141] *Rotuli Parliamentorum*, 1767, vol. 1, pp.112-3.
[142] Stevenson, *Documents*, I, pp.407-7. Walter Cambo, a local man, seems to have been appointed by Edward as keeper of Fife on 20 November 1293, but was only given access to the earldom's revenues by King John at a parliament at Lanark on 16 February 1294.
[143] *CDS* ii no. 698; *Calendar of Close Rolls, 1288-96*, p.295, p.367.
[144] *CDS* ii no.676, no.681; *CCR*, 1288-96, p.328.
[145] *CDS* ii 689; *CCR* 1288-96, p.349. The hunting presumably took place in and around his manor of Hatfield Broad Oak, since he had to be excused from inadvertently taking the king's deer, probably from the neighbouring royal forest of Hatfield Regis.
[146] See Prestwich, *Edward I*, Chapter 15 for an account of the outbreak of war with France in 1294.
[147] See Beam, *The Balliol Dynasy*, pp.89-90 for a discussion on whether or not John Balliol ever took up arms.
[148] *CDS*, v, no.129, no.130, no.131.
[149] *Feodera*, I, p.804.
[150] *Hemingburgh*, p.78.
[151] Bower, *Scotichronicon*, vol. 6, p.43; *Foedera*, I, p.801.
[152] *Hemingburgh*, p.90.
[153] *Foedera*, I, p.800. In the old days, this vast sum would have been owed to the Scottish treasury.
[154] *Foedera*, I, p.804. John Comyn, earl of Buchan, was also summoned as an English landowner [p.803], so it wasn't just the Bruces.
[155] *CDS*, ii, 699.

[156] TNA SC1/15/136.
[157] TNA SC1/25/31.
[158] *CDS* ii nos. 1073 and 1074. Admittedly the Annandale valuation was done in 1304, when the lordship was still to recover from six years of war, so this may not be an entirely fair comparison.
[159] I would argue this, firstly because there is no evidence that he swore homage to King John and secondly because he did not come to an agreement with his detested stepmother, Christina of Ireby, over the income owed to her as her dower [share of her husband's estate] until August 1296 [*CDS*, ii, nos. 826, 828]. Although Annandale was given into the custody of John Comyn of Buchan when both sides finally began to prepare for war in the spring of 1296, there had been time for Robert (6) to settle the issue after his father's death if Annandale had been in his possession. The fact that this agreement included the stipulation that: 'Robert (6) grants her [Christina] dower from the freehold *of his father* in the valleys of Annan and Moffet as in John late King of Scotland's time' [*CDS*, ii, no.826] suggests that he himself had not held that freehold during Balliol's reign. It is true that English sources always describe Robert (6) as earl of Carrick and lord of Annandale after his father's death, but even Edward I could do nothing if homage was not made for these lands.
[160] *CDS*, ii, no.712.
[161] *Close Rolls*, 1288-96, pp.444-5.
[162] *CDS*, ii, no.716, 718, 736.
[163] Stevenson, *Documents*, ii, p.2.
[164] *RPS*, 1293/8/1.
[165] Stevenson, *Documents*, ii, pp.2-3; *RPS*, A1296/1.
[166] Ranald Nicholson, 'The Franco-Scottish and Franco-Norwegian treaties of 1295', pp.114-32.
[167] Prestwich, *Edward I*, p.469.
[168] *Hemingburgh*, p.90, including footnote 5. This seems to be corroborated by TNA SC 1/14/44, and more certainly, for 12 October 1295, at *Rotuli Scotiae*, I, p.21 and *CDS*, v, nos.135-6.
[169] John's wife and Surrey's daughter, Isabella, had died a few years before.
[170] *CDS*, v, nos. 1119, 1120, 2092; *CDS*, ii, no.839. Further safe conducts were issued in early January [*CDS*, v, nos.1121-2], which either means that the embassy was reinforced after it had departed or that it only set off then. Surrey's safe-conduct was dated 30 November 1295, over two weeks before Edward ordered his army to muster the following year.

Given that King John and his nobles were included in the orders to serve, this was also a final test to see if the Scots were indeed preparing to rebel. The last sentences in the first paragraph of *Lanercost*, p.116 must refer to this embassy.

[171] *Lanercost*, pp.115-6.

[172] *RPS*, A1296/2/1.

[173] *Lanercost*, p.128-9. See p.125, which states that the Scots refused to hand the castles over to Edward, but since there is apparently good evidence that they did in October 1295, this perhaps refers to a later rescinding of that agreement early in 1296. It is certainly highly unlikely that there had been time or opportunity for English officials to have been put in place.

[174] *Lanercost*, p.129, pp.138-9; *Miscellany of the Spalding Club*, vol. ii, p.314; *Hemingburgh*, pp.94-6. Sir William Carlisle was described as 'defending Carlisle castle' on 12 April 1296, which is admittedly a couple of weeks later. The reference to him being 'with the earl of Carrick' at the same time does not necessarily mean that Robert (6) was also at Carlisle, but that Sir William was part of his retinue. Other evidence strongly suggests that Bruce - and presumably his son, Robert (7) - were with the king and the main English army throughout this period [*CDS* v, no.1135; no.2130].

[175] Given that, as we will see, both King John's renunciation of his homage and fealty to Edward and the invasion of north-eastern England by the Scottish army did not take place until *after* the English had taken Berwick, Buchan's earlier attack on Carlisle stands out as distinctly odd. It may even have been intended as a warning against any lingering Bruce ambitions towards the Scottish throne rather than as the opening salvo in an Anglo-Scottish war, though that was certainly how it was interpreted.

[176] Stevenson, *Documents*, ii, p.22.

[177] *CDS*, v, no.2109. Cryps – or Crisp as it was written in December – was inadvertently left off the list of safe-conducts and had to be quickly added on 25 March so that Robert (6)'s paperwork could be put in order [*CDS*, ii, 732].

[178] *Knights of Edward I*, vol. iii, p.92; *Knights of Edward I*, vol. i, p.183. Bardolf was a Suffolk knight, with landed interests in Norfolk and across the Midlands [*Knights of Edward I*, vol. i, pp.43-4]; Sir William Bruce inherited lands in Huntingdonshire given to his father by Robert (5) [Blakely, *The Brus Family*, p.107]; Sir Archibald le Breton had been attorney for Carrick's uncle Richard and held lands at Patching Pychot,

which lay only a few miles from Writtle [*Knights of Edward I*, vol. i, p.140; Sir William Rothing held Great Matching Manor roughly mid-way between Writtle and Hatfield [*Knights of Edward I*, vol.iv, p.151, though this must to refer to William's father]; Baddow was a Bruce manor that lay next door to Writtle.

[179] *CDS*, v, no.146. The earls of Angus and the Balliols may have been friendly in the past thanks to their Northumbrian connections, but there doesn't seem to have been any hesitation on the part of the current earl about staying loyal to Edward I [see Beam, *The Balliol Dynasty*, p.155]. The earl of Dunbar did change sides after the battle of Bannockburn in 1314, when it became clear that the English under Edward II had no chance of retaking Scotland, but that was surely understandable. See *CDS*, ii, no.732 for an example of Robert (6) being called earl of Carrick at the same time as his son was accorded that title, but this didn't last too much longer, thank goodness.

[180] TNA C 241/18/59; TNA C241/31/103. Though this last reference states that the merchants were citizens of Winchester, the debts seem to have been incurred in London.

[181] *Langtoft*, volume II, p.235.

[182] Bower, *Scotichronicon*, VI, p.75.

[183] Stevenson, *Documents*, ii, p.33-4.

[184] Stevenson, *Documents*, ii, p.25. See, for example, *Hemingburgh*, pp.96-99 for a description of the capture of Berwick.

[185] Stevenson, *Documents*, ii, p.25; p.37-8. See, for example, *Hemingburgh*, pp.96-99, *Lanercost*, pp.134-5 and Bower, *Scotichronicon*, VI, pp.58-9 for descriptions of the capture of Berwick. Bower states that the town was taken by an English ruse, for which there is no corroborating evidence, but it does let the defenders off the hook for Berwick's fall.

[186] Stones, *Anglo-Scottish Relations*, no.28; *Hemingburgh*, pp.99-101; *Gesta Annalia*, chapter 86 in Fordun, *Chronicle*, p.316, as well as Bower, *Scotichronicon*, VI, p.51. Whoever wrote this was misinformed as to who was sent to deliver King John's renunciation of his homage to Edward – the abbot of Arbroath had been on an earlier mission to England that returned to Scotland in January 1296 [*CDS*, ii no.839].

[187] *CDS* v, no.1135. The issuing of this safe-conduct for Robert (6) does not prove that he was with the king on 5 April, but it is a strong possibility.

[188] *Hemingburgh*, pp.101-2; *Lanercost*, pp.135-9. Lanercost says that Buchan did not raid until 8 April either, but this is contradicted elsewhere.

[189] *Itinerary*, ii, p.140.

[190] The allegation about Berwick comes from a near-contemporary snippet contained within the *Scotichronicon* – Volume V, Book IX, pp.79-81 An entry in the same chronicle written later omits the reference to Robert (6), presumably because it was politically embarrassing to mention it in a Scotland ruled by King Robert's descendants [*Scotichronicon*, VI, p.59]. One well-informed English source - *Hemingburgh*, p.104 - mentions the ruse used to capture Dunbar castle, while a number of Scottish sources do repeat the allegation that friends of the Bruces deserted Balliol's army around the time of the battle of Dunbar [see, for example, Fordun, *Chronicle*, p.319].

[191] *CDS*, ii, no.807; *Hemingburgh*, pp.98-9; *CDS*, ii, no.742; Stevenson, *Documents*, ii, p.62. *Langtoft*, p.255; *CDS*, ii, no.737; *Rotuli Scotiae*, I, p.30, p.31, p.33. Only those directly involved in holding Dunbar against King Edward were imprisoned, so Mar and the senior Comyns were not, while Atholl, along with Comyn of Badenoch's eldest son, were.

[192] Stevenson, *Documents*, ii, p.40. Dunbar is thirty miles from Berwick, where Edward remained, which is perhaps too far for news of the battle to have reached him on the same day. He had probably made up his mind for certain to get rid of the king he himself had made when John sent his renunciation of homage, though it is likely that such an idea had been in his mind for some time even before that.

[193] *Gesta Annalia*, chapter 94, in Fordun, *Chronicle*, p.319; also in Bower, *Scotichronicon*, volume VI, p.75.

[194] There had been a king of Scotland on record since 900 [*Annals of Ulster*, 900.6], but before that there were kings of the Picts in central, eastern and northern Scotland, and kings of Dalriada in the west.

[195] *Itinerary*, ii, pp.140-1.

[196] Stevenson, *Documents*, ii, pp.26-28; *Lanercost*, p.144; *Hemingburgh*, p.105.

[197] *Rotuli Scotiae*, I, p.23; *CDS*, v, no.1148.

[198] They certainly weren't among those who witnessed the homage and fealty sworn by James the Steward at Roxburgh on 13 May, though the earls of Angus and Dunbar, who had sworn homage and fealty to Edward along with the Bruces around 25 March, certainly did [*Instrumenta Publica* pp.60-1]. By 3 July, as we will see, Robert (6) was at his castle of Turnberry [TNA C47/22/9].

[199] *Foedera*, I, pp.841-2.

[200] *Langtoft*, p.255. The first person to renounce the treaty with France was supposedly James the Steward at Roxburgh on 13 May [*CDS*, ii,

no.823, p.193], but the list alleging this was put together some months after the event and so must be treated with caution and is contradicted in another version of the Steward's fealty [*CDS*, ii, no.737; Palgrave, *Documents*, nos.44 and 45, pp.151-3].

[201] Stevenson, *Documents*, ii, pp.59-63. You would have thought that there would be little argument as to the chronology, timing and content of such a carefully crafted series of events, but, alas, there is some disagreement on these points. Professor Barrow puts forward a slightly different version at *Robert Bruce*, p.97.

[202] *Hemingburgh*, p.106; *Gesta Annalia*, chapter 95, in Fordun, *Chronicle*, p.320; also in Bower, *Scotichronicon*, vi, p.77.

[203] TNA C47/22/9.

[204] *Scalachronica*, p.17.

[205] *CDS*, ii, no.1027, pp.264-5; *CDS*, v, no.215.

[206] *Itinerary*, pp.143-4.

[207] *Instrumenta Publica*, pp.176-176b.

[208] He made his homage and fealty on 28 August as 'Robert Bruce the younger, earl of Carrick.'

[209] *Rotuli Scotiae*, I, p.28, 30.

[210] *Rotuli Scotiae*, I, p.31. In addition, in October James the Steward had to hand over the castles of Kirkintilloch and Dumbarton, which he had held since at least his submission [*Rotuli Scotiae*, I, p.35, p.36]. See Watson, *Under the Hammer*, pp.57-8 fn.20 for the convoluted recent history of Cruggleton's ownership.

[211] Henry Percy's mother, Eleanor, was Surrey's daughter. Her sister Isabella had been married to John Balliol.

[212] *Knights of Edward I*, iv, pp.39-40.

[213] Nicholas Harris Nicholas, *The Siege of Caerlaverock*, p.15.

[214] *CDS*, ii, no.850; *CDS* ii, no.852.

[215] *Scalacronica*, p.17.

[216] Fordun, *Chronicle*, pp. 297-8; Paris, *History*, iii, p.205; Prestwich, *Edward I*, p.3; *Chronicles of the Age of Chivalry*, p.107.

[217] *Langtoft*, p.249.

[218] *Heminburgh*, p.127; Prestwich, *Edward I*, p.124, p.476. This sum was only a little less than the entire Scottish crown revenue during Alexander III's reign [Duncan, *The Making of the Kingdom*, p.599].

[219] See Barrow, *Robert Bruce*, p.467, fn.26 for a discussion of Christian of Carrick, who may well have been Bruce's mistress.

[220] *Hemingburgh*, p.119 onwards discusses the 'oppression' felt in England by the wool prise.

[221] *Rotuli Scotiae*, I, p.41 (this was Edward's response); see Watson, *Under the Hammer*, pp.34-37.
[222] *Scalacronica*, p.18; *Gesta Annalia*, chapter 98, in Fordun, *Chronicle*, p.321.
[223] http://www.breakingofbritain.ac.uk/blogs/feature-of-the-month/september-2011-the-guardians-in-1286-and-wallaces-uprising-in-1297/; *Scalacronica*, pp.17-18. This shows that, as in most instances, Wallace was not entirely alone in his exploits, in this case being accompanied by Sir Richard Lundie, whose lands lay north-west of Dundee. Sir Richard seems to have been appalled by the murder of the sheriff, to judge from the fact that he went back to the scene of the crime the next day and saved the life of another English knight, Sir Thomas Gray. Lundie submitted very quickly to the English two months later, presumably well aware that he faced dire penalties if he did not secure good submission terms that would guarantee his life, person and property. At the battle of Stirling Bridge, he attempted to persuade Cressingham, the treasurer, to let him take a force of horsemen across the ford of the River Forth at Kildean so that they might come round behind his erstwhile colleague, Wallace, in a pincer movement but Cressingham vetoed this sensible suggestion.
[224] Stevenson, *Documents*, ii, p.193-4. The 'Scottish sea' was the name commonly used for the River Forth, but here it means beyond Scotland's borders, since up until the later tenth century and the acquisition of Lothian, the northern tip of the kingdom of Northumbria, this was the southernmost limit of the kingdom. So far as the 'middling sort' are concerned, given that Edward issued an unprecedented demand that 'all those with twenty pounds worth of land (£13,700 today)' in England were to muster for the continent, it was men worth a similar amount who no doubt expected to be targeted in Scotland too, along with the equally-abhorrent demand for their wool. [Prestwich, *Edward I*, p.419].
[225] *CDS*, ii, no.887.
[226] *CDS*, ii, no.894.
[227] The word used is 'Galwegians' but the men of Galloway – whose lord had, until recently, been John Balliol – would not have ridden with Robert Bruce. Nor, as we will see, would the men of Annandale, whose lord was still Robert (6). These were presumably Carrick men, the word 'Galwegians' to an English writer perhaps meaning those from south-west Scotland, some of whom might have spoken Gaelic.
[228] *Hemingburgh*, pp.129-130.

229 *Hemingburgh*, p.130. Messengers from these great lords, which must mean Bruce, Wishart and the Steward, came in haste to Wallace at Perth.
230 *CDS*, ii, no.742, p.177. Andrew Murray's father of the same name remained locked up in the Tower of London.
231 Stevenson, *Documents*, ii, pp.211-3; *Hemingburgh*, pp.131-2.
232 *Rotuli Scotiae*, I, 42 44; *CDS*, ii, no.1433.
233 Stevenson, *Documents*, ii, p.193-4; *Hemingburgh*, pp.133-4; *CDS*, ii, no.884.
234 *Heminburgh*, p.134.
235 *Gesta Annalia*, chapter 98 in Fordun, Chronicle, ii, p.321.
236 Stevenson, *Documents*, ii, pp.202-3.
237 Stevenson, *Documents*, ii, pp.206-9
238 *CDS*, ii, no.910. The three were the Steward, the bishop of Glasgow and Sir Alexander Lindsay.
239 Stevenson, *Documents*, ii, pp.215-6; pp.208; pp.226-7.
240 Stevenson, *Documents*, ii, pp.217-8.
241 *Hemingburgh*, p.134. This is usually interpreted as Wallace responding angrily to the capitulation at Irvine [see Andrew Fisher, *William Wallace*, p.45], but the sentence in Hemingburgh comes immediately after reference to the imprisonment of Bishop Wishart and so must surely be a reaction to it, showing the strength of the bonds between the two men. See Palgrave, *Documents*, volume II, p.344 for Wishart being imprisoned because Robert did not hand over his hostages. The sons are actually described as 'nephews,' the standard euphemism for clerical offspring.
242 *Close Rolls, 1296-1302*, p.58.
243 *Rot. Scot.*, I, 44. On 29 July the king granted yet another respite of debts to Robert Bruce, senior, (that is, 6) 'who is about to go beyond seas with him'. [*CDS*, ii, no.926].
244 *Hemingburgh*, pp.124-6.
245 Wyntoun, *Original Chronicle*, volume II, pp.343-4.
246 *Hemingburgh*, pp.135-6.
247 *Scalacronica*, p.19.
248 Stevenson, *Wallace Documents*, p.159; *Hemingburgh*, pp.144-5.
249 See Barrow, *Robert Bruce*, p.445, note 1. It is quite possible that the Scots carried on for a period of time as if Murray was still alive precisely because of the constitutional difficulties in presenting Wallace alone as the ruler of Scotland.
250 We now know, from the seal attached to the letter sent to Lübeck by Wallace and Murray in October 1297 that William's father was called Alan Wallace. A Sir Alan Wallace, royal tenant in Ayrshire, paid homage

and fealty to King Edward in 1296 using a crude seal emblazoned with a curlew with foliage behind it [*CDS*, ii, p.534, Appendix 1, 3(28)]. Unfortunately we cannot with absolute certainty say that this is the same man, but it is certainly possible.

[251] *Rishanger*, p.384.

[252] Barrow, *Robert Bruce*, pp.121-2; Bower, *Scotichronicon*, VI, p.87; see for example *Calendar of Inquisitions Miscellaneous*, no.2367; *CDS*, iii, no.628.

[253] *CDS*, ii, no.961; Palgrave, *Documents*, I, p.344.

[254] *Rotuli Scotiae*, I, p.51; *CDS*, v, no.1173.

[255] TNA E101/6/30, m.3, m.1; *Rotuli Scotiae*, I, p.51; *CDS*, v, no.1173; *Hemingburgh*, pp.146-7. The prior of Carlisle's evidence at *CDS*, iii 524, given nearly twenty years later, is probably a somewhat garbled description of Clifford and Percy's activities in the summer of 1297, leading to Robert (7)'s submission at Irvine, rather than Clifford's foray into Annandale in December. There is certainly no evidence that the later campaign resulted in Robert (7)'s submission.

[256] Prestwich, *Edward I*, Chapter 15; J. Favier, *Philippe le Bel*, Chapter 8.

[257] M. Prestwich, 'The Battle of Stirling Bridge. An English perspective,' pp.73-5.

[258] *Calendar of Patent Rolls, 1292-1301*, p.314; TNA E101/6/35, m.11, 4.

[259] Watson, *Under the Hammer*, pp.53-4.

[260] Prestwich, *Edward I*, pp.479-80. See also *Rishanger*, pp.185-6 and p.388. John Balliol was permanently forfeited in 1296 and William Douglas in 1297, but most Scots had only just received formal confirmation from Edward of the return of their lands in time to be deprived of them again as a prelude to the Falkirk campaign.

[261] *Parliamentary Writs*, I, pp.310-318.

[262] *CDS*, ii, no.987

[263] *CDS*, v, no.1219; *Rotuli Scotiae*, I, p.51.

[264] Watson, *Under the Hammer*, pp.61-2.

[265] Bower, *Scotichronicon*, VI, p.93. Later writers needed to explain Wallace's defeat at Falkirk in July 1298 and so put the blame on fractious nobles. That the Comyns were not great fans of the Guardian is entirely believable but, as we will see, that does not mean they betrayed him at Falkirk.

[266] Watson, *Under the Hammer*, p.62-66.

[267] *Hemingburgh*, p.174.

[268] *Hemingburgh*, p.176.

[269] A league is generally viewed as three miles, making nine miles in total, though Falkirk is double that distance from Kirkliston (called Temple-Liston at this time, since it was owned by the Knights Templar).
[270] *Hemingburgh*, pp.177-9. The chronicler was quite wrong in stating that Falkirk was in Selkirk Forest; in fact it lies in the vicinity of the great Torwood. But Selkirk Forest was clearly the one that had made the most impression on the English.
[271] *Rishanger*, p.187; *Scalacronica*, p.21; *Gesta Annalia*, chapter 101 in Fordun, *Chronicle*, ii, p.323.
[272] See Morris, *Bannockburn*, p.43 for a discussion of Falkirk generally and a comparison with Maes Moydog in particular. However Prestwich (*Edward I*, p.223) is not at all convinced that archers were used to any great extent in the Welsh battle; Fisher, *William Wallace*, p.82.
[273] *Lanercost*, p.167.
[274] It is curious that, according to his itinerary, Edward seems to have come south from Falkirk via Stirling and headed towards Berwick, only to make a quick about-turn on 21 August in order to go straight for Ayr [*Itinerary*, p.168]. Hemingburgh also says that the king deliberately deviated from his intended route, having reached Selkirk Forest, to go to Ayr [*Hemingburgh*, p.181].
[275] *Hemingburgh*, p.181. The English seem to have lumped together all the territory in the hilly lands south of Ayr under the term 'Galloway.' See also *CDS*, ii, 1011. *CDS*, iv, Appendix 1, no.7.
[276] *CDS*, ii, no.1015; *Foedera*, I, p.901.
[277] NRS, GD137/3679.
[278] *CDS*, ii, no.742; *Rishanger*, p.185; *Itinerary*, p.162.
[279] NRS, GD137/1472.
[280] *CDS*, ii, no.993; TNA, SC7/8/4
[281] *CDS*, ii, no.1301. This has been wrongly dated to April 1302, despite the fact that, if that had been the date, the bishop of St Andrews would surely have told Philip that Carrick and Comyn had not been joint guardians, just the two of them, since August 1299. Since Wallace was guardian in April 1298, that only leaves April 1299 as the correct date.
[282] Beam, *The Balliol Dynasty*, pp.169-171.
[283] *Scalacronica*, pp.22-3; Bower, *Scotichronicon*, vi, pp.101-9; *Foedera*, I, pp.897-8, p.907; *Rishanger*, p.185.
[284] Beam, *The Balliol Dynasty*, p.173; p.175; pp.176-7.
[285] *Gascon Calendar of 1322*, No.131.
[286] *CDS*, ii, no.1057.
[287] *CDS*, ii, no.1081; no.1115

[288] *CDS*, ii, no.1071.
[289] TNA E159/72, m.102.
[290] This is mentioned in the charges laid against Bishop Wishart after Bruce became king [Palgrave, *Documents*, volume I, p.344].
[291] *CDS*, ii, no.1949. See also Watson, *Under the Hammer*, p.86.
[292] *National Manuscripts of Scotland*, vol. ii, no.8, summarised in *CDS*, ii, no.1978.
[293] A safe conduct from John Balliol was apparently found among Wallace's belongings when he was captured in 1305. The only time Sir William could have got it was during his continental trip.
[294] *CDS*, ii, no.1978.
[295] *CDS*, ii, no.1115.
[296] In an undated court case before 1304 – but most likely much earlier than that - John Comyn, acting as Guardian, judged against the earl of Strathearn, who had ravaged the lands of one of Comyn's allies on King Edward's behalf 'in the beginning of the war' [probably meaning 1297]. The earl claimed he accepted the judgement and paid the fine demanded only out of 'fear of greater damage' [*CDS*, ii, no.1592]. This certainly suggests that few, if any, could stand up to the power of the Comyns north of the Forth and that the wielding of power and influence there had to be done with their say-so.
[297] *Liber S. Thomas de Aberbrothoc*, vol. 1, no.231.
[298] See Young, *The Comyns*, p.85, p.114. Sir John Maxwell, probably of the Lanarkshire branch of the family, was with John Comyn as part of his inner council in 1304 [*CDS*, ii, no.1741].
[299] *CDS*, ii, no.1101.
[300] J. Viard, *Les Journaux de Tresor de Philippe IV*, pp.526-7, no.3504.
[301] See Barrow, *Robert Bruce*, p.139 for a discussion of the individuals involved.
[302] *Acts of the Parliaments of Scotland*, I, p.98.
[303] Beam, *The Balliol Dynasty*, pp.180-1.
[304] We can deduce this from the fact that, after he submitted to King Edward in 1301/2, he said he would no longer call out the tenants of Melrose abbey in Carrick to perform this service, having previously asked them to do so 'frequently' [*Liber Sancte Marie de Melrose*, I, no.351].
[305] *CDS*, ii, no.1060. Both the de Umfravilles and the Balliols were prominent Northumbrian families, as well as holding lands elsewhere. *CDS*, v, no.220; G.O. Sayles, 'The Guardians of Scotland and a parliament at Rutherglen,' p.246.
[306] *Itinerary*, pp.191-2; Watson, *Under the Hammer*, p.100; p.107 onwards.

[307] See for example *Liber Quotidianus Gardrobae Contrarotulatoris Garderobae*, p.177; *CDS*, ii, no.1147, no.1159.
[308] *CDS*, ii, no.1115, p.282; *CPR*, 1292-1301, pp.536, 537-8; *Liber Quotidianus*, p.81; Stevenson, *Documents*, ii, pp.296-8. This last document is wrongly dated to 1298.
[309] *Chronicles of the Picts and Scots*, ed. W F Skene, pp.216-21.
[310] *Foedera*, I, 924.
[311] *CDS*, ii, no.1191.
[312] *CDS*, ii, no.1190.
[313] TNA E101/358/6.
[314] *Gesta Annalia*, chapter 103 in Fordun, *Chronicle*, ii, p.324.
[315] See Barrow, *Robert Bruce*, pp.150-1 for a discussion of Soules, his background and the implications of his appointment as sole guardian, though I am taking the line that Sir John Comyn continued as Guardian along with Soules.
[316] *Itinerary*, p.178; *CDS*, ii, no.1178.
[317] Stevenson, *Documents*, ii, pp.431-3; pp.434-5.
[318] For an illuminating discussion of both sides' arguments to the pope at this time, see R. James Goldstein, 'The Scottish Mission to Boniface VIII in 1301', pp.1-15.
[319] *CDS*, v, no.262. See also, Watson, *Under the Hammer*, pp.126-34 for a fuller discussion of Edward's financial woes during this campaign.
[320] *CDS*, ii, no.1136.
[321] *CDS*, ii, no.1121. This is wrongly dated.
[322] *CDS*, iv, p.454.
[323] *CDS*, v, no.259 and, in more detail, E L G Stones, 'The submission of Robert Bruce to Edward I, c.1301-2', pp.122-134.
[324] *Foedera*, I, p.936.
[325] *Itinerary*, pp.206-210.
[326] *CDS*, ii, no.1247; *Foedera*, I, p.937.
[327] *CDS*, ii, no.1657.
[328] Stones, 'The submission of Robert Bruce,' p.132, Nicholas Trivet, *Annales*, p.397, n.7, TNA E101/371/21/32; *CDS*, ii, no.1657.
[329] The document had previously dealt with what should happen if Bruce lost his lands so this is unlikely to be what is referred to in terms of his 'right.' The fact that that right is given in the singular also makes it unlikely to refer to his lands which, as their lord, he would have had many rights over.
[330] *CDS*, iv, p.376.
[331] *CDS*, ii, no.1291; E101/10/18, part 2, m.170

[332] *Liber Sancte Marie de Melrose*, I, no.351.

[333] See TNA E 213/329 and Penman, *Robert Bruce*, p.71. There had been a mutiny at Berwick over lack of pay and supplies in late August 1301 [see Watson, *Under the Hammer*, pp.126-7].

[334] Maurice Keen, ed., *Medieval Warfare: A History*, pp.113-4; p.203; Contamine, *War in the Middle Ages*, p.258.

[335] TNA, SC7/7/6.

[336] *Les Journaux de Tresor*, no.1106, no.2640, no.3520, no.4138, no.4149, no.4823, no.5322, no.5421. There are missing sections, which may well serve to obscure Bishop Crambeth's presence in France between 1301 and 1302.

[337] RPS, 1302/9/1; E L G Stones, 'An Undelivered Letter from Paris to Scotland [1303]?', pp.86-88.

[338] As we will see, this delegation addressed a letter to their colleagues back home led by John Comyn, guardian of Scotland in May 1303 [*Foedera*, I, pp.955-6].

[339] Stevenson, *Documents*, ii, pp.449-50.

[340] Beam, *The Balliol Dynasty* pp.187-8; *Journaux de Trésor*, no.5917.

[341] *Calendar of Close Rolls*, 1302-1307, pp.65-6.

[342] See E L G Stones, 'The submission of Robert Bruce to Edward I', p.132 for two unequivocal references to Scotland as a kingdom.

[343] *CDS*, ii, no.1334; no.1356; Stevenson, *Documents*, ii, p.178. This last is wrongly dated to 1297. The letter to Carrick heads a long list of similar requests, none of which mention Annandale, so it is possible that Robert was being given some responsibility in his father's lordship, even if Edward kept hold of Lochmaben and the crucial port at Annan.

[344] See Watson, *Under the Hammer*, pp.168-70. However, despite what I say there, based on English sources, it is clear that Sir John Segrave languished in Scottish prison until July/August, when he was probably released as part of a prisoner exchange [See *CDS*, iv, no.1833; *CDS*, ii, no.1375, no.1379, no.1388].

[345] *The Book of Pluscardine*, ed. F J H Skene, volume ii, p.169; *Gesta Annalia*, chapters 107-8 in Fordun, *Chronicle*, ii, pp.325-328; also in Bower, *Scotichronicon*, vi, pp.295-7.

[346] *Itinerary*, p.225; *Foedera*, I, pp.952-4.

[347] *Foedera*, I, pp.955-6.

[348] Bower, *Scotichronicon*, vi, p.297.

[349] *CDS*, ii, no.1375; *Calendar of Close Rolls, 1302-1307*, p.91.

[350] *CDS*, ii, no.1385; *CDS*, v, no.1466, no.2450; *CDS* ii, no. 1424; no.1516, p.394.

[351] TNA E159/76, m.18. See also Watson, *Under the Hammer*, pp.174-177.
[352] *CDS*, ii, no.1385.
[353] TNA E101/11/21, mm.55-59; *CDS*, ii, no.1390, no.1392.
[354] *Itinerary*, pp.229-30. See for example Haskell, *The Scottish campaign of Edward I, 1303-4*, p.28, for an engagement between the Prince of Wales's force and the Scots.
[355] TNA SC8/9/444.
[356] *CDS*, ii, no.1393.
[357] Stevenson, *Documents*, ii, p.453.
[358] *CDS*, iv, p.487.
[359] CDS, ii, pp.392-3; *CDS*, v, no.346.
[360] *CDS*, ii, p.394; *CDS*, v, no.346.
[361] See Watson, *Under the Hammer*, pp.185-8 and Watson, 'Settling the stalemate: Edward I's Peace in Scotland, 1303-1305' for more detailed accounts of the submissions of 1304.
[362] *Langtoft*, ii, p.353. It surely does not diminish the great Scottish patriot to suggest that he, like the other Scottish leaders, would wish to submit on terms and it was only when he was refused them that he went on the run. I am aware that there will be some who would argue that one cannot believe an English source which is consistently hostile to Wallace and that is fair enough, but I am willing, on the balance of probability, to believe Langtoft that Sir William did send envoys to the English king along these lines, because of the strength and longevity of the story of Wallace and his mother associated with Dunfermline, which is both an embellishment and misunderstanding of Langtoft's account (it was Edward who was at Dunfermline, as we know, not Wallace, who, we might presume, would certainly not have brought his mother so perilously close to the enemy).
[363] TNA E101/11/9, m.4 CDS, ii, no.1420, no.1437, no. 1657, no.1658, no.1420; TNA E101/101/15.
[364] *CDS*, ii, no.1465; 1466.
[365] *CDS*, iv, p.482.
[366] Stevenson, *Documents*, ii, p.478; pp.481-3.
[367] The order to inquire into the extent of the Bruce lands in England was issued on 1 May at Stirling [*CDS*, ii, no.1540]. Robert (6) was, most unusually, buried at the abbey of Holmcultram, rather than at Guisborough [*Hemingburgh*, p.240].
[368] *CDS*, ii, no.1531; Palgrave, *Documents*, i, pp.323-4; *CDS*, ii, no.1546.
[369] *CDS*, ii, no.1540; no.1548.

[370] *CDS*, ii, no.1560; *Foedera*, I, p.966; *Calendar of Close Rolls, 1302-1307*, p.217.
[371] For a blow-by-blow account of this long and winding process, see Watson, 'Settling the stalemate: Edward I's Peace in Scotland, 1303-1305'.
[372] See Prestwich, *Edward I*, pp.258-64 for a discussion of the *Quo Warranto* inquiries.
[373] *CDS*, ii, no.1588. King William's time – a good century before – was probably as far back as people's memories, remembering also what their fathers and grandfathers had said, could safely take them.
[374] *CDS*, ii, no.1604.
[375] *CDS*, ii, no.1608; no.1115, p.282; nos.1657-8.
[376] See, for example, *Parliamentary Writs*, I, p.159.
[377] *Calendar of Close Rolls, 1302-1307*, p.223; *Langtoft*, p.359.
[378] *Calendar of Charter Rolls*, iii, p.93, p.115; *CDS*, ii, no.1606.
[379] *Calendar of Close Rolls, 1302-1307*, p.247.
[380] *The Parliamentary Writs and Writs of Military Summons*, I, pp.155-6. This provides a fascinating insight into contemporary Scottish parliaments, most particularly that they were composed of two each from among the bishops, earls and barons, and ten from among the abbots and the same number to be chosen by the community of Scotland. This was a much smaller assembly than English ones, but was nonetheless clearly meant to be representative. See also Prestwich, *Edward I*, p.507. *Calendar of Close Rolls, 1302-1307*, p.336; p.340.
[381] *Parliamentary Writs*, I, p.156; *CDS*, ii, no.1669; no.1678.
[382] *CDS*, ii, no.1713.
[383] See T M Smallwood, 'An unpublished early account of Bruce's murder of Comyn,' pp.1-10. Smallwood suggests that this parliament was called just to choose the delegates to be sent to the Westminster parliament in September, which it was, but that doesn't preclude the possibility that Bruce met up 'on the side' with key men whose support he would want to canvas.
[384] Dr Alexander Grant was the first to make this point clearly and persuasively in his seminal article 'The death of John Comyn: what was it about?,' pp. 176-224. The three qualifications for kingship – blood, assent and fitness to rule – were used subsequently, but with far less justification, by King Robert, most famously in the Declaration of Arbroath.

[385] See, for example, Barbour, *The Brus*, pp.68-72 for one version of this agreement and also Grant, 'The death of John Comyn,' p.193 onwards for a discussion of more Scottish sources that claimed this.

[386] *CDS*, iv, no.477; *CDS*, ii, no.1424; TNA E101/364/13, m.9. When Wallace was finally captured, he was found with a number of safe conducts in his possession, suggesting that he was trying to get back to the continent, there being no obvious other reason as to why he would carry these documents with him.

[387] See, for example, *Flores Historiarum*, iii, pp.123-4; *Langtoft*, ii, pp.363-5.

[388] Palgrave, *Documents*, i, pp.293-4; *CDS*, ii, no.1691 (9).

[389] *Calendar of Close Rolls, 1302-1307*, p.349.

[390] *CDS*, v, no.353; *CDS*, ii, no.1646, p.443; no.1617; *CDS*, ii, no.1694.

[391] *CDS*, v, no.472 (y), p.205.

[392] *CDS*, ii, no.1745.

[393] *Flores Historiarum*, iii, p.128.

[394] *Gesta Annalia*, chapter 112, in Fordun, *Chronicle*, ii, p.330, but quoting the more modern translation at Bower, *Scotichronicon*, vi, p.301.

[395] See *CDS*, ii, no.1694.

[396] *CDS*, ii, nos.1734-5.

[397] *CDS*, ii, no.1726.

[398] Barbour, *The Brus*, p.80.

[399] See Grant, 'The death of John Comyn' and Barbour, *The Brus,* pp.69-80, including the notes, for summaries of the various versions of this infamous murder. King Edward names those who were known to have been at the murder as Robert himself, Lindsay and the three Setons, presumably on the testimony of Comyn's valet, Galbraith, who survived [*CDS*, v, no.472(r) and (u). Kirkpatrick isn't mentioned, though, as we will see, he soon plays his part in the story. With regard to an agreement between Bruce and Comyn, I have already dismissed the stories told in some of the chronicles, but there is one point at which there might have been discussions between them as to the future of an independent Scotland. Later writers mention an agreement made between the two former Guardians 'as they came riding from Stirling,' which could only have been in the aftermath of the siege of 1304 [*The Brus*, p.68]. Comyn stayed away from the siege in its early stages, pleading illness in mid-April, but this was not a reason/excuse that could have kept him from playing his part in the final act of Edward's reconquest of Scotland forever [*CDS*, v, no.368]. Perhaps there were some tentative discussions along the same lines as those that had led to the formal agreement with Bishop Lamberton – at that point Robert, as one of Edward's right-hand

men, was in a much more powerful position than John, who had only just submitted. But I still think it unlikely, given Comyn's continuing influence within Scotland itself, even if he wasn't yet in a position to make much of it. In any case, within the year, once the assembly at Scone/Perth had sat, it was Comyn who was in the ascendancy and any notion that Bruce's ambitions might be taken seriously were cast right out of the window. As for killing Comyn and dumping his body in front of the altar [*Hemingburgh*, p.246], even Edward I admitted the murder took place in the cloisters, adding that this was 'near the high altar', which is no doubt true, given that the church was presumably nearby, but not quite the same thing [Palgrave, *Documents*, I, p.346].

[400] The earliest version of this story is probably *Gesta Annalia*, chapter 113, in Fordun, *Chronicle*, ii, pp.330-1.

[401] See Grant, 'The death of John Comyn', p.200 onwards for this important discussion.

[402] *Annals of the Four Masters*, 1274.1; 1277.2.

[403] *Annals of Ulster*, 1295.1; *Annals of the Four Masters*, 1299.3.

[404] Barbour, *The Brus*, p.144, note to lines 659-78; p.80; *CDS*, ii, no.1811, p.486 [most historians have interpreted this last entry as saying that Siward was captured in his own castle, but the entry suggests he was at Dumfries when the castle was taken immediately after the murder]; Stones, *Anglo-Scottish Relations*, no.34.

[405] *Calendar of Patent Rolls, 1301-1307*, p.417; *Calendar of Close Rolls, 1302-1307*, pp.369-71; *CDS*, v, no.471.

[406] *CDS*, ii, no.1747, with a more accurate rendering of it at Grant, 'The murder of John Comyn,' p.180 fn10.

[407] *CDS*, v, no.472, p.199.

[408] Stones, *Anglo-Scottish relations*, no.34, p133.

[409] The source of this information [see previous endnote] stated that this meeting happened 'The Saturday before this letter was written' (the letter itself is undated) and goes on to say that Bruce, having left Glasgow, was en route north across the River Forth via Dumbarton, presumably to his inauguration at Scone, which took place on 25 March. Though the meeting could conceivably have taken place the next Saturday, 12 March, the timings fit better with the earlier date, giving Robert 2-3 weeks to take a circuitous route to Scone and get ready to be made king. Edward also seems to have reacted to these warnings by 20 March – five days *before* Bruce's inauguration - taking action against 'the infidelity, rebellion and premeditated iniquity of Robert Bruce and his followers.' If the report giving these warnings was only written in the

week following Saturday 12 March, there would not be enough time for it to have reached the king, who was at Winchester in the far south of England.

[410] See Barbour, *The Brus*, p.88 notes referring to lines 175-77.

[411] Palgrave, *Documents*, pp.348-9

[412] Palgrave, *Documents*, p.347.

[413] *Gesta Annalia*, chapter 118, in Fordun, *Chronicle*, ii, p.333, as well as at Bower, *Scotichronicon*, VI, p.317.

[414] See for example, *Hemingburgh*, p.247 and the rather garbled account in *Scalacronica*, pp.30-1 (it was Isabella's husband, John of Buchan, who must have been at his manor of Whitwick in Leicestershire) and the current earl of Fife, who lived in England, was her nephew. See *CDS*, ii, no.1914 for a reference to the gold coronet.

[415] Palgrave, *Documents*, I, p.336, p.337. Bishop *Lamberton* seems to have been given young Andrew Stewart as, in effect, a hostage while Edward negotiated with his father as to suitable guarantees for James the Steward's loyalty.

[416] See Barrow, *Robert Bruce*, Appendix, p.421 onwards for a list of the kind of men who came out for Bruce in the first few months. *Calendar of Patent Rolls, 1303-1307*, p.482.

[417] Barbour, *The Brus*, p.88 and also p.89 footnote to line 187.

[418] *CDS*, iv, no.68.

[419] This is made clear in the plaintive and peevish iteration of the many occasions on which Bishop Wishart had sworn homage and fealty to King Edward on various holy relics [Palgrave, *Documents*, I, p.340 onwards].

[420] *CDS*, ii, no.1757. See also, for example, *CDS*, ii, nos.1771, 1775 and 1776.

[421] Barbour, *The Brus*, p.90; *CDS*, v, no.472 (u).

[422] *CDS*, ii, no.1753.

[423] *Calendar of Close Rolls, 1302-1307*, p.374; *Calendar of Patent Rolls*, 1301-1307, p.426; *CDS*, v, no.419; *Calendar of Close Rolls, 1302-1307*, p.433.

[424] *Calendar of Patent Rolls, 1301-1307*, p.426.

[425] See Watson, *Under the Hammer*, p.116, p.159.

[426] Palgrave, *Documents*, I, pp.320-1.

[427] *CDS*, ii, no.1773; *Hemingburgh*, p.248; *Langtoft*, ii, pp.369-70.

[428] *Hemingburgh*, p.247; *CDS*, v, no.492 (v-x).

[429] *CDS*, ii, no.1782.

[430] *CDS*, ii, nos.1780-1. Valence could have captured Wishart – who may at that point have been besieging Cupar castle – himself, though that would have meant a detour away from Perth.

[431] *Hemingburgh*, p.248; *Scalacronica*, p.31. The story told by the earl of Strathearn makes clear that he was first approached to swear homage and fealty to King Robert by the earl of Atholl, but was later coerced into it by Atholl's men along with Sir Neil Campbell, Sir Walter Logan and Sir Robert Boyd [Palgrave, *Documents*, I, pp.320-1].

[432] *Hemingburgh*, pp.248-9; *Scalacronica*, pp.31-2; Barbour, *The Brus*, p.92.

[433] Barbour, *The Brus*, pp.100-102; Gray, *Scalacronica*, p.32; *CDS*, ii, no.1807. Both English and Scottish sources agree that the Scots were not that numerous.

[434] Barbour, *The Brus*, p.102; *CDS*, ii, 1811; *Flores Historiarum*, iii, p.133. It is not clear whether the marshal – called Hutting – was executed and presumably the chaplain was saved by his holy orders.

[435] Bower, *Scotichronicon*, p.323; Barbour, *The Brus*, p.104-6.

[436] *CDS*, ii, no.472, p.202.

[437] *CDS*, v, no.472, p.200; *TNA* SC 1/47/85

[438] Barbour, *The Brus*, p.108. Barbour says that it was the 'worthy James Douglas' who did all this hunting and fishing. Douglas would become one of Bruce's most trusted commanders and close friend, but, despite Barbour's assertion that he was at Methven, the evidence suggests that he hadn't yet decided to join the Scottish king.

[439] *CDS*, ii, no.1803; *CDS*, ii, no.1811; *Rishanger*, p.230.

[440] *Flores Historiarum*, iii, p.130.

[441] Barbour, *The Brus*, pp.112-4. Professor Duncan disputes that the skirmish at Dalrigh was between Bruce and the Macdougalls and he may well be right. However, on 18 August – a week later – King Edward received two messengers from 'John Dargail' [John of Argyll, which was another name for Macdougall of Lorne] while he was at Newbrough in Northumberland. The messengers were John's chaplain and his clerk, so Macdougall clearly had something of importance to tell the king [*CDS*, v, no.427, p.203]. The legend of the brooch is, alas, just that – legend [Barbour, *The Brus*, p.118 note 146].

[442] *Scotichronicon*, vi, p.323.

[443] *Langtoft*, ii, p.373; *Flores Historiarum*, iii, p.134; *CDS*, v, no.471, p. 197, p.198.

[444] *Flores Historiarum*, iii, p.324-5; *Scotichronicon*, vi, p.323.

[445] Palgrave, *Documents*, i, pp.356-9; *CDS*, ii, no.1910.

[446] *CDS*, v, no. p.472, p.199; *Itinerary*, pp.264-5.

[447] Barbour, *The Brus*, pp.156-8, including note to line 172.
[448] *CDS*, ii, no.1829.
[449] Barbour, *The Brus*, p.130.
[450] *CDS*, v, no.492, p.212; *CDS*, ii, no.1808, no.1845; *CDS*, v, no.472, p.199, p.203; Barbour, *The Brus*, p150, including note to lines 16-19.
[451] Barbour digresses so awkwardly into a discussion of crying [p.136] - beginning 'Although I say that they wept, truthfully it wasn't real crying,' essentially because that's what women do, 'who can wet their cheeks with tears whenever they like, even though very often nothing is hurting them' – that the reader is left with the feeling that he protests too much. It is tempting to wonder if social pressure on men to keep a stiff upper lip grew in the fifty years between the events described here and when they were written down. We are almost totally reliant on Barbour (from p.130) for what Bruce got up to in the months after Dalrigh, for no-one else knew for sure where he was, though rumours abounded.
[452] Barbour, *The Brus*, p.140.
[453] *CDS*, v, no.472, p.202.
[454] CDS, v, no.492, p.212; no.472, p.199, p.202; no.457; *CDS*, ii, no.1833, 1834; *Hemingburgh*, p.249. Hemingburgh actually says that the besieging force believed Bruce to be inside Dunaverty castle, but that he had gone away to the furthest away islands [extremas insulas], which is certainly not Rathlin right next to the northernmost tip of the Irish mainland. He also says [p.251] that Bruce left Kintyre on 29 September, which he certainly can't have done unless he really had been inside the castle, so this suggests that the chronicler has confused the Scottish king's flight with the day on which Dunaverty fell to the English.
[455] Barbour, *The Brus*, p.144.
[456] Walter Scott, *Tales of a Grandfather*, pp.63-5. In any case, it is not clear what Bruce could have done if he'd attempted to go to the Holy Land, because, since the fall of Acre in 1291, all the Christian crusader states in the Middle East had been recaptured by 'the Saracens' and there was no Crusade currently either taking place or being planned.
[457] *Hemingburgh*, p.251.

Printed in Great Britain
by Amazon